competitive
INTELLIGENCE

CREATE AN INTELLIGENT ORGANIZATION
AND COMPETE TO WIN

Michelle & Curtis Cook

**KOGAN
PAGE**

First published in 2000

Kogan Page Limited
120 Pentonville Road
London
N1 9JN

Kogan Page US
163 Central Avenue, Suite 2
Dover NH 03820
USA

British Library Cataloguing in Publication Data

A CIP record for this book is available from the British Library.

ISBN 0 7494 3312 4

Typeset by Jean Cussons Typesetting, Diss, Norfolk
Printed and bound in Great Britain by Bell & Bain Ltd, Glasgow

Whatever our souls are made of, yours and mine are the same stuff.

Contents

Acknowledgments

We would like to acknowledge the many people who assisted us in the writing of this book, namely: Victoria Groom, Pauline Goodwin, Heather Langridge, Henry Watson and everyone else at Kogan Page that participated in the production of our book. Thanks also to Helen Moss, Hendry Martinez Leon and the advance reviewers Jim Cummings and David Hartman.

introduction

I am enough of an artist to draw freely upon my imagination. Imagination is more important than knowledge. Knowledge is limited. Imagination encircles the world.

ALBERT EINSTEIN

Welcome to the intelligence age. In this age, business success is dependent on knowing how to cultivate intelligence and use it to your advantage. It is a time of gathering and developing quality information, rather than hoarding a vast quantity of information. It is a truly global age in which an entrepreneurial spirit drives the new economy in ways that have not been witnessed in previous times. It is a renaissance of human intervention that, paradoxically, enhances the importance of technology. It is also an age where 'intelligence innovators' are the most valuable assets of an organization. In this age, it is necessary for an organization to become an intelligent organization.

In the intelligence age, truly competitive companies will become increasingly sophisticated at collecting and processing information to churn out intelligence. They will need it to survive. Businesses will learn that their greatest assets are the sharp minds of their employees, their analysis tools and their ability to make effective decisions. They will need intelligence to compete. In the information age, organizations were consumed with the idea of acquiring information and data. An intelligent organization is one that goes well beyond information and knows that information is not nearly as valuable as the intelligence within the company and the capacity to generate or access intelligence.

Knowing the right things at the right time and acting on them is critical to success. There is a dawning of awareness that information as a commodity has little value to an organization, regardless of quantity. Rather, what is needed is the type of alchemy that transforms information into intelligence. This is competitive intelligence – a metamorphosis of data to information to knowledge to intelligence. Few organizations have mastered this transformation. Typically, they get stuck at some point along the way. Information or knowledge is no longer sufficient for competing in the intelligence age. Companies need intelligence.

Over the past decade there have been volumes written about the impact of the information age on businesses. The information age was spawned from a long industrial period, in which manufacturing and production ruled. The 'more is better' mentality ruled. This carried over into the realm of information. Companies have collected vast quantities of data and information in an effort to learn more or know more than their competitors. The reality is that very little of that information is used or, for that matter, has any value. Our obsession with information has, however, created some wonderful and useful tools. Consider the Internet. It has changed and will continue to change virtually every aspect of life, including the way we conduct business. The quantity of information on the Internet continues to grow at a mind-boggling pace. While there is extraordinary value in the information that resides on the Internet, companies will never be able to access all of it, nor is it necessary to do so. Companies have built up massive networks, databases and repositories simply to house and manage all the information they may never use. That does not take into consideration all the more traditional sources of information like reports, publications and surveys that gather dust in filing cabinets. In today's business world, the 'more is better' mentality does not work well with information. What companies really need to succeed is intelligence, not information.

Global competitiveness is crucial in the intelligence age. Companies can no longer rely on domestic markets for success. There really is no such thing any more. As markets become increasingly global in nature, so too must the businesses that want to succeed. In the information age we saw this trend growing. With international trade agreements and the removal of tariffs and protectionist policies, exports continue to grow. Organizations that fail to consider their opportunities in the global marketplace will go the way of the dinosaur. Global intelligence cannot be confused with its domestic counterpart. The ability to compete in one market does not ensure success internationally. In fact, many companies have learnt the hard way that there are unique circumstances in world markets. Conducting business as usual may be a recipe for disaster. In the intelligence age, the development of global intelligence skills is vital.

Entrepreneurial spirit is also driving the intelligence age. This entrepreneurialism runs rampant in the new economy. An economy that is fuelled by innovation, creativity, risk, technology and intelligence. The 'business as war' mentality has also gone the way of the dinosaur. Many companies have left that notion behind to adopt far more constructive strategic concepts of business as partnership, alliance and innovation, all of which generate healthy competition. Winning in the intelligence age does not necessarily mean that everyone else loses. Merger mania has shown that the fiercest of competitors quickly become allies when analysis shows benefits to the bottom line. Your 'enemies' may be your strongest allies. War rooms are replaced by 'intelligence innovation' rooms where a more ethical approach to business yields better results. We saw the beginnings of this trend in the information age, where companies started to become more socially conscious. Organizations that became environmentally aware and/or affiliated with diverse social causes often saw increased revenues as these efforts became public. As more information becomes more available to more people, companies' actions become more transparent. Increasingly, information finds its way into the public domain. This is a concept that businesses must fully grasp in the intelligence age.

We are experiencing a renaissance of human intervention in the world of strategic analysis for corporate planning. Technology has overshadowed the relevance of human analysis in recent years. The resurgence of the human touch does not mean that technology loses its importance. On the contrary, when people apply their skills in combination with technology, they take the technology to new and greater levels. Where technology was in the hands of information technology people in the intelligence age, it will become integrated into all functions and be further developed by this greater exposure to business developers, strategic planners, financial people and other key minds within an organization. That ensures that its uses become greater because of the blend of advanced technology and skilled human intervention.

This renaissance of human intervention will give rise to a new breed of businesspeople. They will be intelligence innovators. Well beyond the 'knowledge workers' of the information age, these innovators will use competitive intelligence to develop new lines of business, methods of research and technology applications. Knowledge workers were custodians of information like worker bees or squirrels – gathering and storing nourishment away. As custodians of information, they guarded and hoarded information often to the detriment of the company. While they recognized the intrinsic value of knowledge, they were oblivious to the real power of information – its synthesis into intelligence for the benefit of the company. Intelligence innovators in the intelligence age will have the skills to synthesize information and knowledge into intelligence and recognize the implications of it to their organization. Competitive intelligence has the capacity to effect change and alter the reality of an organization.

Throughout history we have seen the commodity of choice evolve and change, and the lengths to which leaders of empires would go to attain the silks of China, the spices of India, the olives of Greece or the wines of France knew no bounds. That is the value of intelligence in the creation of today's empire. Intelligence is coveted like the silk, spices, olives or wines that helped these empires flourish. Business empires will rise or fall based on the foundation of intelligence. Intelligent organizations will succeed not only when presented with opportunity, but also in the face of obstacles or opposition. They will have an uncanny ability to recognize opportunity and capitalize on it, while bypassing obstacles and opposition. Perhaps, most importantly, the intelligent organization and intelligence innovators will know how to create opportunity where before there was none. Organizations that recognize true intelligence and cultivate it will be tomorrow's leaders. All the rest will fall by the wayside.

Our vision for this book is to offer you a very practical approach to cultivating intelligence within your organization and using it effectively to become more competitive. Competitive intelligence is not going to go away. It will become increasingly necessary to competing in the intelligence age. This book will provide you with the tools and techniques you need to master your business environment through better preparation and sound strategic decisions. We have attempted to give this book an international perspective and to do justice to the increasingly significant role of technology in the conduct of business. We have tried to keep the book concise, interesting and non-theoretical to make it more relevant to the harried executive or entrepreneur of today's economy. Everyone can benefit from competitive intelligence. Ignore it at your own risk.

competitive intelligence

Hell is truth seen too late.

THOMAS HOBBES

You have turned off the computer, switched off the lights and locked the door to the office. You have even activated the security system, but before you go home and relax at the end of a long work-day, consider this: one of your rivals has just spent half an hour on the phone to your receptionist to gain that last puzzle piece of your business strategy for the next year. Over the last month, they have crawled your Web site, searched online databases, pored over scores of newspaper and trade journal articles, searched government filings and talked to your customers and former customers, employees, distributors and maybe even you. All the information they have gleaned has contributed to their coup. Think this is unlikely? Think again. Every day, businesses large and small are exposed in exactly this manner and the companies doing the digging have done nothing illegal or unethical.

What they have done is implement a process called competitive intelligence (CI), one of the most valuable business management tools at a company's disposal. Competitive intelligence is organized, structured information gathering, analysis and processing to enhance strategic decision-making. It is used by businesses to gain a competitive edge by learning about suppliers, customers, regulators and, of course, competitors. It is used by businesspeople looking to gain insight into the future of their businesses, make more effective decisions and sleep soundly at night after a long day at the office. Sleeping comfortably at night is not always easy in today's competitive marketplace. Your rivals are no longer just around the corner; they are around the world.

The CIA describes the intelligence cycle as 'the process by which raw information is acquired, gathered, transmitted, evaluated, analysed and made available as finished intelligence for policymakers to use in decision making and action'. It is a cycle consisting of five steps that are repeated to address specific business problems. They include planning and direction, collection and research, processing and storage, analysis and production, and dissemination and delivery.

But good CI is more than just information gathering. Its real strength lies in analysis of the information and making it useful to a decision-maker. Throughout this book, we will use several terms that are commonly, although not correctly, used interchangeably: 'data', 'information', 'analysis' and 'intelligence'. It is important to understand the differences between the terms to understand fully how to create intelligence.

Data are seemingly unrelated pieces of information. They could take the form of inflation rates, employment levels, number of cars in a car park, earnings, sales figures or names of corporate executives. There is an infinite amount of data. This book will show you how to get the data you need.

Information is a composite of data pieced together to make connections. Information may appear to be valuable, but on its own it is not actionable. Many companies believe that when they have pooled their data into oceans of information, they have intelligence. Actually, they are probably just drowning. For example, information might be, 'Based on decreasing product prices, fewer cars in their car park and a decline in employment, the competitor seems to be in trouble.' This information has little value on its own.

Knowledge is analysed information. Using the above information, an example of knowledge might be, 'Declining employment levels and fewer cars in the car park indicate that Competitor B has become a leaner, meaner organization and is not struggling at all.'

Intelligence is a collection of knowledge that has been verified, analysed and applied to your business to make a decision. Intelligence is often about forecasting or predicting some future event or change in the marketplace or business environment. However, intelligence is useless unless it is acted upon by a decision-maker. An example of intelligence might be, 'Based on the competitor's leaner, meaner operations in a complementary business, Competitor B is a merger candidate.'

These are very simplified examples, but they help to differentiate between data, information, knowledge and intelligence.

A dozen myths about competitive intelligence

There are many myths about competitive intelligence circulating in the business world. We outline a dozen of the most common myths, and explain the lesser-known reality behind them.

1. Competitive intelligence is spying.
2. CI is the same as market research, therefore it is not necessary to do both.
3. Business intelligence software gives you competitive intelligence or business intelligence.
4. Regular Web surfing about your competitors gives you competitive intelligence.
5. Gathering information from newspapers, magazines and journals constitutes CI.
6. Database searching is the same as competitive intelligence.
7. Industry leaders are not at risk from competitors.
8. Competitive intelligence is expensive.
9. Small businesses do not need competitive intelligence.
10. Competitive intelligence requires volumes of data.
11. CI is for businesses only.
12. CI is reserved for business crises.

Myth number 1: Competitive intelligence is spying

Competitive intelligence is more like good investigative journalism than spying. However, many companies cross the line into corporate espionage. It is important for CI practitioners to adhere to strict ethical behaviour and to be aware of the difference between legal and illegal ways of gathering information, because the penalties for breaking laws in certain jurisdictions are severe. Gathering information using spying or other illegal means is considered the failure of CI. An intelligence innovator will be able to find 95 per cent of the information a company needs from legal sources using ethical means.

Intelligent organizations and effective CI professionals never engage in acts of blackmail, bribery, extortion or other criminal behaviour. In the digital age, some companies have moved their spying efforts into the electronic realm. CI does not advocate hacking computers, intercepting secure transmissions or stealing e-mail.

Being legal and not misrepresenting yourself are fundamental principles of CI, and that is about as far from espionage or spying as you can get. We will explore the legal and ethical issues pertaining to this profession in greater detail in Chapter 10.

Myth number 2: Competitive intelligence is the same as market research, therefore it is not necessary to do both

Competitive intelligence is not market research. While the two disciplines share many similarities, they are not the same. Market research usually involves some degree of information gathering about competitors. Competitive intelligence includes this type of information gathering, but also includes much more. For example, it may comprise analysis of financial statements, executive profiling or analysis of plant operations and manufacturing processes. Market research is rarely as expansive. Market research typically supports the marketing process or details particular markets or market segments. Market research may come in a pre-packaged report about a particular industry, market or market segment. Many government bodies partake in market research on behalf of their countries' businesses. Some have even taken to calling it competitive intelligence. Competitive intelligence, however, is never pre-packaged information, no matter how valuable the information may be. Keep in mind that some governments conduct competitive intelligence to support domestic business; others conduct espionage. Businesses looking to expand into new territories should be aware of this fact, as it may affect their competitiveness.

Myth number 3: Business intelligence software gives you competitive intelligence or business intelligence

Lately, there has been a surge of business intelligence software in the marketplace. These products are generally built around two concepts: data warehousing and data mining. Data warehousing provides access to logical structured data buried within databases and electronic files within an organization. It is only as good as the data you have in it and the functions you have in place to pull the data out for analysis. These systems help you transform data into potentially interesting associations that you could define as information, but you still have to do all of the intelligent work – the real analysis that makes the information actionable. Perhaps you have heard of the expression 'GIGO': garbage in, garbage out. This is especially true of data warehousing software. It is only as good as its contents.

Data mining is the process of finding, exploring and modelling data to reveal potential patterns or associations. With the growth of database software use and the warehousing of data in quantities most humans cannot comprehend, let alone access, data mining tools are becoming increasingly common as a way to extract interesting patterns or relationships between data. By using sophisticated statistical analysis, data mining applications uncover relationships that would be missed using more traditional methods. Data mining finds these relationships using various modelling techniques, some of which are patterned around the neural networks of the brain. Of course, the models you create with this information are only valuable if they can help you make better business decisions. Human intervention is still required to analyse the information, turn it into intelligence and actually make the decisions.

But there is plenty of value in the software as well. Because it stores and organizes vast amounts of data and extricates it in a format that shows associations and provides some useful information, the software is an excellent addition to an overall competitive intelligence function.

Most of the software developers claiming to create business intelligence applications have really created little more than sophisticated database software that gathers data and draws some loose connections. Put simply, it takes raw data and turns it into information, not intelligence.

Myth number 4: Regular Web surfing about your competitors gives you competitive intelligence

Web surfing is just that, Web surfing. It is not competitive intelligence. While an intelligent organization can uncover a large amount of valuable information about its competitors from the Web, relying solely on it is risky. The data may be inaccurate, it may be outdated or it may even be intentionally misleading. We will be discussing more about online information in Chapter 5.

Myth number 5: Gathering information from newspapers, magazines and journals constitutes competitive intelligence

By the time you have found the article in your local newspaper, clipped it out, filed it and maybe even sent the information it contained around the office as a memo, it is too late. The whole point of competitive intelligence is to figure the news out *before* the newspaper does. The situation is even worse with magazines and journals that have copy deadlines many months in advance. The value of the news is lost, or at least greatly diminished. You are still just reacting. That is not to diminish the value of creating an office clipping system. In fact, it can be a valuable tool, particularly over time, to create a historical profile of your competitor. But a media monitoring system is just the tip of the iceberg when it comes to CI. Keep doing it if you have already started; start doing it if you have not already; but add the remaining functions necessary for obtaining CI.

Myth number 6: Database searching is the same as competitive intelligence

We recently read an article in a library science journal in which the author stated that librarians have always been conducting competitive intelligence, but they just did not use the term to describe it. Librarians, library scientists, library technicians and library researchers often perform an invaluable function in the CI process. They can make the information-gathering portion of CI efficient through their knowledge of and experience with online and electronic databases. Few librarians conduct expansive analysis such as financial ratio analysis, benchmarking, SWOT analysis or the many other CI analysis techniques. While corporate librarians play a vital role in the competitive intelligence process by streamlining the gathering of published information, their role is really just the beginning of the CI process.

There are many databases for conducting secondary research available to the CI professional. They will often provide plenty of background information. However, primary research is crucial to effective competitive intelligence.

Myth number 7: Industry leaders are not at risk from competitors

You might think that corporate powerhouses like Microsoft, Motorola and IBM defy competition. In fact, these companies are ranked as leaders in making good use of competitive intelligence. They have been able to build and maintain dominant positions in their industries because they recognized the value of analysing the competitors. Consider how IBM has turned its operations around by competing in new and different arenas.

Still there are many corporations who believe that intelligence techniques have never been used against them. This would indicate a high level of naïvety in the intelligence age when competition is fierce.

Many executives make the assumption that accurate competitor analysis is not possible and feel that simply being in the same marketplace, competing day to day, gives them everything they need to do so effectively. This is a simplified and inaccurate view of the competitive environment.

Myth number 8: Competitive intelligence is expensive

That depends. Is it more expensive than being the by-product of a merger, or worse yet, than watching your customers gradually decline and your new products being beaten to the shelf for every product launch?

A marketing executive of a company afraid of its competitor's power position in the marketplace once told us that he had $2 million to spend on advertising to combat the competitor, yet he could not find any resources to allocate to competitive intelligence to understand his competitor's strategy better. That is like going into battle blindfolded and carrying a gun with blanks instead of ammunition. It does not matter how big your gun or how much noise you make, you are still going to lose.

The competitive intelligence function within your company does not have to be huge, glamorous and costly to be effective, but it needs to exist. It can be as small as one or two people dedicated to the process, particularly if everyone in the organization understands the significance of it, or it can be a full team effort where everyone adds a small component to the CI process. An intelligence innovator is able to obtain the intelligence necessary to succeed within budgetary constraints. Setting up a CI function is covered in more detail in Chapter 3.

Myth number 9: Small businesses do not need competitive intelligence

The only business that does not need CI is one that has no competitors. If you think you have no competitors, think again.

You may be the only printing company in a small town, but you still have competitors. There is currently a company on the Internet that receives files electronically, prints them on demand and ships them back to the clients. Its office may be right across the country, but it is still a competitor. That is not to mention that you compete with all the hardware and software companies that provide increasingly powerful and inexpensive printing solutions for the home office and small business. They may not be printing companies; however, they are still competing in your market.

While many companies are starting to recognize the value of competitive intelligence to their organizations, they have often been slow to adopt it. Large businesses have typically been the first companies to embrace CI, but in the intelligence age it is equally important that small and medium-sized companies recognize the value in allotting a portion of their resources to the CI function. In an increasingly competitive business arena where companies large and small coexist, businesses of all sizes need to stay competitive. To remain or become successful, small companies need to be aware of their competitors' strengths and weaknesses and know their competitors' existing and future strategies.

Myth number 10: Competitive intelligence requires volumes of data

There are executives who do not discourage CI, but perceive tremendous difficulty in conducting effective competitive intelligence. They may believe that a phenomenal amount of data is required to analyse a competitor thoroughly. As a result, decisions on ways to compete in the marketplace are made in an *ad hoc* fashion or by gut feelings. This book will illustrate that analysing a competitor does not have to be a complex and onerous task.

The world's entire printed information doubles every nine months (at the time of this printing), but that does not mean your company needs all of it to be effective. In fact, one of the greatest downfalls of the competitive intelligence process is unfocused and excessive information gathering. You do not need a lot of information; you just need the right information. The 'more is better' mentality of the information age proved ineffective in competitive intelligence.

Knowing where and how to obtain information is half the battle, but it should not take half the time. In fact, CI experts agree that the information-gathering process should take about 20–25 per cent of the time spent on a CI project. That frees up considerably more time for analysis and dissemination, among other things. North American CI practitioners have a notorious reputation for spending too much time (up to 70 per cent according to some studies) collecting information they will never be able to use. Chapter 2 discusses the CI cycle and the competitive intelligence process, including information gathering.

Myth number 11: Competitive **intelligence is for businesses only**

Competitive intelligence is not just for businesses. Non-profit and not-for-profit organizations, government departments and trade associations can also benefit from using the processes and techniques of CI to become intelligent organizations. They all compete for limited audiences, exposure and resources. Government departments and trade associations in particular need to be up to date with their stakeholders in order to serve them better. This is best accomplished using CI to learn about customers, marketplace trends and opportunities to improve services or to advance the organization's agenda. Throughout this book, we look at the advantages of CI both for commercial and non-commercial entities.

Myth number 12: Competitive **intelligence is reserved for business crises**

CI may be your best weapon in a crisis; however, using it on an ongoing basis will ensure that you avoid crises in the first place. While it is essential for overcoming business threats such as a potential takeover scheme, the emergence of a new competitor, substantial loss in market share and numerous other business concerns, it can be used on an ongoing basis to anticipate situations before they become crises.

CI works with and supports the other business processes within an intelligent organization. It is a cycle that begins with a needs analysis, moves into a task assessment and is followed by focused data gathering. From there, it involves organizing the data into information, analysing it to create intelligence and disseminating the intelligence to decision-makers, who then use it to make strategic business moves. It becomes a cycle when the outcome of those moves is analysed again to determine their effectiveness and the next requirements. You are back to defining your needs. This cycle is discussed in Chapter 2.

Why competitive **intelligence is important to an organization**

The 12 myths above have probably provided you with a good idea about how CI can benefit you and your company, whether you are in sales, marketing, operations, manufacturing or finance, or whether you are the CEO of the company. Competitive intelligence helps you:

- understand the business environment better;
- understand your industry better;
- learn about your competitors' corporate and business strategies;
- forecast opportunities and threats;
- anticipate competitors' research and development strategies;
- reconstruct a competitor's, supplier's or customer's financial, marketing and operational information;
- validate or invalidate industry rumours;
- create a company information library;
- plug information leaks within your organization;
- make effective decisions; and
- act rather than react.

Competitive intelligence also provides a company with an opportunity to compare its operation, or specific functions within its operation, against 'best-in-class' organizations. Competitive benchmarking is a type of competitive analysis. It is a process for measuring performance against those companies that are recognized for excellence in certain aspects of their business. A benchmarking study and analysis of the way these leaders operate illustrates not only how to improve, but also how much to improve. The strength of competitive benchmarking is that you do not have to do it against your competitors. Chapter 7 discusses this type of analysis in greater detail.

Before you race back to the office to implement a competitive intelligence strategy, there is more you need to know to make your company an intelligent organization using competitive intelligence.

setting up a competitive intelligence project

A journey of a thousand miles must begin with a single step.

LAO-TSU, *THE WAY OF LAO-TSU*

Beginning any competitive intelligence project may seem like a daunting task, regardless of whether your organization is just starting CI for the first time or has been at it for a while. Although there are many factors to consider, the process can be streamlined by following the models and checklists we provide in this chapter.

Few construction companies would start building a house without first obtaining architectural blueprints, lot measurements, building permits or written specifications. The planning stage is integral to a structurally sound and attractive home that meets the owner's standards, the city's regulatory requirements and the architect's vision. The same is true of competitive intelligence. Taking the time to draw the CI project blueprints at the outset can help ensure you obtain what you need, guarantee that everyone is working toward the same goals, make sure that your company stays on time and on budget, and streamline the overall process.

This chapter explains the process involved in a competitive intelligence project. It provides tools and techniques that a corporate executive, a competitive intelligence practitioner, a researcher or anyone else involved can use to start a CI project for the first time or enhance the effectiveness of existing projects. Regardless of the size of the organization, following the competitive intelligence model can make the project run smoothly.

The competitive **intelligence model**

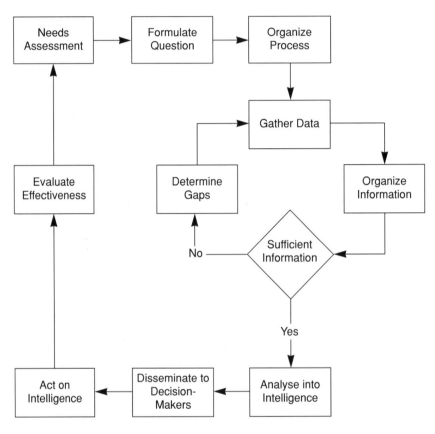

Figure 2.1   The competitive intelligence model

Figure 2.1 illustrates the competitive intelligence model that we have found most effective. It begins with a needs assessment to determine why you need to begin a CI project at this time. The second phase is to formulate a question based on your discussion in Phase 1. Phase 3 entails organizing the process so that your resources are used most effectively, and providing a 'map' of the process so you are aware of all the upcoming aspects of the project. In Phase 4, the researcher or research team begins to gather data. After collection, the data is organized into information in Phase 5. In Phase 6 it is assessed to determine its quality, accuracy, reliability and sufficiency. If the information is inadequate in this phase, the research team moves back to Phase 4 and continues to gather data. If the information is adequate, then the information moves along to Phase 7 where it is analysed into intelligence. This is a key component of the whole research process and therefore 35 per cent of the time allotted for the project should be left for this phase. After the information has been sufficiently analysed into intelligence, it gets disseminated to decision-makers in Phase 8. If the value of the intelligence is understood by the executives and if they have sufficient buy-in for the overall process, then they should make a strategic decision in Phase 9, after which the outcome can be evaluated for effectiveness in Phase 10. Any lessons learnt through this evaluation can then be incorporated into the next CI project, which takes us back to Phase 1, and the competitive intelligence project process begins again.

Phase 1

The first phase in any project is to determine your precise need for undertaking it. While this may seem obvious, sometimes it is not. There are, typically, four areas to address in your needs assessment. They are competitive threats, industry, market and duration. First consider the competitive threats that have prompted you to start the competitive intelligence project. Each threat may determine a different strategy for the research and analysis, so it is important to consider the threat at this stage. Besides, it helps to write it down for use during the project to keep you on target. Some examples of reasons why your organization might begin a CI project are: to help you take advantage of market opportunities; to determine likely merger or acquisition candidates; and to identify and determine the strength of partners for joint ventures in foreign markets. There may also be a new competitive threat to consider: a new competitor might have entered your industry and you are not sure what this means to you, an existing corporation might have launched a product that could substitute for yours, or your industry may be scheduled for government deregulation. There are many other valid reasons to begin the process. By better understanding why you need CI at this time, your organization will be more capable of meeting those requirements throughout the process and ending with satisfactory results.

Often the need for a competitive intelligence project is brought to the attention of executives by the front-line or operational-level staff. Typically, salespeople are in contact with suppliers, distributors, customers and sometimes even competitors, who may inform them of changes or advances in the industry that your company needs to be aware of. Or the employees working at the operational level may find weaknesses in manufacturing technology. Having a means in place to draw feedback from these employees can help management identify problems or weak spots to be addressed through competitive intelligence.

After determining the precise reason you are beginning your CI project now, ask yourself which industries you need to look at more closely. Before you scoff and answer, 'Obviously, the industry I'm in', consider that the activities in other industries could have repercussions on your competitive position in your existing industry. Start by considering technological advances. Advances in technology have ramifications in virtually every industry. We call this the 'law of technological influence' and we discuss it further in Chapter 6. Basically we are suggesting that technological advancements affect every industry sector. The higher the level of technology use within a market, the more influence it has on an industry or organization. Technology use tends to be directly proportional to its influence. An example of how this law works is: the consumer goods industry may be impacted by the services offered by US-based Accompany, which offers significantly lower-than-suggested retail prices through volume purchases of products advertised on its Web site. The company lists available products, suggested retail prices, discount offered, the number of people needed to purchase the item to receive the discount and the buying cycle for each product. The price keeps dropping as more people sign up to purchase a product. On the last date of the buying cycle, the final price that consumers will be paying is calculated. Should this type of service take off, it could have significant consequences on traditional retail shops and approaches for e-commerce.

Once you have established your needs at the industry level, it is time to consider which markets you need to learn more about for the particular project. This usually entails several levels. Consider the country, and then the region within that country if necessary, as well as the market or market segment you need to understand. This will better enable you to determine the resources you need in Phase 3.

Finally, consider the duration for which you need to forecast. Do you need to predict advancements for six months from the start of undertaking this project, or for three years? Do you need an answer right away for a very specific and urgent situation? Assessing your exact requirements will ensure you meet your needs at the end of the project.

To be effective in Phase 1, company executives and all people on the CI team need to work together. The respective roles and commitments of the various individuals involved in a CI project are discussed in greater detail in Chapter 12.

Phase 2

Phase 2 focuses on the formulation of a specific question, the end product of all the effort put into Phase 1. This question clearly addresses the primary requirement of the business at that point in time, for example, 'Is our competitor a lower-cost manufacturer than us?' and, if so, 'How are they doing it?' or 'Who would make an ideal merger candidate for us?' or 'Should we expand our wireless operations in the United States?' Phase 2 is successfully completed when everyone involved in the competitive intelligence project leaves the boardroom with one question that needs to be answered. With everyone on the same page, working toward a clearly defined, common goal, the CI process continues forward.

Phase 3

Phase 3 involves organizing the research and analysis process. This part of the process is typically best left in the hands of the CI practitioners and not dictated by management. This process should cover all the resources currently available, and those that will be needed, including human, financial, technological and informational resources. Table 2.1 provides a checklist of the skill sets your organization may need throughout the competitive intelligence project process.

Table 2.1   Assessing your organization's resources

Human resources
Does your organization have access to the following skills, either through people within the company or external contractors or consultants?

	Internal	External
Library research		
Internet research		
Database research		
Interviewing		
Company analysis		
Industry analysis		
Market analysis		
Languages (all that apply to the CI project you're working on)		
Project management skills		
Information technology skills (data management)		
Communications		

Table 2.1 *(contd)*

	Internal	External

Presentation
Decision-making ability

Financial resources
Do you have sufficient funds to cover the following?
Market studies
Industry studies
Databases/directories
Membership in strategically beneficial associations
Publications
Salaries
Consulting costs
Database or data warehousing software (if necessary)
Data mining or Web crawling software (if necessary)

Technological resources
Do you have sufficient technological resources in the
    following areas?
Internet access (number of lines and adequate access
    speeds)
Commercial databases
Software to store data (database or data warehouse
    software)
Software to organize or sift through data
(data mining or Web crawling software)

Informational resources
Have you obtained information from the following sources?
General
Commercial databases
Internet access
Publications of all trade or industry associations
Relevant market studies
Relevant industry studies

Competitors:
Annual reports of all key public competitors
Financial information of all relevant competitors
Marketing information of all relevant competitors
Operations information of all relevant competitors

Table 2.1 *(contd)*

	Internal	External
Distribution information of all relevant competitors		
Strategy information of all relevant competitors		
Suppliers:		
Annual reports of all key public suppliers		
Financial information of all relevant suppliers		
Marketing information of all relevant suppliers		
Operations information of all relevant suppliers		
Distribution information of all relevant suppliers		
Strategy information of all relevant suppliers		
Distributors:		
Annual reports of all public distributors		
Financial information of all relevant distributors		
Marketing information of all relevant distributors		
Operations information of all relevant distributors		
Distribution information of all relevant distributors		
Strategy information of all relevant distributors		
Government:		
Filings required by law		
Country studies		
Industry studies		
Market studies		
Economic statistics		
Demographic information		

Chapters 3, 4 and 5 look at finding the information you need, sources of information and electronic and online information resources respectively.

Typically we find that most companies do not assess their status and requirements in each of these categories. In some cases, they are extremely technologically astute corporations that do not recognize the extensive human role in the CI process. These same companies often mistakenly believe that they have all the information they need within their data warehouses (more on this topic in Chapter 9) and do not need to acquire more or go outside the organization to fill gaps; or they may be companies that are aware of the other aspects of the process but overlook technology's role altogether. By breaking this phase into four distinct categories, it is much simpler to determine any gaps that currently exist, how they can be filled and how to make the most effective use of the organization's resources.

The consideration of human resources should go beyond counting the numbe. ... people your organization can allot for the project. There should be a small intelligence audit of the skill sets of all the individuals who will be working on the project, so that their skills can be more effectively used. There should also be consideration given to people outside the company whose talents can be drawn on to fill gaps in skills at the organization. For example, is there someone within the organization who can accurately translate any foreign information that the researcher(s) come across? Some of the likely skills your organization will need to conduct an effective competitive intelligence project are: library research; Internet research; commercial database research; interviewing; company, industry and market analysis; the ability to speak or understand languages relevant to the project; project management skills; information technology skills; and communications and presentation skills.

Library research, or secondary research as it is also called, includes all the more traditional published sources of information. A corporate librarian, library technician or skilled researcher who is familiar with the many and varied published sources of information is a great asset to the competitive intelligence team. His or her library research skills help ensure that adequate data is gathered within the time constraints of the project.

Someone who is versed in **Internet research** is essential to most CI projects. Keep in mind that Internet research goes well beyond just 'surfing' the Net; it is actually knowing how to take advantage of all the resources above and beyond the Web, such as newsgroups, search engines and wire services. (This topic is discussed further in Chapter 5.)

Commercial database research is often a necessary part of conducting research for competitive intelligence projects. Because databases like Lexis, Dialog and the many other databases that exist have a steep learning curve, it helps to have someone who is already skilled in this area. This could not only save a significant amount of time, but also save money involved in accessing these databases.

Effective **interviewing** skills are critical to the overall process. Because so much of the valuable information gathered in CI comes directly from conducting primary research, an interviewer who has the skills to get people to open up is essential. This goes beyond just making phone calls and asking questions. Most highly skilled interviewers have journalistic backgrounds or have adopted journalistic techniques and therefore know how to get people to talk. They usually know the best ways to word questions to get information that is not tainted with interviewers' opinions. Executives who have had media training will probably be aware that there is far more to interviewing than meets the eye. Having someone on your team who has these skills ensures that your organization has adequate information to analyse in later stages of the project.

While it may not be fair to suggest that there is a single most important skill to the competitive intelligence conducted at an organization, if there is one skill that stands out, it is **analysis**. It is through analysis that information or knowledge transforms into intelligence. A skilled analyst is comparable to an alchemist – someone who is capable of taking valueless materials and turning them into gold. The analyst takes information and assists in its metamorphosis into intelligence. Company, industry and market analysis is essential to most CI projects. Analysis in competitive intelligence is diverse. For example, a market analyst may be very skilled in the examination and forecasting of a particular market. However, he or she may not be versed in the other analysis techniques, which may be more significant for a CI project answering a financial or operational question. In fact, the analysis portion of the process is so critical to the success of the project that a team of analysts experienced in using the many analysis tools may be necessary. (Company, industry and market analysis are discussed in Chapter 6.)

If your organization is operating in different countries or has multi-ethnic customers, there may be a need to understand the **languages** of the people or research you come into contact with in the competitive intelligence project. You will want to have people on your CI team who have a written and/or verbal comprehension of those languages.

Like other projects, the competitive intelligence process typically requires **project management skills**. The project will probably flow better if there is a project leader with the skills and experience in competitive intelligence to guide the project through to a successful completion. The project leader may be an analyst working on the analysis phase or an outside consultant who lacks an internal bias and who may have worked on many different types of CI project.

Information technology skills such as data management experience with databases, data warehouses, data mining, Web crawling or 'business intelligence' software may be necessary for sifting through large quantities of data. A person (or people) with these skills assists in organizing and finding trends or patterns in the data you use in your project.

Communications and presentation skills are necessary to present the intelligence to decision-makers in the most timely and effective manner.

This is not the same as report-writing skills. Typically, a voluminous report is counter-productive to the project, so the person you choose should have the capacity to be concise and to separate the wheat from the chaff in the information gathered. It may be necessary for this person to be able to produce a visual presentation of the findings if this is how management will gain the most from the information presented. (Presenting and using your findings is discussed in Chapter 8.)

You also need strong decision-making ability at the executive level in your organization. The entire process is wasted if there is no buy-in and decisiveness on the part of management.

After you have assessed your human resources for the project, it is important to consider your budgetary constraints. Competitive intelligence projects vary in the amount of funds required to fulfil the desired outcome. You should consider whether you have sufficient funds to cover market or industry studies, databases or directories, membership in strategically beneficial associations, publications or reports, salaries of the people you choose for your CI team and any consulting costs that may be necessary.

There are also technological considerations that you should assess. Consider whether you have sufficient technology in the areas of Internet access (both in the number of lines and adequate access speeds), commercial databases, storage software (like database or data warehouse software) and software to organize or sift through the data (such as data mining or Web crawling software).

Consider your informational resources as well. There are many different types of information or data that may be necessary for your project. You should consider the types that are critical to the success of your particular project. Typically, there is information that pertains to specific industry players, like competitors, suppliers or distributors. There is also government information and more general industry information. Be sure to consider the scope of your project from the perspective of your informational requirements. Some of the more general types of informational resources include commercial databases, Internet (World Wide Web and other online resources), trade or industry association publications, and market or industry studies. If your project requires information on specific companies like competitors, suppliers or distributors, determine whether you have all the information required on these companies or whether it needs to be gathered. Some of the information that you may need could be in the form of annual reports, or financial, marketing, operations, distribution or strategy information. Keep in mind that your particular project may demand more unique and innovative sources. If so, consider what they may be and whether you currently have access to them.

It is only after you've determined your organization's existing resources that you can adequately allot them to the competitive intelligence project. If there are any gaps, you can obtain the resources in each of the four categories to balance the needs of the project. Effective allotment of the human, financial, technological and informational resources at this stage will better enable the entire project to flow smoothly. Keep in mind that each project is unique and may require different resources. Some projects do not need much in the area of technological resources; others can be accomplished on a low budget. All projects, however, require sufficient human resources.

Phase 4

Gathering the data your organization needs to complete the competitive intelligence project effectively takes place in Phase 4. There are two main types of data collection that should be done simultaneously. They are: library research, which includes the collection of all print or electronically published data; and field research, which is also called interviewing. By conducting both types of data collection at the same time, you will be able to make more effective use of all the data you gather. For example, some of the print publications may lead you to industry experts whom you can call to interview. Conversely, by being aware of a particular market study when you call an interviewee, he or she may take you more seriously and offer more valuable data.

Phase 5

The fifth phase entails organizing the data into information. You may recall that in Chapter 1 we discussed the flow of data into information and further into intelligence. It helps to start drawing some loose connections between the data before taking it into the heavier, more analysis-intensive phase of turning it into intelligence. You have not actually put the puzzle pieces together, but you are more aware that there may be pieces that could be combined.

Phase 6

In Phase 6, you begin to assess the quality, quantity, reliability and accuracy of the information you've gathered. This is an especially important phase when conducting international competitive intelligence projects, since you may be stepping outside your area of knowledge and depending on sources whose reliability may be uncertain. This is also a particularly important phase when using the Internet for research, since the origin of the information may also be unknown, and its validity may be questionable.

Phase 6A

This phase is only relevant if you determine that you lack the information needed to analyse sufficiently and complete your competitive intelligence project. If you answered 'No' to the question 'Do you have sufficient information?' then you move to Phase 6A, which involves determining gaps – you need to consider any gaps in your information at this point. We have seen that companies that are new to the CI process or those that do not understand it often have difficulty in determining if they have sufficient information. This may be the result of inexperience and fear of making a premature decision. It may also be a symptom of the 'more is better' mentality that pervades many information-intensive pursuits. The former is often resolved through experience, evaluation and feedback from completed CI projects. The latter requires a paradigm shift. It requires an acceptance of the intelligence age.

You may discover that you are consistently running into problems in trying to collect a particular type of information. At this stage, you evaluate the possible reasons and attempt to come up with a different strategy to fill any gaps in information. You then return to Phase 4 to gather the data you need to continue the project.

Phase 7

In Phase 7, analysis techniques are used to convert information into knowledge and, further, into the intelligence your business requires. Table 2.2 (see later in chapter) illustrates that 35 per cent of all time devoted to a competitive intelligence project should be spent conducting analysis of information to turn it into intelligence. We have witnessed many organizations spending only about 10 per cent of their time on this phase, typically because they are unsure of how to do analysis. In Chapter 6, we examine a number of different analysis techniques, including corporate, industry and market analysis. New analysis techniques, as well as methods borrowed from other disciplines, are finding their way into competitive analysis projects all the time.

Phase 8

After the analysis is complete, the intelligence is disseminated to the decision-makers in Phase 8. It must be presented succinctly and effectively to ensure that executives understand the consequences of not acting upon the intelligence. Chapter 8 is devoted to the presentation and use of your competitive intelligence findings.

Phase 9

Phase 9 comprises making a strategic decision and acting upon it. The real value of competitive intelligence only occurs if it is applied to the actual competitive threat or other situation that has prompted the organization to pursue a competitive intelligence project. Surprisingly, many organizations conduct competitive intelligence only to 'sit' on their findings and procrastinate at moving the organization in a strategic direction. There are many stages at which a project can fall apart. It is amazing how often a competitive intelligence project can stay on track only to be derailed at the penultimate stage.

Phase 10

The decision, resulting activities and competitive intelligence process are evaluated for effectiveness in Phase 10, the final phase of the initial project. Some of the questions to consider in this phase are:

1. What resulted in the industry as a result of the decision we made? This applies to a specific competitor as well.
2. Were the results beneficial to our organization? If so, how? If not, in what ways?
3. Could we have made a better decision? What would it have been?
4. What information could have been used that was not found for this project?
5. What information or analysis could have been done to lead us to a better decision?
6. How can we improve the competitive intelligence process for future use?
7. What can we do to improve the results of the decision we made (to our organization)?

Any lessons that are learnt from evaluating the process, decision and results can be incorporated into future competitive intelligence projects. Thus the competitive intelligence model starts again, only with more intelligence than before.

Problem areas

Throughout the competitive intelligence model, keep in mind that there are phases that most people and organizations get stuck in to the detriment of the rest of the process and, ultimately, of their competitiveness. Table 2.2 outlines the recommended amount of time that should be devoted to any one phase of the competitive intelligence project. It is contrasted by the time utilization we have discovered following the evaluation of many companies' CI project efforts.

Most organizations spend almost 20 per cent of their time in the first two phases: assessing requirements and formulating the question. We suggest that these two phases combined should take only about 5 per cent of the overall time. Many organizations use the planning phases as opportunities to procrastinate. There are many other distractions; assessing requirements to proceed need not be a cumbersome ordeal. Often, we find that organizations do not ever formulate a question. We have found that by having a question in mind throughout the whole process, the CI project flows better, the resulting intelligence is practical and on target, and the intelligence is easier to disseminate to decision-makers, who are then more likely to be able to guide the organization in a strategic decision.

Another problem spot that most organizations find while completing competitive intelligence projects is their ability to know when to stop gathering data. In the information age, particularly since the onset of the Internet, there are immeasurable amounts of data available to us. Knowing when to stop gathering data to move on to other phases is crucial. Usually the analysis phase suffers for the data gathering compulsion. You can see in Figure 2.1 that Phases 4, 5 and 6 create a loop. If you repeatedly organize the data into information and assess the value of the information while gathering the data, you are more likely to be aware of when you have gathered sufficient data to proceed to begin analysis.

Acting upon the intelligence is crucial, yet it is often not completed. This is unfortunately the case with the final phase as well, when your organization is evaluating the effectiveness of the whole project and its results. Successful completion of these phases can guide your organiza-

Table 2.2 Typical amount of time spent on phase of a competitive
intelligence project (in percentages) compared to the preferred amount
of time spent on phases

Task	Typical % of Time Spent	Preferred % of Time Spent
Assess Requirements	15	<5
Formulate Question	<5	<5
Organize Process	5	5
Gather Data	60	25
Organize Information into Intelligence	0	10
Assess Information	0	5
Analyse into Intelligence	10	35
Disseminate to Decision-Makers	5	5
Make Strategic Decisions	<5	5
Evaluate Effectiveness	0	5
TOTAL	**100**	**100**

tion into a more competitive position within a particular industry or
market. If the phases are not completed, you are effectively crippling your
CI efforts and will probably have wasted considerable time and effort. If
your organization does not even start, however, the consequences are far
more serious.

finding the information you need

Information is everywhere. That is one of the greatest problems when conducting a competitive-intelligence project. The key to survival in the intelligence age is knowing where and how to get started so you are not inundated with valueless information. Knowing where to start will vary from one project to another, depending on the type of intelligence you require. For example, if you are looking for a publicly traded company's marketing strategies, you will start in a completely different manner from that in which you would start if you were looking for a private company's financial information. Determining an organized approach to finding the information can save you countless hours of research time. However, if new or different sources become available, your strategy must be flexible enough to incorporate them.

Where do you start? Where do you look? What is valuable? What is reliable? In the information age, we have been overwhelmed by the rate at which information grows. Some estimates suggest that online information alone is doubling every six months. It is impossible to comprehend just how much information is actually floating around the globe, but it makes the odds of the information you need existing very reasonable. Finding it is the real task. You need to know where to look and how to sift through the information, recognizing what you need and discarding that which lacks value to you.

This chapter teaches you how to find the information you need while making the most efficient use of your time. It explains the differences between primary and secondary sources of information, and encourages you to find innovative sources that go beyond the Internet, paid databases, market studies and other 'first choices' of information. It explains some fundamentals of effective interviewing, and teaches you how to find experts on virtually any topic, market or industry sector. It also discusses the differences between finding information on public and private companies and how you can overcome any obstacles that exist.

Researching companies

Conducting research on a company is one of the most common competitive intelligence tasks. Perhaps that is why CI is so often confused with competitor intelligence, which is really a subset of competitive intelligence. Every organization has competitors, whether it is a small or large company, a government department, or a non-profit association or charitable organization. If you think your company or organization does not have any competitors, think again. Even seemingly non-competing companies compete. For example, telephone companies and cable television companies never considered each other as competitors at one time, yet as a result of technological innovation they are now fiercely competitive. The entrepreneurial spirit that continues to grow globally means that more new companies form every day, presenting new competitive challenges to your organization. Knowing your competition is crucial for success. While it is possible to conduct business blindly in a vacuum, it is rarely the route to long-term business success. It is important, therefore, to be effective in researching competing organizations. While we have called this section 'Researching companies', many of the same rules apply to other types of organization as well. Many of the same approaches can be used regardless of whether you are researching a company, business unit, government department or non-profit (or not-for-profit) group.

Public and private company information

Finding information about public companies can be a rather simplistic task, since so much information is made available through government filings like those required by the US Securities and Exchange Commission (SEC). However, finding information on private companies can be a difficult and sometimes daunting challenge.

There are many different definitions as to what constitutes public, as opposed to private, companies. For the purpose of our book, we define public companies as any companies that sell securities or shares on an exchange to the public. Private companies, conversely, are those companies that do not sell securities on a public exchange.

Many organizations overlook the value in finding information about their private competitors. They reason that these companies are simply too small and not worth the investigative effort. They assume that conducting competitive intelligence to research private companies is best left for other small, competing private firms. That would be an oversimplification. While many privately held companies are small, not all are. People also wrongly assume that all private companies tend to be restricted to a particular market. In fact, many private companies are international in nature. Additionally, many private companies fulfil key competitive roles by providing valuable add-on niche services to their publicly traded counterparts. It is also very common for businesses to overlook that many private companies could make excellent merger, acquisition or investment targets.

While it is true that it is more difficult (for the most part) to find information on privately held companies, if you are creative and diligent this task can be simplified. The methods that we are suggesting here are applicable to any industry research regarding privately or publicly held companies.

Many people get 'bogged down' with thinking that their industry is different and much more difficult to research than any other. Do not fall into this trap. While it is true that each industry has its own particular nuances and variations, this type of mentality only promotes frustration and procrastination. All industries can be researched effectively, regardless of their complexity.

The techniques for researching private or public companies, for the most part, are very similar. Public company research gives you greater options and, perhaps, more accuracy in your findings. Most of the techniques we are supplying here can be used regardless of the type of company you are researching. The most critical part of company research is to think in creative terms.

Conducting your needs assessment – what types of company information do you need?

It is important first to conduct a small needs assessment to determine what types of information are really most crucial to you, regardless of whether you are researching a public or private company. We divide the types of information you may want to gather into 10 key areas to help you define your needs. These include company background, management information, corporate strategy, financial information, operational information, marketing information, sales and customer service information, product information, distribution information and employee information. The approach you take in your research efforts may vary depending on the type of information you want. For example, if you want marketing information on your competitor, you will not take the same approach as if you were looking for financial information. The same is true of company background information or operational information.

The same is also true if you need to conduct 'due diligence' on a particular competitor. The term 'due diligence' has its genesis in the legal world, but has come to mean something less technical in the world of competitive intelligence. 'Diligence' may be defined as giving reasonable care or attention to a matter, which is good enough to avoid a claim of negligence. While that may still sound like legal garble, it really means watching out for your own best interests. This is obviously essential when you are taking on a partner or looking to acquire a competitor.

The business world is full of horror stories of profitable, growing businesses brought to their knees because their principals did not do their homework when it came to foreign expansion, or partnering with companies or individuals with whom they were not familiar. You wouldn't leave your spouse or child in the hands of strangers, and it makes sense to take the same approach with your business. There are a number of ways to find out more about third parties anxious to help you succeed.

If you are conducting due diligence on a company, your research approach might be to find out its history and to talk to customers and business bureaux if they exist. Do background checks on the principals as well, to find out where they came from and whether they left a path of success or destruction in their wake. Check the company financial information, and determine whether there is a history of litigation. The actual news on the company may not seem too bad, but you should make sure that it is not. You should also remember that being diligent when you are considering business dealings beyond your familiar territory means checking on the government and judicial systems for evidence of corruption as well. From a competitive intelligence perspective, due diligence is a fancy way of saying, 'Prepare thoroughly before you make your next move.'

Once you have determined the key areas in which you want to find information, the next step is to break your needs down even further. In this case, if you want company background information, you could consider the different types of information falling within the category of company background that might interest you, such as the corporate history, ownership, key industry sectors or the perception of the company by the media or customers. The boxed section, 'Types of company information', will help you identify your information needs. At this stage, consider whether your research target is a public or privately held company (if you already know) and whether it is a foreign or globally operating company. We discuss the implications and unique challenges arising from researching foreign or global companies later in this chapter.

TYPES OF COMPANY INFORMATION

Company background

History of the company
Key ownership of the company
Key industry sector(s) the company is involved in
Perception of the company by media, customers, etc
Exchange on which securities are traded

Management information

Background of key corporate executives and advisers – there are typically six key levels of corporate executives and advisers to consider in the management of a company:

1. president, chief executive officer (CEO), chief operations officer (COO), chief financial officer (CFO), chief marketing officer (CMO) and chief information officer (CIO);

---

2. senior or executive vice-president;
3. vice-president of operations, vice-president of finance, vice-president of marketing, vice-president of informatics, etc;
4. board of directors;
5. legal adviser(s) – this may be a legal firm;
6. accounting adviser(s) – the person or company that audits the company's financial information.

The outside legal or accounting firm that is involved in the company may have key advisory roles that will enable you to know the company's approach. Consider whether the company is receiving advice from a law firm that has a reputation for being very aggressive in its legal stance. The company may also assume this posture in any of its legal and contractual dealings or other aspects of its business.

Company strategy

Company's focus (past, present and future)
Corporate culture
New product developments
Market entry strategies/new markets

Financial information

Revenues
Profitability
Fixed costs
Variable costs

Operational information

Facility information:
    Number of facilities
        Their location
        Size

Condition of facilities
New/upcoming/expanding facilities
Technology used in operations
Operational output

Marketing information

Key markets served
Market share in each market
Marketing and advertising strategies
Market entry strategies
Customers/clients served in each market

Sales information

Number of people on sales force
Key sales channels
Customer service information
Sales force compensation methods

Product information

Major product lines
Minor product lines
Sales information by key product lines
Specifications on products
Suppliers of raw materials, parts, labour or intellectual capital

Distribution information

Supply chain used
Shipping methods
Suppliers

Employee information

Number of employees

Number of employees in major employment categories (ie marketing, human resources, accounting, etc)

Salaries of major employment groups

Union information/collective bargaining agreements

Other information

Specify

Formulate your question

As we mentioned in Chapter 2, after you finish your needs assessment, you should formulate a specific, targeted question. For example, you may want to find employee information about your competitor: how many employees it has, how much employees in the accounting department earn, and how your employment contracts and benefits programmes differ from its programmes. Your question might be, 'Should we match our competitors' employment programmes?' As you can see, this is a very simple question, yet the answer is a decision that can be acted upon, once the data is collected. If you determine through your research that your competitor pays higher salaries and better benefits, you can decide if this is an action you want to compete with. If, on the other hand, you discover that your competitor pays less and offers fewer benefits to its employees, you can also decide if you want to maintain your position with regard to employment issues or lessen your programmes and salaries. Your decision may differ depending on the issues your organization is facing. For example, if your company is consistently losing employees from its accounting department to your competitor and you discover that the competitor's benefits and salaries are actually less than you offer, you might decide to maintain them and start focusing your attention on other issues that have been arising. Perhaps there are employee morale issues or management–employee conflicts that need to be addressed.

Organizing the process

Before you dive right into the research by gathering data to answer your question, consider spending a few moments organizing the whole research and analysis process. The time spent in this phase will save you countless hours of work created by not having any focus or organization in your data gathering efforts.

Once you are ready to start researching, take inventory of the things you already know about the company or industry you are researching. You may find that you know much more than you originally anticipated. Consider whether you know any of the key sources of information in the industry you are examining or, more specifically, if you know sources of information on your target company. You may already be aware of key associations and trade journals, for example.

Then consider what is available to you within the company you are working for. If you are researching a competitor, there is probably already a fair bit of information floating around your co-workers' offices or their minds. Take stock of that information or knowledge as well. There are many people in most companies who have relevant information for most competitor research projects. Your credit or accounting department may be aware of financial news that also affects your competitor. Your company library probably keeps files on your competition. Your labour union (if you have one) will definitely be up to date about any labour issues at your competitor's organization. Your personnel or human resources department may know salary information in the industry (which may translate into your competitor's personnel costs). It is also very likely that your competitor's employees send in CVs to this department, so there may be some understanding of the work environment at their organization. Typically, CVs indicate information about specific projects, budgets, number of staff being managed and more. If your company has a purchasing office, you will probably find that its staff already know a great deal about your competitor's suppliers or specific information about their purchases. Your public relations department may know your competitor's key media announcements. Your organization's sales force probably has a gold mine of information about your competitor's products, sales force and customers. They are typically in contact with all of them on a regular basis. Likewise, your marketing department may have some familiarity with your competitor's marketing plans and advertising campaigns.

Once you have determined what you already know, it is time to start filling in the gaps in your information by conducting research. Before getting too far, consider who else would have or need the kind of information that you are looking for. If you consistently ask yourself, 'Who else needs this?' you may be led to some very innovative sources and save yourself a fair bit of time and energy.

In this phase, you consider likely sources that might provide answers to your questions, and whether you would be more successful starting on the Internet, a paid database or by jumping into field research. In competitive intelligence, field research is also called 'primary research'. It is important to understand the difference between primary and secondary sources of information because they lend themselves differently to the outcome of your project.

Primary and secondary sources

Primary sources are those that have not been tampered with, are unedited and unaltered. Secondary sources are edited in some way. Examples of primary sources include speeches (unedited), phone interviews, annual reports and media releases. Secondary sources include magazine articles, edited speeches, rumours and analyst reports.

There are countless published sources of information available for competitive research: newspapers, magazines, trade journals, directories, books and reports on virtually any industry sector or aspect of business. Some of our favourite business periodicals for finding information on large multinational corporations include: *Bloomberg, Business 2.0, The Economist, Eurobusiness, Journal of Commerce* and *The Wall Street Journal.*

Typically, by the time news hits the news-stands, it is too late to help an intelligent organization act, instead of react; however, this is not always the case. A national newspaper in Canada released a story about the creation of a new regional airline as part of the fallout from the Air Canada/Canadian Airlines/Onex fiasco. Any existing carrier that gathered this news from the newspaper found out too late that new players were emerging in the regional airline markets. Yet an extremely valuable piece of information regarding an upcoming government hearing was mentioned in the article. This new player was about to discuss its proposal for entry into the regional airline industry in Canada. Access to the summary or minutes of this hearing would yield considerable intelligence about the strategies of the new competitor. It would just be a matter of finding out if the information was made available to the public.

It is important to attempt to confirm any information from published or secondary sources with primary or field research. Field research is significantly more important than research from published materials. It offers far more timely insight than can possibly be obtained from published sources, which by their very nature tend to be out of date quickly. There are countless field research sources that you can use. You probably do not want to use all of them in any particular project since you would be at the mercy of information overload. However, it is important to keep the many possible sources of information in mind as you are researching so that if you come to any dead ends, you may quickly discover an alternative route to getting the information you need.

The following sections outline some of the most valuable field research sources. Keep in mind that this is only a partial list. The actual research project you are working on may offer clues into other innovative sources. Each industry is different and may present unique sources as a result. It is important to stay creative in the completion of your research in CI. Some of the possible field research sources include the various advisers to your organization, colleges and universities, competitors, customers, departments within your own organization, distributors, embassies, government departments, industry analysts, investors, venture capitalists, industry associations, labour unions, librarians, media personalities, seminars, suppliers, temporary job placement agencies and trade shows. It is important to understand the types of information each of these sources may be able to provide you with, as well as their unique strengths and weaknesses with regard to information collection. It is also important to understand some basics about interviewing for any field research you may be conducting.

Advisers to your organization

Does your organization rely on any external legal, accounting, consulting or other type of assistance from advisers? If so, they may become a real asset to your organization's competitive intelligence efforts. Your lawyer, for example, will probably know of any lawsuits pertaining to your competitors and would therefore be an excellent source with regard to such matters. Similarly, your accountant or auditor may be able to explain the significance of fluctuations in your competitor's earnings, expenses, costs or other numerical data.

Colleges and universities

Colleges and universities are often hotbeds of research, which businesses can access. People there typically collect and produce both business and industry information. It is usually not difficult to find someone at a college or university who will be happy to impart his or her research or knowledge.

Competitors

Who would know your competitor better than your competitor? Much of the information you might need can be culled directly from your competitor. If a customer phones your competitor, he or she will probably get a fair bit of information on its products and services, or other relevant company information. While many companies will not divulge information directly to competitors, it can be gathered from them. If you are interested in learning about a particular company, you may consider, for example, becoming a shareholder and attending shareholders' meetings. Third-party research is also effective for gathering information from competitors. Many companies are willing to share information with their competitors in exchange for other information that might be of interest to them – all in the good name of healthy competition.

Customers

Customers or clients are great sources of field data since they are often in contact with your competition or know the flaws of your products or services. They are a great source of competitive intelligence. Typically, they are also very reliable sources, provided you are not prompting them with misleading questions. *Anything* can be proved in research. That is not what you are trying to do; it is far more valuable to use non-biased questions, which do not lead your interviewees into the answers you want from them.

Departments within your organization

Your company may be an excellent source for starting to find the intelligence you need for your projects or decisions. Consider the information that may be stored away in the minds of the people in personnel or human resources, marketing, sales, purchasing, operations, finance and engineering. They each have different strengths that could potentially add value to your research, depending on the nature of your particular project.

Distributors

Distributors, either yours or your competitors', often have some valuable input with regard to supply chain management.

Embassies, consulates and high commissions

Do not mistake these government institutions as useless sources of diplomatic rhetoric and foreign policy. These offices can provide leads to valuable industry or business contacts, assist in arranging meetings and, in some cases, produce detailed reports on domestic and foreign markets and industry sectors.

Government departments

Government organizations often have a great deal of information that you can use in your competitive intelligence activities. Which departments you approach will depend largely on the type of information you require in your research. Government departments typically have information on companies or industries regardless of whether they regulate them. They may only regulate particular activities or processes. Either way, they are great sources of information. If the company you are interested in is a supplier to the government, much information is typically available for public consumption under various laws like those on access to information or freedom of information. There are government records pertaining to procurement that may provide insight into your industry or its players. Ask yourself if your research target is in a regulated industry and, if so, find out which organization regulates it. Consider if your target has employees, since in many nations, information pertaining to labour is revealed. This could include working conditions or union disputes, for example. Emerging technologies are often registered with the applicable government departments. If the company you are researching emits potentially dangerous pollutants in its processes, it typically must file reports or obtain permits that government departments maintain. If your target manufactures consumer products, it may be monitored by a government department that oversees the safety of consumer products. If the trade is governed by measurable quantities, there are departments that ensure companies are supplying the quantity listed on labels. If the work environment at your competitor's company is potentially damaging or hazardous to employees, this type of information must be filed with the government in many countries. Companies or individuals are also required to register any patents or trademarks in the countries where they plan to use them. The appropriate government departments that register intellectual property keep files the public can search through for further information about the patents or trademarks. If your research target has been involved in any lawsuits, the courts monitor the results or progress. Typically, quite a lot of information that might be considered 'secretive' gets released during lawsuits. If a company is planning to expand its facilities, it usually must file building permits. When a company 'goes public', it opens up some of its information to government officials who regulate and monitor securities and exchanges of stock. Non-profit groups must usually file tax returns, which are made available to the public. If your research target is a non-profit group, this kind of information may be valuable to you.

Industry analysts/investors/venture capitalists

Industry analysts, investors and venture capitalists typically keep a close eye on certain companies or particular industries. As a result, they may have a fair amount of 'inside' information that may be valuable to your research efforts. Analysts tend to be conservative in their estimates, should they quote specific statistics to you. Keep that in mind as you are researching. They must make recommendations to investors, and are therefore often more conservative than other sources of information. Venture capitalists often keep their eyes on up-and-coming players within an industry. They may also have passed up the opportunity to invest in particular companies and this may provide you with some insight as well.

Industry associations

Most industries have associations promoting their interests and the interests of their members. While you may not be able to get specific information on a member from an association, they tend to be valuable sources of general information. They often publish directories of their member companies or individuals, and magazines, journals or newsletters. (We go into more detail on published sources of information later in this chapter.)

Labour unions

Labour unions can be valuable sources of information in the area of wage statistics, working conditions, contracts and collective bargaining disputes if you can find a contact who will speak freely on these subjects. This is more likely to occur if the contact feels that divulging such information will help further the union's agenda.

Librarians

Clearly, a skilled librarian will not only be familiar with using various information resources and tools, but he or she will also retain some of the contents and help point you in the right direction from the start. There are librarians at business libraries, academic libraries and archives; even municipal or local libraries have access to information you might need and can be valuable sources.

Media: journalists, editors, advertising executives

Media personalities can be valuable resources in your research. They tend to be less biased than other sources and usually have a 'beat' in which they are quite familiar. For example, there is usually a technology journalist or editor for most daily newspapers. The same is usually true of business. Often, journalists or editors have many contacts as well and, even if they cannot provide you with a lot of information, they can usually refer you to someone. Keep in mind when you work with the media, however, that media people tend to be extremely busy. This is especially true of mass media, particularly daily newspapers. Editors of smaller, industry-specific publications can usually offer leads into many up-and-coming companies, merger and acquisition candidates, financial information of companies and much more. If you are going to consult the journalists or editors, be sure to respect their time considerations. Ask for the editor or journalist who handles the specific topic of information you are looking for. If you are not sure who that is, call the 'newsroom'. Do not forget to ask if there are any special issues pertaining to the industry you are interested in. Be prepared to offer some valuable information in return, which could take the form of industry insight, trends you have followed, upcoming industry events or industry rumours.

Seminars/workshops

Seminars and workshops are often hosted by businesses or organizations that are looking for an audience of potential customers for a new product or service. Attending this type of seminar can yield valuable information. Conversely, the presenter may be an expert on a company or an expert from a company. He or she may also be an expert at leaking information, a talent that many people have but do not recognize.

Suppliers

Your company may have the same suppliers as your competitors. These suppliers may be very candid when they discuss their business with you. If you want to find out why your competitor uses a different supplier, it is perfectly acceptable to approach this business to find out the benefits of working with them. In doing so, you may discover some competitive advantage for your company by switching or you may gain some insight into the benefits or disadvantages that this relationship gives to your rival.

Temporary job placement agencies

'Temps' know a fair bit about many different companies since they have typically worked in so many. This makes them a valuable source of information about your competitors.

Trade shows or conferences

Trade shows are great places for really researching an industry or its many players, finding experts on a particular topic or following industry trends. All year long the same companies that attend the trade shows have typically been trying to protect their company information as confidential. Then, at the conferences, they reveal all the information that has been hidden the rest of the year. You find salespeople bragging about their products, marketing people revealing their upcoming marketing strategies, engineers or scientists speaking amongst their peers to reveal their research and top executives speaking about their corporate strategies, successes and failures at keynotes, seminars or in hospitality suites.

We define trade show competitive intelligence or trade show CI as 'the effective use of trade shows to gather intelligence about an industry or its players'. We cannot stress enough the value of trade shows to a competitive intelligence project or overall function. There are so many reasons why you should consider attending industry trade shows to conduct CI:

- Your competitors are probably already conducting CI at trade shows.
- You need to understand the many ways to protect your company at trade shows.
- You can make new and valuable contacts that may lead to 'inside' information about your industry. These contacts may be suppliers, distributors, manufacturers, competitors, media, analysts, researchers and others.
- Trade shows are among the best sources of competitive intelligence, such as:
  - general industry information;
  - industry trends;
  - discovering new competitors; and

     – finding information about existing competitors' marketing plans, financial information, distribution methods, operational information, management changes and overall company strategy.

We break trade show CI into three main stages of participation:

1. pre-show preparation;
2. trade show activities;
3. post-show analysis, dissemination, action and evaluation.

Few organizations ever really maximize their trade show participation from a competitive intelligence perspective. They spend far more time developing their booth, advertising and trying to identify sales leads.

Pre-show preparation

What you do prior to attending the trade shows can really determine your level of success while at the shows. Here is a checklist of the key things to do before you head to your next trade show:

- Find out who attended the previous year's show.
- Find out who is attending this year.
- Find out how the show is being promoted.
- Find out if the show has a theme.
- Identify key activities in addition to exhibit booths. These activities typically include keynote speeches, seminars, round tables, hospitality suites, gala events, cocktail parties and other networking events.
- Ask if there are any media/press conferences being held at the show.
- Determine your objectives for the show. These could take the form of 'to learn more about trends and other developments in our industry', or 'to learn more about a specific competitor', or 'to create a specific impression or deliver a specific message'.
- Prepare your questions and the approach you will take in advance of attending the show.
- Prioritize the information you want to learn about specific targets, which may include:
  - financial status;

- marketing strategies;
- sales techniques;
- product developments;
- technology use;
- personnel; and
- company expansion plans.

You should also put together a trade show CI team, which will work together to maximize the value your organization derives from the show. It should include people who can best help you meet your particular information-gathering needs. For example, if you are looking to speak to a key engineer at your competitor's firm to learn more about his or her research, you may want an engineer from your firm to participate on the team, as an engineer would be more likely to understand your competitor's engineer. The same is true if you are looking for financial information: you should then include a financially minded person on the trade show CI team. Consider personnel from marketing, sales, operations, technical, engineering and senior management, as well as outside assistance (if necessary), to participate on your team.

If you have opted to find specific information about a key company within your industry, such as a competitor, supplier or distributor, consider conducting a small-scale intelligence audit on both the target company and the individuals who may be attending the show. Then prepare key questions for the competitors' staff who will be attending the show, based on your needs. Afterward, assign the tasks to the appropriate team members. The small-scale intelligence audit could be as simple as determining the key people who will be attending the show, their department, their position and any critical information about management who will be attending the show.

Trade show activities

Once you have put together your trade show CI team and prepared all the tasks for the upcoming show, it is time to conduct those activities at the trade show. You should establish a team meeting place, preferably not at your own booth or display. We regularly observe companies whose staff always meet at their own booth. This really has the potential to give your competitors a great deal of information about your company, should their employees be taking note. The meeting place should be close to the exhibit floor, however, to allow for regular updates between your team members. Set consistent times to compare notes, look for any information gaps and plan the next steps. There is real value in scheduling these regular times, as it enables people on your team to share their findings, shed light on one another's ideas and better understand the significance of any research that's been done. This, in turn, enables the same people to build on that information while the show is still under way, rather than finding gaps when they get back to the office.

There are so many things to consider while observing the competitor's display that we have included a checklist you can use as a starting point. It is found in the accompanying box.

TRADE SHOW COMPETITIVE INTELLIGENCE TEAM TASK ASSIGNMENT WORKSHEET

Team member:

Area of specialization:

Trade show or conference:

Date:

Location:

Target company:

Booth location:

Description of the company:

Contact information:

Key questions to ask:

Responses/insights:

COMPETITOR/TARGET WORKSHEET

Name of competitor/customer/supplier/distributor:

Booth location and size:

Number of personnel at the booth:

Position (level of seniority) of personnel:

Advertising themes/slogans:

Types of graphic displays:

Types of literature provided:

Price sheets:

Media releases:

Business cards:

News clippings:

Description of new product demo:

Describe level of technical sophistication at the booth:

Interest of trade show crowd:

Types of question asked by attendees:

Seminars:

Title:

Theme:

Level of attendance and perceived interest:

Questions asked (by whom?):

Product demonstrations:

Product name and presenter name:

Product specifications:

Questions asked (by whom?)

Start by considering advertising slogans, graphic displays, types of literature provided, the overall booth 'theme', price sheets, new product demos and the level of technology and sophistication. Some of the things we have included seem obvious or unimportant; however, consider their value from a different perspective, perhaps the perspective of an outsider looking into the industry. You may discover a lot more value in information you might otherwise have overlooked. Consider regular sales pitches that coincide with the theme and slogan on the booth display. They might give you insight into an overall new marketing plan the company is starting to implement. As another example, if you found there were seven people operating the booth, of which six were key executives at the company, you could deduce that the company is not merely seeking sales leads from this show, but rather that it has some other motive and considers the show significant enough to send management.

Beyond all the visual clues to watch for, there are also many things to listen for. Listen to the questions being asked by others, to the boasting of speakers, references to future plans, recurring sales pitches, any competitor bashing, mention of any media or press conferences, and referrals to the hospitality suites.

When you are approaching the booths, do not misrepresent yourself. It has become so common for people to take off their badges to hide their identities that most exhibitors become immediately suspicious of anyone doing so. On the other hand, do not give away any more information than you need to. If you are asked your name, simply give your first name, not your full name and company information. If someone wants to ask you for more, he or she can do so. Knowing some key interviewing techniques can be especially valuable in culling information from key people at trade shows. Consider obtaining third-party assistance in gathering information at shows as well, since third parties will be less well known to your competitors.

Keep in mind that not all information may seem valuable at first. It is not necessarily what you are looking for. Rather, it may be a lead to more information. There are many leads to further information at conferences, for which you should keep your ears and eyes open. Consider that new products or services may be mentioned but not yet displayed, or there may be references to important future dates, or names mentioned of key or new personnel in the company. Other leads to further information may include mention of expansion plans, views about competitors and competing products, referrals to other people who might be considered 'experts' and, as mentioned above, keynote speeches, seminars, workshops and hospitality suites, all of which may be leads to further information.

As part of your meetings with your team you should ensure regular, timely exchanges of information with all the trade show CI team members to discuss the implications of findings and identify information voids that need to be addressed. Be sure that everyone retains their findings somewhere other than in their heads. While the findings may seem memorable at the time, they may be easily forgotten once everyone is inundated with more information from the show. There are usually so many names of people discussed throughout the duration of a trade show that even remembering them may be difficult once you are back in your office. If everyone on the team makes short (one page or less) notes on key findings, the information can easily be shared with other members of the team.

One of the things we tell people in our seminars is to act as though they know nothing while attending trade shows. They will then be far more likely to learn about the industry and its players than if they assume they already know most of the information presented to them.

Pay close attention to the level of interest of people visiting your competitor's booth. Do they regularly seem disinterested in the features of a new product your competitor has unveiled? If so, this might suggest features that hold little or no value to consumers or potential customers. If you talk to some of the same people (obviously, not at your competitor's booth) you might learn that they have a greater interest in some other possible feature that your company could work toward developing. You might find that you could learn what is really valuable to these customers and target your marketing strategies to suit them.

You should also look well beyond the booth displays while attending trade shows. Valuable information can be gleaned from hospitality suites, keynote speeches, seminars and workshops, cocktail parties, gala events, networking opportunities and other informal 'post-event' discussions that take place.

Remember, as far as seminars, workshops and other speeches are concerned, typically, the best information is provided after any formal talks have ended. Remain in the presentation location to hear the questions being asked by people in the audience. The answers may be more revealing than the information the speaker delivered during the formal speech or presentation.

Post-show analysis, dissemination, action and evaluation

The real value of all the information culled from the trade show experience is apparent when everyone returns to their offices. Remember that it does not matter what you do at the show or how much information you gather if you do not do several things when you return:

1. Analyse your findings.
2. Confirm your findings by using other sources.
3. Share your analysis with decision-makers.
4. The decision-makers need to act on the findings in a manner that improves the overall competitive position.
5. Evaluate the actions of the team to determine ways to improve upon each trade show experience.
6. Evaluate the effectiveness of the actions taken by the decision-makers to the overall competitive position.

So what exactly are you analysing? That really depends on the goals and objectives you set for yourself and your team in your pre-show activities. If your goal was to gather financial information on your key competitor, your analysis should be financial in nature and should cover whether you met your goals. You should conduct further research of a financial nature to substantiate or disqualify any research you gathered at the show. The same is true if your goal is to gather technology information. Your analysis will cover that aspect of your research. We discuss analysis in greater detail in Chapter 6.

Always consider alternative sources for any information you gather at trade shows to qualify the data further. Often salespeople embellish their products while speaking about them, especially while they are attending conferences. You should consider validating this type of information with non-trade-show-specific information sources.

If you begin to conduct analysis of findings from each trade show you attend, you can start to analyse how the competition or industry has evolved since your last analysis. You might also learn how your company has evolved during the same time. If you notice that a key competitor is evolving and growing much more rapidly than your company, you may need to determine the ways in which you can counter the competitive repercussions of this phenomenon.

Once your analysis is conducted, you should share your findings with key decision-makers within your organization. The best way to do this is to keep it short and to the point, since wishy-washy suggestions or long reports rarely result in action. The decision-makers will want to incorporate the findings into their corporate strategies to ensure that there is value from competitive intelligence efforts.

After action has been taken, there should be sufficient evaluation to determine the effectiveness of the overall approach taken in gathering the data at trade shows, as well as the resulting actions made by the company to incorporate the findings into the corporate strategy. Identify areas that could use improvement for any upcoming trade shows your company will participate in, as well as goals and objectives that may be helpful for the next show. Ongoing data gathering and analysis afterward may also prove to be beneficial at this time.

Trade shows are so valuable that we have developed several worksheets you can use to maximize your trade show participation. They include a trade show CI team task assignment worksheet, a competitor/target worksheet and a trade show CI evaluation report (see box). You will also learn some basics for protecting your company at trade shows in Chapter 13, 'Counter-intelligence: protecting your company from competitors'.

TRADE SHOW COMPETITIVE INTELLIGENCE EVALUATION REPORT

Brief review of trade show goals/objectives:
Level of success meeting goals/objectives:
Additional information collected:
Outstanding questions/concerns:
Potential solutions/follow-up:
Recommendations for future improvement

Researching private companies

The key things to consider when conducting research on private companies include:

- Typically, there are no single sources for information on private companies.
- There are no guarantees – only approximations. Finding information on private companies usually means estimating and making inferences, and is not likely to yield information that is down to the last decimal point. Instead, you get data that is approximate.
- Diligence is crucial. Getting the information you need typically means piecing it together from many diverse sources. This requires patience and diligence.

Researching public companies

Finding information on public companies is a much simpler task. In most countries there are organizations similar to the United States Securities and Exchange Commission (SEC). This government body regulates and standardizes information filings from both US and foreign public companies that trade on the US national stock exchanges. Some of the information available to you from the US SEC filings includes:

- the nature of the business and some background information about it;

- the types of products and services offered;
- the number of employees the company hires;
- the company's revenues;
- the markets the company sells to and the methods of distribution used in each;
- the names of the company's directors, officers and major shareholders;
- two years' balance sheets (that have been audited);
- three years' income statements (that have been audited as well);
- five years' net sales and operating revenues; and
- the company's total assets.

The states of the US also have their own regulations for firms selling stocks only within the state boundaries, which the SEC does not regulate, so remember to search at state level for any company information in the US.

Innovative sources

There are many very valuable sources of information that will be helpful to you regardless of whether you are researching a private or a public company. Consider how valuable the supplier to your competitor might be in providing you with key information about the company's raw materials. Who would know this information better than the company's own supplier? What if you wanted to know about the sales force at your competitor's company? Try asking your sales force. Typically, they will be in regular contact with customers who have also been approached by your competitor's sales team. Speak with customers directly. They are often more than happy to share their disgruntled dealings with your competition's salespeople with you.

It is important to be very creative in finding valuable sources of intelligence. Here is one example. A residential real estate investor, Sam Kolias, recently made the news for being innovative in finding investment properties. He made fantastic use of some unlikely sources to scout out apartment buildings and condominium properties that would be likely candidates for purchasing through his company, Boardwalk Equities Inc. Kolias hired former police officers and taxi drivers from the cities he was targeting to videotape and describe the neighbourhoods and buildings. Who would know the history, safety and general appeal of a location better than people who spent a great deal of time living and working in the area? His company purchased apartments that were in great neighbourhoods but needed improvements to maximize the value of his investment.

There is no single formula that can provide you with effective competitive intelligence. The key is to be creative, or to find someone who can be creative on your behalf. Working with 'experts' does not necessarily mean high-priced help, if for example you want to secure the kind of information this real estate investor needed. He asked a simple question: 'Who would know this neighbourhood's reputation for safety, security and appeal?' The responses he received helped his company determine its strategy for new purchases, renovations and rental prices, for example.

Information is everywhere, including the street. Harnessing it will help your business too.

Interviewing 101

It is valuable to learn some effective interviewing techniques to maximize the information culled from your field research efforts. It is not merely a matter of asking questions to get what you need. Getting people to open up to you to provide you with information that may not be available elsewhere is an important skill to master. Doing so helps the overall competitive intelligence process. Here are 10 tips to help you learn some of the basics of effective interviewing:

1. Maintain a friendly and casual tone. Never grill the person you are interviewing. In fact, the person should never feel as though he or she is being interviewed. The questions can be asked as though it is simply a friendly conversation. Salespeople have some insight in this regard. They have a common expression, 'Smile as you dial.' There is definitely value in this for interviewing.

2. Volunteer something of value in exchange for the information you would like. This is not about bribery. Rather, if you have some information that may be of interest, or a contact person that your interviewee might find interesting, make mention of it in exchange for the information you are looking to obtain. This should never be a negotiation or come across as bartering. Instead, you may wish to volunteer the information you have up front so that the interviewee feels more comfortable with you.

Never volunteer information that is confidential or that would cause damage if revealed.

3. Act as though you know very little. Often the best interviews are conducted by skilled interviewers who have little knowledge or experience within the industry in which they are conducting the interviews. This lack of knowledge can translate into people sharing or explaining more of what they know. Keep this in mind even if you are experienced within a particular industry. Do not assume that you know what your interviewee is discussing with you. You will glean far more valuable information if you do not interrupt or assume things that have never been spoken.

4. Do not ask yes or no questions. Yes or no questions will result in yes or no answers. In other words, you will obtain very little valuable information. By asking questions that require longer answers, the resulting information will be far more valuable.

5. Ask the same question in different ways. If your interviewee answers a question without providing much of the information you need, try asking the same question in a different way. This may result in the interviewee discussing the topic further with you and may lead to greater information.

6. Do not ask leading questions. Leading questions are those that imply a personal bias and may 'lead' the interviewee to give you the answer he or she thinks you want to hear and not the actual answer. An example is, 'Do you think Company X is experiencing financial difficulties?' By asking this type of question, you imply that you think the company may be experiencing problems.

7. Make mention of rumours or other information you have gleaned elsewhere. If your interviewee does not have the answers or information you are looking for, he or she may remember more if you mention some news pertaining to the topic that you heard elsewhere.

8. Pause. If you are doing all the talking, your interviewee cannot. Let the interviewee speak without cutting him or her off. If he or she is speaking about something that interests you but stops prematurely, simply pause. Typically, people try to fill the 'uncomfortable silences' in conversation. If you just wait, the interviewee may feel inclined to share more information with you.

9. Sometimes the best information comes from informal discussion after the questions have been asked. If you maintain 'small talk' afterward, the interviewee may 'open up' more.

10. Ask for leads to more information sources. At the end of every interview, always ask if the interviewee knows anyone else you should speak to or any other publications that might be of value to you. In this way, your interviews will not be 'dead end streets'; rather, they will lead to more information.

Always keep in mind that people have prejudices based on their experiences. An engineer who developed a new technology is likely to view it as superior to other similar technologies in the marketplace. Industry associations try to speak positively about the industry. Media or analysts, on the other hand, tend to be highly critical. Intelligent organizations must consider the motives behind the data provider. For example, why would the executive director of a prominent industry association refer to glowing growth statistics for the industry? Perhaps the individual's vested interest in the industry introduces a bias regarding actual growth potential in a specific market. It would be best to find an alternative source to verify the executive director's statistics, at the very least. An editor at a trade publication, a journalist specializing in the industry or even a market analyst may have less of a bias with regard to the subject. A quick cross-reference to confirm the data you have collected will increase your confidence in relying on that information. The more valuable the sources at your disposal, the greater the number of options you have.

It is also important to understand some of the uniqueness of interviewing people of differing cultures.

Tips for interviewing across borders

Competition is no longer confined within country borders. As a result, it is important for an organization to learn about its counterparts and competition in other nations. This may lead you to communicate with people who are proficient in different languages. Here are some pointers for improving your chances of getting the information you need by ensuring clear communication:

1. Prepare – conduct your research in advance. Learn the proper pronunciation of names, countries, cities or other places you will be mentioning. In this way, you are less likely to insult the person you are interviewing.

2. Avoid slang or industry jargon. It may be a regional term that is not understood by other cultures. Worse yet, it may have a different meaning altogether that may lead to confusion.

3. Avoid getting too personal too quickly. For example, North Americans have a reputation for moving business discussions to a personal level faster than many other cultures. If you get too personal with someone you are interviewing, you may insult him or her.

4. If you are communicating in person, observe the individual's body language. Body language often says more than most people realize. It may indicate when someone is uncomfortable or trying to hide something.

5. Be patient and be polite. If you are on the telephone, ask if it is a good time to speak – if not, ask to make alternative arrangements. People will be more likely to partake of your interview if you respect their time.

6. Pace your speech to make it easier for the person who is trying to understand you. This is particularly true if you are speaking with someone whose mother tongue is different from the language in which you are conducting the interview. He or she may need to think about what you are saying to understand it better. Many people have a tendency to mumble or speak too quickly. By making a concerted effort to pace your speech, you will probably find that you speak more clearly.

7. Respect age and rank. In many nations, age (older rather than younger) and hierarchical position in an organization are the gauges for respect. You may not get an audience with the person you need to speak with if you do not come across as a peer or equal.

8. Determine job responsibility in advance of your discussion. Jobs and titles differ all around the world and you want to be speaking to the right person.

9. Restate your questions using alternative wording. This helps ensure there has been no miscommunication. When conducting cross-cultural interviews, it is extremely important to restate some of your questions in different ways. In this way, you avoid misinterpretations.

sources of **information**

Knowledge is of two kinds: we know a subject ourselves, or we know where we can find information upon it.

SAMUEL JOHNSON

The previous chapter examined the different types of information sources available and provided some techniques for effective and efficient information gathering. This chapter looks at specific sources from around the globe that can help you with the information phase of your CI project. By now, we have probably convinced you that there is a massive supply of information at the corporate level, the industry level, the market level and the country level. When you factor in the global level, the sources of information seem limitless. We have chosen international sources of information from nine different countries: Brazil, Canada, China, France, Germany, Italy, Japan, the United Kingdom and the United States. Additionally, we limited our choices to easily accessible information sources: government and government-related organizations, associations and chambers of commerce. These sources are often excellent points of departure for more intensive information gathering within each nation. To go into greater detail would require nine more books, each dedicated entirely to information sources within that one country.

We chose the countries for various reasons. The US, Japan, UK, Germany and France are economic powerhouses, world leaders in a number of industries, and innovators. Japan and the US are renowned for their expertise in competitive intelligence, while France and Italy are more renowned for their reputation for espionage and government/industry collaboration in intelligence gathering on foreign firms. Brazil has the largest economy in Latin America, a very attractive and growing regional market. It is struggling with a number of issues that affect its development into a truly competitive economy in which foreign businesses are comfortable investing. China is a powerhouse waiting to happen. Like Brazil, it must get its house in order to be truly competitive in the global economy. Canada is the home of the authors and very representative of the level of acceptance and use of CI in more technologically advanced and industrialized economies: that is, most companies are not using it or believe they are using it when they are in fact conducting market research or information hoarding. The one common denominator among these nations is that they all are, or will be, very lucrative markets for businesses looking to expand. Competition from domestic and foreign competitors will become increasingly fierce. Knowing where to find valuable information in these countries will become essential.

There are a number of factors to consider when using international information sources. Depending on the country, the amount of data you find from diverse sources varies. Some countries, like the United States and the United Kingdom, produce a seemingly infinite supply of data on everything you could possibly imagine. This creates another set of concerns that we addressed in the previous chapter. Yet consider the difficulty you might run into as you attempt to develop a profile of the potential laptop computer market in China. Is there any historical information available to use for forecasting? Is there market research identifying computing preferences or technology users? Has anyone in the government or industry delivered a speech on the topic? Are there companies manufacturing laptops in China? Do they know the numbers? Will they share the information?

Information collection from international sources raises a number of issues. You may find that data from a particular international source is neither current nor accurate enough to be valid for your project. Motives for producing and providing information for public consumption also vary from nation to nation. A state-controlled media may sing the praises of industry growth within a country, but is virtually useless as an information source on businesses. Consequently, interviews and face-to-face research take on even more value in these situations. This brings up the issue of language constraints, which make certain international sources of information less accessible but no less valuable. Overcoming this potential obstacle is discussed further in Chapter 11. Despite these obstacles, an intelligent organization can make international intelligence efforts work. These sources are a good place to start.

Government sources

Despite a seemingly worldwide reputation for inefficiency and frustrating bureaucracy, many governments do manage one task very well – gathering information. This does not necessarily mean a government knows how to organize and use that information effectively for its own purposes, but it often provides a windfall for anyone looking for specific data on the competitive environment in which it operates, or for specific competitor information. Government departments and agencies that are responsible for patents, trade marks, licences, financial regulations and marketplace protection are valuable sources of information that is available to the public. Whether by telephone enquiry, formal request through access to information or freedom of information channels or some method in between, the government can deliver a wealth of information for your intelligence needs. The following sections indicate government offices, departments and agencies worth considering.

Ministries or departments of industry or commerce

Often considered the economic flagships of national governments, these organizations are responsible for supporting and promoting the national marketplace and driving investment in different industry sectors. As a result, they collect and produce huge volumes of economic data and statistics about national industry sectors, as well as information about foreign markets and industry sectors. The information may be somewhat dated, but is generally reliable and provides a solid historical overview for CI projects that require industry-level analysis. Often the reports or information provided from these departments also include contact information for industry experts or further more detailed sources, which further enhances the value of contacting these organizations first.

Ministries or departments of international trade or foreign affairs

The name generally says it all for these organizations; however, some play a greater role in the actual international trade and investment arena while others focus more on the diplomacy and policy issues. These organizations often maintain large and fairly current collections of market reports and studies, industry competitiveness reports and other trade data that focuses on countries, regions or industry sectors. Often these departments employ regional and industry analysts whose expertise can be yours with a simple telephone call. If they do not have the information you require, they may be able to give you leads to people or information that can help you. These organizations often serve as the home base for the embassies, consulates and high commissions located around the world. They serve as a clearing-house for the information that is gathered from these various markets and can direct you to an individual specialist in a country and industry who can provide you with more specific information, or direct you to a local expert in your area of interest.

General information offices

Many governments have set up agencies that act as information clearing-houses or guides to more specific offices where your information requests can be handled. While the individuals operating these services cannot be expected to know everything, they may be able to save you a considerable amount of time by directing you within range of the people you need to reach. In Canada, for example, you might consider contacting the Canada Business Service Centres (CBSC) located in each of the provinces. Typically, the CBSC can help you track down both federal and provincial government contacts in your area of interest. If nothing else, they can help narrow your search considerably, saving you time and effort.

Industry-specific and industry-regulating government departments

Many businesses have very specific information needs related to an aspect of their business. Perhaps your competitive advantage in an agricultural industry is compromised by a proposed change in agricultural and environmental legislation. You have a number of options at your disposal. You can contact the government organizations responsible for agricultural matters or environmental matters, as well as the legal body that reviews proposed changes to legislation. You may be able to speak directly with regulatory affairs specialists or individuals working directly on the project. They may also be able to inform you about the nature of the consultation (if any), the driving forces behind the change and your rights as part of the process.

Other levels of government

While the sources above are generally found at the national or federal level of governments, it is important to recognize the potential of municipal, county, provincial, state and other regional levels of government as valuable information sources. Businesses and individuals are required to file information at all these levels and many of the records are in the public domain. As hard as it may be to believe, you can benefit from the assistance of the public sector. After all, they are paid to deliver service to you.

One level of government that is often overlooked by North American information-gatherers is the European Commission. The concept of a transnational governing body with such an integral economic and social role is still relatively new to many information-gatherers in the United States, Canada and Mexico. The EC has been very public in providing information on policy directives, strategies and plans for its members and their interactions with one other. Any CI project that involves an industry-level or market-level analysis in Europe or in any of the EU Member States requires information gathering at the EC level as well.

Industry associations

Most countries have associations that represent the major industries within the nation. Some countries seem to have an association for every industry sector you could possibly imagine. The typical role of an industry association is to further its interests and the interests of its members within the nation and within the industry on an international scale. Individuals working at these associations, and the publications they produce, can be great sources of information in the area of industry developments and trends. Unless you are a member, however, it is unlikely that you will be provided with more specific information, such as details about a specific company. If you approach an association with a genuine interest in their agenda, you will probably gain some valuable insight, and perhaps leads to the more detailed information you require.

Chambers of commerce

Chambers of commerce work with businesses in their respective countries to help foster growth, profitability and competitiveness. In some instances, they wield considerable influence and can be invaluable sources of information. The difficulty is how to approach them if you are not a member. Some of the techniques described in Chapter 3 are certainly useful and you should never underestimate the value of joining a chamber of commerce to gain greater access to contacts and information. Remember, however, that business relationships must be built on trust and mutual benefit. You may find your involvement in a chamber of commerce provides you with great opportunities to gather information. Use it wisely and respectfully, and give something of value in return.

Sources of information by country

If your CI project requires information gathering in any of the nine countries we chose to examine in this book, here are some information sources you may want to explore. We have added more detailed descriptions to a select few, when we felt the name was not self-explanatory or the information source was very diverse, such as a multi-functional government department.

Brazil

Government and government-related organizations

Ministry of Industry and Commerce
EMBRATUR
SCN – Q2 – Bloco G – 3rd Floor
70710-500 Brasilia, DF
Tel: 55 61 224 9100
Fax: 55 61 322 2486

Brazilian Industrial Property Institute
Instituto Nacional da Propriedade Industrial (INPI)
18 Floor – Centro
20081-240 Rio de Janeiro, RJ
Tel: 55 21 291 1223
Fax: 55 21 263 2539

Secretariat of Foreign Trade
Secretaria de Commercio Exterior (SECEX-MICT)
Esplanada dos Ministerios, Bloco J, 8th Floor, Sala 812

70056-900 Brasilia, DF
Tel: 55 61 329 7085
Fax: 55 61 329 7075

Ministry of Foreign Relations
Ministerio das Relacoes Exteriores
Esplanada dos Ministerios, Palacio do Itamaraty
70170-900 Brasilia, DF
Tel: 55 61 211 6161
Fax: 55 61 223 7362

Associations

National Confederation of Industry
Avenida Nilo Pecanha, 50-s/2601 – Centro
20044-900 Rio de Janeiro, RJ
Tel: 55 21 534 8156
Fax: 55 21 534 8003

FIESP – Federation of the Industries of the State of São Paulo
Avenida Paulista, 1313, 5th Floor, Sala 505
01311-923 São Paulo, SP
Tel: 55 11 251 3522
Fax: 55 11 284 3971

Chambers of commerce

Brazil Chamber of Commerce
Avenida General Justo, 307-4
20-022 Rio de Janeiro, RJ
Tel: 55 21 240 7070
Fax: 55 21 533 1295

Canada

Government and government-related organizations

Department of Foreign Affairs and International Trade (DFAIT)
Lester B Pearson Building
125 Sussex Drive
Ottawa, ON, K1A 0G2
Tel: 1 613 944 4000
Fax: 1 613 944 6500

Industry Canada
235 Queen Street
Ottawa, ON, K1A 0H5
Tel: 1 613 954 2788
Fax: 1 613 954 2303

Industry Canada is the federal government's macro-economic flagship department, covering virtually every aspect of Canada's economy. It includes a number of marketplace regulatory agencies, as well as the Canadian Intellectual Property Office (CIPO). It also boasts a great business Web site called Strategis, which is discussed in Chapter 5.

Statistics Canada
RH Coats Building
Tunneys Pasture
Ottawa, ON, K1A 0T6
Tel: 1 613 951 8116
Fax: 1 613 951 0581

Standards Council of Canada
45 O'Connor Street, Suite 1200
Ottawa, ON, K1P 6N7
Tel: 1 613 238 3222
Fax: 1 613 995 4564

Canada Business Service Centres
230 Richmond Street West, 9th Floor
Toronto, ON, M5V 3E5
Tel: 1 416 954 4636
Fax: 1 416 954 8597

Associations

Alliance of Manufacturers and Exporters Canada
75 International Boulevard, 4th Floor
Etobicoke, ON, M9W 6L9
Tel: 1 416 798 8000
Fax: 1 416 798 8050

Canadian Advanced Technology Association (CATA)
388 Albert Street
Ottawa, ON, K1R 5B2
Tel: 1 613 236 6550
Fax: 1 613 236 8189

Canadian Council for International Business
350 Sparks Street, Suite 501
Ottawa, ON, K1R 7S8
Tel: 1 613 230 5462
Fax: 1 613 230 7087

Conference Board of Canada
255 Smythe Road
Ottawa, ON, K1N 6C3
Tel: 1 613 526 3280
Fax: 1 613 526 4857

Chambers of commerce

Canadian Chamber of Commerce
350 Sparks Street, Suite 501
Ottawa, ON, K1R 7S8
Tel: 1 613 238 4000
Fax: 1 613 238 7643

China

Government and government-related organizations

State Economic and Trade Commission
26 Xuanwumen Xidajie
Beijing 100053
Tel: 86 10 6304 5328
Fax: 86 10 6304 5326

Ministry of Foreign Affairs
2 Chaoneidajie
Dongcheng District
Beijing 100701
Tel: 86 10 6596 1114

Ministry of Foreign Trade and Economic Cooperation
2 Dongchang'an Jie
Beijing 100731
Tel: 86 10 6519 8804
Fax: 86 10 6519 8904

Ministry of Information Industry
13 Xichang'anjie
Beijing 100804
Tel: 86 10 6603 8848
Fax: 86 10 6201 6362

People's Bank of China
32 Chengfangjie
Xicheng District
Beijing 100800
Tel: 86 10 6619 4114
Fax: 86 10 6601 5346

State Administration for Industry and Commerce
8 Sanlihe Donglu
Xicheng District
Beijing 100820
Tel: 86 10 6801 0463
Fax: 86 10 6801 0463

State Intellectual Property Office
6 Xituchenglu
Jimenqiao
Haidian District
Beijing 100088
Tel: 86 10 6209 3276
Fax: 86 10 6201 9615

State Administration for Inspection of Import and Export Commodities
Jia 10 Chaowai Dajie
Beijing 100020
Tel: 86 10 6599 4329
Fax: 86 10 6500 2163

Associations

China Council for the Promotion of International Trade
1 Fuxingmenwai Street
Beijing 100860
Tel: 86 10 6801 2867
Fax: 86 10 6801 1370

Chambers of commerce

China Chamber of International Commerce
1 Fuxingmenwai Street
Beijing 100860
Tel: 86 10 6851 3344
Fax: 86 10 6851 1370

France

Government and government-related organizations

French Industrial Development Agency (DATAR)
23 rue Docteur Finlay
75015 Paris
Tel: 33 1 44 37 05 81
Fax: 33 1 44 37 05 90

French Statistical Institute
INSEE INFOS Services
Tour Gamma A
195 rue de Bercy
75012 Paris
Tel: 33 1 41 17 50 50
Fax: 33 1 53 17 88 09

French Foreign Investment Control Agency
Ministére de l'Economie, des Finances et des Industries
Direction du Trésor
Service des Participations et Financements
Bureau D3 Investissements Etrangers en France
Télédoc 267
139 rue de Bercy
75572 Paris Cedex 12
Tel: 33 1 40 04 04 04
Fax: 33 1 40 04 29 71

Invest in France Mission
Ministère de l'Economie et des Finances
139 rue de Bercy
75572 Paris Cedex 12
Tel: 33 1 44 87 70 21
Fax: 33 1 44 87 70 26

National Institute of Industrial Property (INPI)
26 bis rue de Saint Petersbourg
75800 Paris Cedex 08
Tel: 33 1 53 04 57 19
Fax: 33 1 43 87 74 68

Associations

French International Trade Association
Confédération Français de Commerce de Gros Interentreprises et du
Commerce International (CGI)
18 rue des Pyramides
75001 Paris
Tel: 33 1 44 55 35 00
Fax: 33 1 42 86 01 83

Chambers of commerce

Chamber of Commerce and Industry of Paris (CCIP)
2 rue de Viarmes
75001 Paris
Tel: 33 1 55 65 35 68
Fax: 33 1 55 65 36 92

Chamber of Commerce and Industry of Val D'Oise – Yvelines
21 avenue de Paris
78021 Versailles Cedex
Tel: 33 1 30 84 79 79
Fax: 33 1 30 38 57 34

Germany

Government and government-related organizations

Federal Bureau for Foreign Trade Information
Bundesstelle für Aussenhandelsinformation
Agrippastrasse 87–93
50676 Köln
Tel: 49 221 2057 249
Fax: 49 221 2057 212

Federal Ministry of Economics
Bundesministerium für Wirtschaft
Villemombler Strasse 76
D-53123 Bonn
Tel: 49 228 615 2158
Fax: 49 228 615 2652

Federal Cartel Office
Bundeskartellamt
Kaiser-Friedrich-Strasse 16
D-53113 Bonn
Tel: 49 228 9499 0
Fax: 49 228 9499 400

The Bundeskartellamt (Federal Cartel Office) is an independent higher federal authority that reports to the Federal Ministry of Economics. It is responsible for enforcing the ban on cartels and exercising the control of abusive practices, as well as merger control. For example, the Bundeskartellamt prohibits a merger if it is likely that a market-dominating position will be created or strengthened as a result of a merger, unless the firms involved prove that the merger will lead to improvements in the conditions of competition and that these improvements will outweigh the disadvantages of market domination.

Foreign Investor Information Centre
Scharnhorst Strasse 36
10115 Berlin
Tel: 49 30 2014 7753
Fax: 49 30 2014 7036

Associations

Federation of German Industries
Bundesverband der Deutschen Industrie eV (BDI)
Gustav-Heinemann-Ufer 84–88
50968 Köln
Tel: 49 221 3708 00
Fax: 49 221 3708 730

Chambers of commerce

Federation of German Chambers of Industry and Commerce
Deutscher Industrie und Handelstag (DIHT)
Adenauerallee 148
53113 Bonn
Tel: 49 228 104 0
Fax: 49 228 104 158

Italy

Government and government-related organizations

Italian Trade Commission
Instituto Nazionale per il Commercio Estero
Viale Liszt 21
00144 Rome
Tel: 39 06 59921
Fax: 39 06 5992 6899

Ministero dell'Industria e Commercio Ufficio Centrale Brevetti per
Invenzioni Modelli e Marchi
Via Molise 19
00187 Rome
Telephone: 39 06 488 0321
This deals with patent and trademark enquiries.

Presidenza del Consiglio dei Ministri Ufficio del Propriet Letteraria,
Artistica e Scientifica
Via Boncompagni 15
00187 Rome
Tel: 39 06 487 971
Fax: 39 06 4879 7727
This deals with applications and enquiries concerning copyrights.

Italian Anti-trust Authority
Autorità garante della concorrenza e del mercato
Via Liguria 26
00187 Rome
Tel: 39 06 481 621
Fax: 39 06 4816 2256
The Anti-trust Authority is an 'independent authority' instituted by law
in 1990. This means it acts independently, without interference from the
Italian government or parliament. In addition to its role regarding anti-
trust issues, it also has responsibility for ruling on misleading advertising.

Associations

National Association for Foreign Trade
Associazione Nazionale del Commercio con l'Estero (ANCE)
Corso Venezia 49
20121 Milan
Tel: 39 02 775 0320
Fax: 39 02 775 0329

Confederazione Generale dell'Industria (Confindustria)
Viale dell'Astronomia 30
00144 Rome
Tel: 39 06 59031
Fax: 39 06 591 9615
This is the principal trade association in Italy, covering diverse industry
associations.

Confederazione Generale Italiana del Commercio e del Turismo
(Confcommercio)
Pazza GG Belli 2
00153 Rome
Tel: 39 06 58661
Fax: 39 06 580 9425
This organization represents diverse industry groups in commerce and
tourism.

Confederazione Italiana della Piccola e Media Industria (CONFAPI)
Via della Colonna Antonina 52
00186 Rome
Tel: 39 06 699 1530
Fax: 39 06 679 1488

This industry association represents the interests of small and medium-sized businesses.

Chambers of commerce

Unione Italiana delle Camere di Commercio Industria Artigianato e Agricoltura
Piazza Sallustio 21
00187 Rome
Tel: 39 06 47041
Fax: 39 06 470 4342
This organization represents all chambers of commerce in Italy.

Japan

Government and government-related organizations

Ministry of International Trade and Industry (MITI)
1-3-1 Kasumigaseki
Chiyoda-ku
Tokyo 100-8901
Tel: 81 33 501 1659
Fax: 81 33 501 5997
The Ministry of International Trade and Industry (MITI) is responsible for all policies covering Japan's industries and foreign trade, with the exception of agricultural products and foods. MITI comprises three industrial bureaux – Basic Industries Bureau (iron and steel, and chemicals); Machinery and Information Industries Bureau (electronics, machinery and automobiles); and Consumer Goods and Service Industries Bureau (textiles, paper, housing and services). Additionally, the Industrial Policy Bureau promotes Japanese industries in general, and the International Trade Policy Bureau negotiates bilateral and multilateral issues in the international arena. Other bureaux include the International Trade Administration Bureau, and the Environmental Protection and Industrial Location Bureau. A number of agencies and organizations are affiliated with MITI, including the Patent Office. Here are some key contact points:

Research Institute of International Trade and Industry
Ministry of International Trade and Industry
1-3-1 Kasumigaseki
Chiyoda-ku

Tokyo 100
Research Division
Tel: 81 33 501 1511 ext 5123-7
Fax: 81 33 501 8577

Japanese Patent Office
International Affairs Division
General Administration Department
Japanese Patent Office
3-4-3 Kasumigaseki
Chiyoda-ku
Tokyo 100-8915
Fax: 81 33 581 0762
The Japanese Patent Office examines and approves (or rejects) patent applications for inventions, utility models, design patents and trademarks. Apparently Japan was the first country in the world to computerize the patent-application system. In addition to computerized patent filing and database searches, the Office also provides technical information, including advice on patents not yet being used, in order to stimulate industrialists to create new businesses.

Fair Trade Commission
International Affairs Division
1-1-1 Kasumigaseki
Chiyoda-ku
Tokyo 100
Tel: 81 33 581 1998
Fax: 81 33 581 1944

Japan External Trade Organization (JETRO)
Business Support Center
ATT Main Building 2F
2-17-22 Akasaka
Minato-ku
Tokyo 107-0052
Tel: 81 33 5562 3131
Fax: 81 33 5562 3100

Trade associations

Japan Federation of Economic Organizations
KEIDANREN
International Relations Bureau
1-9-4 Ohtemachi
Chiyoda-ku
Tokyo 100-8188
Tel: 81 33 3279 1411
Fax: 81 33 5255 6255

KEIDANREN is a national organization comprising over 1,000 of Japan's leading corporations (including more than 60 foreign firms) and over 100 industry-wide groups representing such major sectors as manufacturing, trade, distribution, finance and energy. It focuses on issues relating to the business community in Japan and abroad, and works toward furthering the development of the Japanese and international economies.

Japan Foreign Trade Council, Inc
International Affairs Department
World Trade Center Building
2-4-1 Hamamatsu-cho
Minato-ku
Tokyo 105-6106
Tel: 81 33 3455 5950
Fax: 81 33 3435 5979

Chambers of commerce

Japan Chamber of Commerce and Industry
International Division
Tosho Building
3-2-2 Maranouchi
Chiyoda-ku
Tokyo 100-0005
Tel: 81 33 3283 7607
Fax: 81 33 3216 6497

United Kingdom

Government and government-related organizations

Department of Trade and Industry (DTI)
123 Victoria Street
London SW1H 0NN
Tel: 44 020 7215 5000
Fax: 44 020 7215 6739
In the same vein as Industry Canada mentioned above, the DTI is the UK's full service government department. It seems to have its fingers in every pie that relates to economic development in the UK.

Central Office of Information
Hercules Road
London SE1 7DU
Tel: 44 020 7928 2345
Fax: 44 020 7928 5037

Central Statistical Office
Great George Street
London SW1P 3AQ
Tel: 44 020 7270 3000

Patent and Trademark Office
Concept House
Cardiff Road
Newport NP9 1RH
Tel: 44 1645 5005

Associations

Association of British Chambers of Commerce
9 Tufton Street
London SW1P 3QB
Tel: 44 020 7565 2000
Fax: 44 020 7565 2049

Confederation of British Industry
Centre Point
103 New Oxford Street
London WC1A 1DU
Tel: 44 020 7379 7400
Fax: 44 020 7240 1578

Chambers of commerce

The British Chambers of Commerce
Manning House
22 Carlisle Place
London SW1P 1JA
Tel: 44 020 7565 2000

International Chamber of Commerce
14–15 Belgrave Square
London SW1X 8PS
Tel: 44 020 7823 2811
Fax: 44 020 7235 5447

London Chamber of Commerce and Industry
33 Queen Street
London EC4R 1AP
Tel: 44 020 7248 4444
Fax: 44 020 7489 0391

United States

Government and government-related organizations

US Department of Commerce
14th Street and Constitution Avenue, NW
Washington, DC 20230
Business Liaison Office
Tel: 1 202 482 1360
Fax: 1 202 482 4054
This is the primary contact point for services offered by the Department of Commerce. It is another example of one of these government institutions that addresses so many information needs that it is hard to know where to look first. Here are some of the offices and agencies that fall under its umbrella.

Economic and Statistics Administration (ESA)
HCHB Room 4858
Washington, DC 20230
Tel: 1 202 482 1986
This is a collection of offices that handle statistical information gathered by the US government. Much of this information is made available to the public through the following agencies:

- The Bureau of the Census – conducts most surveys of both businesses and households to create economic indicators.
- The Bureau of Economic Analysis – analyses data to develop an overall picture of the US economy. The Bureau has information on economic growth, regional development and the US position *vis-à-vis* the rest of the world.
- STAT-USA – an information service for economic, business and social/environmental programme data produced by more than 50 federal sources.

US Patent and Trademark Office (PTO)
General Information Services
Crystal Plaza 3, Room 2C02
Washington, DC 20231
Tel: 1 703 308 4357
Fax: 1 703 305 7786
The PTO is a non-commercial federal entity that employs over 5,000 full-time staff to run its operations, consisting primarily of the examination and issuance of patents and trademarks. Of course the PTO also shares patent and trademark information. While they do this 'to promote an understanding of intellectual property protection and facilitate the developments and sharing of new technologies world wide', it can also provide you with some valuable information in your information-gathering efforts.

International Trade Administration
14th Street and Constitution Avenue, NW
Washington, DC 20230
Tel: 1 203 377 4767
With offices across the US and the world, the ITA mandate is to help US businesses succeed globally. There is a considerable amount of information available to anyone who wants to ask for it.

Securities Exchange Commission
SEC Headquarters
450 Fifth Street, NW
Washington, DC 20549
Tel: 1 202 942 7040
Electronic Data Gathering Analysis and Retrieval System (EDGAR)
Tel: 1 203 852 5666
Fax: 1 203 852 5667

Central Intelligence Agency (CIA)
Do not be alarmed. The CIA publishes a document entitled *The World Factbook* in printed, CD ROM and Internet versions. It is chock-full of interesting information on numerous countries, and serves as a great background document when researching and analysing industries or markets in specific countries. It can be obtained from the following sources:

Superintendent of Documents
PO Box 371954
Pittsburgh PA 15250-7954 T
Tel: 1 202 512 1800
Fax: 1 202 512 2250

National Technical Information Service
5285 Port Royal Road
Springfield VA 22161
Tel: 800 553 6847 (only in the US) or 1 703 605 6000 (for outside US)
Fax: 1 703 605 6900

You can also link directly to the CIA Web site at http://www.cia.gov for the online version.

Associations

Encyclopedia of Associations
This publication contains data on over 22,000 trade, business and commercial associations in the United States. It includes short descriptions of each association and provides the address, name of the executive director, number of members and the organization's publications. It is updated annually. It is published by the Gale Research Company, Detroit, MI, and edited by Frederick Ruffner.

National Trade and Professional Associations of the United States
This publication lists trade associations, technology organizations, labour unions (with national membership) and professional societies that are located in the United States. It is indexed by subject, geographical location, budget, executives and acronyms. It is published by Columbia Books, Washington, DC.

Chambers of commerce

There are chambers of commerce in most major cities throughout the United States. To find a particular US chapter, contact:
United States Chamber of Commerce
1615 H St NW
Washington, DC 20062
Tel: 1 202 659 6000
Fax: 1 202 463 3190

Other sources of information

In this chapter, we have touched on a few important sources of information in these various countries. However, we have barely scratched the surface of international sources of information. Regardless of the country in which you are conducting your research and information gathering, you can look for comparable sources to those listed above in any nation around the globe. Additionally, you can find the national equivalents of the other primary and secondary sources we mentioned in the previous chapter, but which are too numerous to list in detail. These include:

- advisers to your international operations;
- affiliates of your organization around the world;
- analysts and consultants with expertise in international markets and businesses;
- business publications and periodicals from various countries;
- colleges, universities and other academic institutions in other countries;
- competitors in other countries;
- customers in other countries;
- directories of international business;
- distributors handling your foreign distribution channels;
- embassies, consulates and high commissions;
- industry analysts, investors and venture capitalists in foreign markets;
- labour unions in other countries;

- libraries in other countries;
- suppliers in other countries;
- telephone directories and the Yellow Pages; and
- trade shows in other countries.

online and electronic
sources of information

Truly great madness cannot be achieved without significant intelligence.

HENRIK TIKKANEN

This chapter is about mastering the Internet in your research efforts, instead of letting it master you. With the exorbitant amount of information at your disposal online, it is important to have a thorough grasp of some of the key sources and techniques to use, otherwise you may find the whole experience of being online maddening.

If you rely heavily on the Internet for your 'intelligence'-gathering, keep in mind that whoever nicknamed it the 'information superhighway' seemed to have understood how far along in the process the information on the Net is – it really is just information, not intelligence.

However, there is plenty of value in using the Internet during competitive intelligence projects. We discuss some essentials to maximize your effective use of the Internet: techniques and sources to consider while researching companies or industries; Web sites to locate media publications, wire services or e-newsletters; some government sites; sites that can assist you while trying to find people for your field research efforts; sites that can help you locate industry associations and non-profit organizations or consumer and industry discussion groups; places to identify trade shows and conferences pertaining to specific industries; and stock markets online. As well, we describe search engines and directories, agents and bots, sources to use to stay abreast of developments in competitive intelligence and ways to retain your anonymity while researching online. The list of sources is in no way complete, as an effort of that magnitude could only be housed online; rather, it is a starting point to help you use the Internet more effectively in all your competitive research projects.

Internet essentials

Here are some general considerations to keep in mind when using the Net for your CI research:

1. Stay focused. The volume of data and information available online makes it more important than ever to be very specific about what you are trying to achieve and exactly what type of information will enable you to meet that goal. Otherwise, you may find yourself stranded in cyberspace with stacks of printouts from Web pages to your credit at the end of many hours online. Focus your needs into a specific question that you can keep in mind throughout the process of gathering data. Turning your objectives into a single, focused question will help you to clarify your needs, enabling you to stay on target while surfing online. The same is true if you are using commercial electronic databases. However, people are more inclined to stay focused when using Dialog, Lexis/Nexis, Dow Jones, Hoovers or any of the other paid services simply because they are paying for the information available to them.
2. Consider the accuracy of the sites you are visiting. There are many 'spoof' sites online hosted by people trying to deflect attention from the real Web sites. There may be people posting misinformation to newsgroups. Take a close look at the accuracy of the information.
3. How reliable is your source? Look into the reliability of the market studies, white papers or other information circulating on the Web.
4. Verify any facts you are using in your CI project with non-Internet (preferably non-published) sources. This is an extremely important component of competitive intelligence – that the data and information being used to analyse organizations be reliable.
5. Know when to stop. While there is a significant amount of information online, beware that there is a significant amount

of information online. That fact is both an advantage and a disadvantage to the competitive intelligence process. You may find plenty of information that will be helpful, but knowing when to stop and move to the next phase of the project is also very important, particularly because information becomes stale very quickly. Decision-makers at organizations need to make strategic decisions in the most timely and effective manner. Wasting time trying to exhaust all the sources of information on a topic is counterproductive.

6. Try different search engines and databases. Not all search engines are equal. Not all engines are even engines. Some are more like databases. Get to know how to use them effectively, but don't get stuck on one or two. Move around between them. This is especially crucial if you are gathering data from international sources. Some of the engines just don't scan as much of the Web outside the United States.

7. If you're conducting competitive intelligence research about international organizations and need translations of the material, start with an engine like Alta Vista that offers this service (unless you have an existing system in place for translating sites).

8. Keep in mind the types of information you may be missing. In some parts of the world, the Internet has not become a part of everyday life. It's not good enough to know the kind of information you've obtained; you must also be aware of the relevance of what you don't have.

9. There are many different types of places to start searching for information online, including: government sites and databases; company Web sites (including competitors, of course); trade associations; online corporate directories; various publications like newspapers, magazines and trade journals; trademark repositories; paid news services; wire services for media releases that didn't make it to publication; career sites for job listings (these are becoming more common); newsgroups; and forums.

While many competitive intelligence practitioners still consider the Internet *passé* when it comes to conducting valuable research, it offers the skilled online researcher valuable data in many different forms. It is crucial to understand some essentials of researching online to benefit fully from its vast resources. The Net can enable you to locate contact information for people or businesses, find your competitors' financial information, monitor the news for any advances in the industry, identify key associations and publications that may have inside information on your industry or specific companies within it, or learn what consumers are saying that may be disparaging to your reputation. This is just the tip of the iceberg. The Internet offers so many other opportunities to give your organization the competitive edge it needs; it is merely knowing how to wade through the vast amount of fool's gold to find the real gems.

Finding information on companies

The first place most researchers find themselves online is on their competitors' Web sites. While this may seem like an obvious and rather basic source of information, none the less it is still very valuable. Most organizations use their Web site as a promotional tool where they host the most current announcements, provide information to keep their customers and shareholders satisfied, and often to generate new business as well. As a result, many corporate sites provide their annual reports, product specifications, news articles, media releases, information about partnerships, strategies and company principals.

If you are unsure of where to find your competitors' Web sites, you can find out rather simply by just calling the organization itself, or try visiting the sites that list domain name registrations like Network Solutions or Whois.net. Obviously you can also try guessing. Just keep in mind the many different extensions currently in use online, such as .com, .net, .org, .web and .gov. There are also many different country extensions being used with domain names. In the United States, there is rarely a country extension, but in Canada, the .ca extension is often used. In the United Kingdom, you may see .uk, or in Japan you will typically see .jp in use.

Network Solutions

You can also search through Network Solutions' 'Who Is' database to find out when a company registered its domain name, the name of the person responsible for its administration, the person responsible for technical maintenance, phone, fax, address and information about the company's server. Or, conversely, enter the company name to learn all the domain names that are registered to it and whether or not each domain is being used. This information can actually provide some understanding of the company's strategic direction. Organizations typically register a domain name when they have plans to unveil a new product, product line, service, business unit or subsidiary. Many companies buy domain names for generic products that they may be focusing on. Here are some examples of companies that own more than one Web site domain:

- Procter and Gamble owns criscokitchen.com and total-affect.com.
- IBM owns www.torolab, www.ibm.com, www.kewleststuff.com, www.gateway.boulder.ibm.com and www.wwwibm.com.
- Toshiba owns www.toshiba-europe.com, www.toshiba-tuk.com (UK), www.tacp.com (Toshiba America Consumer Products), www.lvlalliance.com (Toshiba America Electronic Components, Inc), www.beyondmobile.com (Toshiba America Information Systems, Inc), www.toshiba-copier.com and www.copiersandfax. com. Toshiba America Inc owns www.dvdcca.org. Toshiba America Medical Systems owns www.yes-you-can.com, and also www. networkcopiers.com, which was registered in February 1999. When you visit that Web site, it automatically transfers you to www.toshiba.com on their copier and fax page. When you visit the site and conduct a search on network copier, you learn about a copier that allows users to configure the copier from their desktops (which are, of course, hooked up to a network). An analyst could have guessed what a network copier was and determined from the fact that Toshiba registered the domain name that they expect it to be a relatively large line of copiers at some point; they expect people to guess at a Web site address for one as www.networkcopiers.com, at which point they are sent directly to Toshiba.

Keep in mind that you should use the full name of the company when you are searching for domain names or you may end up with irrelevant ones. The Web site address for Network Solutions is www. networksolutions.com. The direct address of its 'Who Is' database is www.networksolutions.com/cgi-bin/whois/whois.

There are many other great Web sites where you can find valuable information about specific companies, particularly if you are looking for publicly traded companies. However, don't give up if you are looking for information about a private company or a subsidiary of a company. Information on these types of companies can often still be found online. Since public companies must report certain financial information to their shareholders and organizations similar to the United States Securities and Exchange Commission (SEC), it is much easier to find information about them. Identify the stock ticker symbol for the public company you are researching. This will better enable you to locate the company on the sites you visit afterward.

Many international companies do not have their ticker symbols listed on such sites, but you can usually find this type of information on the Web sites of the major international stock exchanges as well, or you can sometimes find this type of information on sites like Yahoo! For US sites you can also visit the Web site for the US SEC, where it has a database of the companies who file reports with them, called EDGAR or the 10K Wizard (after the name of the annual reports that companies must file, called 10K reports). Most countries have a government department that is comparable to the US SEC.

Yahoo! Ticker Symbol Lookup

Yahoo! Ticker Symbol Lookup allows you to search for a company's ticker using any part of the company's name, mutual fund, market index or corporate bond information. If that fails, it also provides an alphabetical listing of companies.

Once you have identified the ticker symbol, it is much easier to locate the information you want on a particular company. There are many great Web sites that host information about thousands of companies. They include sites like Hoover's Online, CorpTech Database of High-Tech Companies, Invest-O-Rama Company Research or Quotes, Infoseek's Industry Watch, Kompass, Wright Research Center, Yahoo! Finance and many others. We list some of the sites you can use below.

Companies Online

Companies Online hosts a database of companies who have registered on the site. It enables you to search for companies by industry type, geographic area or ticker symbols. It includes over 100,000 companies, both private and public, and links to the companies' Web sites.

Web site: www.companiesonline.com

CorpTech Database of High-Tech Companies

CorpTech collects company research on over 50,000 high-tech manufacturers and developers. It is a great place to find information on privately held technology firms since 80 per cent of its database consists of private companies. You can also search this database by product code.

Web site: www.corptech.com

Daily Stocks

If you are looking for information about stocks, here is the Web site for you. It contains countless links to many different stock-related Web sites.

Web site: www.dailystocks.com

Dun & Bradstreet

If you are looking for financial information about a company, try the well-reputed Dun & Bradstreet credit checks and company reports available for purchase through its Web site. The site also hosts economic analyses and industry surveys.

Web site: http://dnb.com

Hoover's Online

Hoover's Online is a paid database and we therefore include information about it in the section below, 'Paid commercial databases'; however, since it also includes some free company profiles that can be quite valuable, it is a useful site to add here. Hoover's Online UK is comparable to the North American counterpart.

Web sites: www.hoovers.com and www.hoovers.co.uk

Infoseek's Industry Watch

Not just another search tool, Infoseek has a valuable section on industry information called Industry Watch that provides you with current headlines, stock information, company information and more.

Web site: http://infoseek.newsreal.com

Invest-O-Rama Company Research and Invest-O-Rama Quotes

Invest-O-Rama Company Research provides links to SEC filings, articles, stock quotations and more for many companies. Its Quotes section allows you to search for numerous stock quotes at the same time, displaying the results in a visual format for easy comparison.

Web site: www.moneynet.com

Kompass

Kompass allows you to search from its databases of over 1.5 million companies in 66 countries, 23 million products and services, 2.7 million executives' names and over 400,000 trade and brand names. What more can we say?

Web site: www.kompass.com

US Public Registrar's Annual Report Service

The US Public Registrar's Annual Report Service offers thousands of US annual reports available free of charge directly from the Web site at www.prars.com.

Wright Research Center

Wright Research Center's Web site provides detailed analysis on over 18,000 companies worldwide, whether they be in Egypt, Hong Kong, Venezuela or Zimbabwe. You can search by country for over 50 different nations or search by company name or search by industry to obtain company profiles. The site lets you choose from over 20 industries. Your output can be received in any of seven different languages including German, English, Italian and Spanish.

Web site: http://profiles.wisi.com

Yahoo!

Yahoo! has a company listings subdirectory, which links to approximately 500,000 company Web sites. For each, the site attempts to include address, phone numbers of the company offices and, sometimes, annual reports, financial statements and media releases.

Web site: http://dir.yahoo.com/Business_and_Economy/Companies

Industry information

Getting an overview of the industry is a crucial part of any business research and a better understanding of the industry will certainly help an organization define its place within it. There are countless sources of general industry information, but here are several well-known ones, including Dow Jones Business Directory, the Federation of International Trade Associations, Hoover's Industry Snapshots, Industry Research Desk, the Michigan Electronic Library, Tradeport and Yahoo! Industry News.

Dow Jones Business Directory

Dow Jones Business Directory offers a set of reviews of what it considers the top Web sites for business information, broken down by industry sector.

Web site: http://bd.dowjones.com

The Federation of International Trade Associations

Looking for international trade associations? Look no further than the Federation of International Trade Associations. It is a network of over 300,000 companies from 300 international trade associations in the United States, Canada and Mexico. The site provides a directory of its member associations, a searchable database of upcoming events, listings of trade opportunity leads and an index of over a thousand international trade Web sites.

Web site: www.fita.org

Global Trade Point Network

This site hosts a wealth of information about trade opportunities, trade regulations, banking practices and market intelligence. It also provides information about global electronic commerce and other trade-related news.

Web site: www.unicc.org/untpdc/gtpnet

Glocom

This is a site that was developed by the Center for Global Communications, International University of Japan. It gives you access to current news that is relevant to the world of global communications and even provides several years of archived news. It also provides valuable information about the Japanese business environment through its section entitled 'Views from Japan', which attempts to provide a forum for the perspectives of Japanese businesspeople, government officials, social critics and academics.

Web site: www.glocom.ac.jp

Hoover's Industry Snapshots

Hoover's Industry Snapshots is an overview of certain industries with links to other sites.

Web site: www.hoovers.com/sector

Industry Research Desk

This site provides links to many Web sites, broken down by industry categories.

Web site: www.virtualpet.com/industry/mfg/mfg.htm

Michigan Electronic Library

The Michigan Electronic Library houses links to many publications by industry sector.

Web site: http://mel.lib.mi.us/business/BU-IPmenu.htm

Tradeport

Tradeport offers the electronic equivalent of volumes of information on its site. Consider that you can start your search in its Country Library by choosing from over 200 countries. One of the world's largest sources of international industry information, Tradeport is worth a look.

   Web site: www.tradeport.or/ts/countries/index.htm

Yahoo! Industry News

Yahoo! Industry News houses industry media releases and news.

   Web site: http://biz.yahoo.com/industry

Media online

There are also many publishers that offer their newspapers, magazines, trade journals or other publications for viewing or searching online. Some of the best sites that host links to many media organizations worldwide include the ones detailed below.

Africa News Online

This site is a news service that lists African news by region, country or topic.

   Web site: http://africanews.org

Arab World Online

This site has plenty of news and information about the Middle East. It lists current events, travel information and, of course, business information. There are links to some Arab and other international organizations.

   Web site: www.awo.net

Asia Inc. Online

This Web site delivers news predominantly for Asian executives, typically from a financial slant, but it also hosts features on trends, technology and lifestyle topics that may be of interest to the competitive researcher. One area of particular interest is the Who's Who of Business in Asia, which will certainly help in personality profiling.

   Web site: www.asia-inc.com

AsiaOne

AsiaOne calls itself the site where you can find 'news about Asia from Asia'. It is an extensive site that hosts plenty of information about the region in general, information technology and general business news. It also has links to many other key Asian sites as well.

Web site: www.asia1.com.sg

Business 2.0

The trend-setting publication and follower of cutting-edge ideas in the world of the new economy, Business 2.0 is a print and online magazine to keep your eyes on.

Web site: www.business2.com

China Economic News Service Online

This site is a great place to start when looking for information about China or Taiwan.

Web site: http://cens.com

China News Digest

This is another Asian news source that offers international updates and plenty of information about China.

Web site: www.cnd.org

China Newspapers

If you are trying to find newspapers in China, visit www. east.net/China.Newspapers.htm first. It host links to China's leading newspapers online, which include *Beijing Daily Media Group, China News, China Youth News, Commodity Purchasing News, Fuzhou Daily, Green Times, Hua Sheng News, Network World, Ming Sheng News, Xinming Evening News, Wen Hui Newspaper* and *Yangcheng Evening News.* The site also hosts journals, links to businesses, chat groups, market studies, other news sources, mailing lists, links to Chinese Internet service providers and more.

CNN Interactive World News

CNN lists its world news stories by geographic region. Its top news stories are updated hourly with links to the full stories. One impressive feature about this site is its links to relevant Web sites directly from the main stories. This feature is certainly of utmost importance to competitive researchers examining world news.

Web site: www.cnn.com/WORLD

E & P Media Info Links

E & P Media Info Links offers many options in searching the site. You can search by regional maps, media type and region. It offers links to many international media.
Web site: http://emedia1.mediainfo.com/emedia

The Economist

The popular business magazine has a great Web site for gathering business information from around the world.
Web site: www.economist.com

GLOBEnet

One of the two main national newspapers in Canada, GLOBEnet is the electronic edition of the *Globe and Mail*. It provides plenty of information about what's happening in Canada.
Web site: www.globeandmail.ca

International Herald Tribune

This site calls itself 'the World's Daily Newspaper'. The Paris-based site contains top world headlines, market reports and travel information.
Web site: www.iht.com

Lycos News World Headlines

This news site on Lycos provides top headlines from around the world as well as links to technology, business, political and other news categories.
Web site: http://news.lycos.com/headlines/World

MSNBC-World

This US-based news site claims to be the best. It offers world news, obviously from a US perspective.
Web site: www.msnbc.com/news/INTLNEWS_Front.asp

Nando Times Global

This site is updated on an ongoing basis and tends to contain international news stories that reflect this fact. Its Global Briefs section provides summaries of the hour's top news stories with links to the full-text versions. The list of the headlines and the attached news stories are updated every three to six minutes, with the most recent ones at the top of the list.
Web site: www.nando.net/nt/world

News Alert

News Alert is the name of an interesting site for current business and financial news. The site offers free, subscriber and pay-per-view levels of service, which are detailed on the site. News Alert is divided into four main areas:

1. News and Analysis provides the user with current events from the business and financial world. Intelligence seekers will find news on specific industries, international business news and more specific offerings like corporate earnings and forecasts, mergers and acquisitions, and initial public offerings (IPOs).
2. Quotes and Research is the place to go to find company profiles, SEC filings, earnings estimates and analyst recommendations.
3. Personalize is the section on News Alert that allows the user to track specific topics of interest, whether they be news-related or stocks.
4. News Alert is a global information source. It incorporates sources such as Business Wire, CBS MarketWatch, M2 Newswires, Financial World News and Reuters NA Securities, as well as press releases from over 15,000 companies.

 Web site: www.newsalert.com

NewsCentral

NewsCentral is a great US site that links to more than 3,500 international newspapers. It is one of the best spots online to find international news links.

 Web site: www.all-links.com/newscentral

The Online-News Page

This site hosts archived news from around the world. You can conduct searches on its archives to find historical news that might assist you with conducting historical analysis of companies or industries.

 Web site: www.journalist.org/cgi-bin/online-news/online_news/index.html

Powerize

Powerize tracks news from over 10,000 publications and other sources of international news. Much of the information is accessed free. The registration arrangement is interesting – simply conduct 30 or more searches using Powerize each month and it remains free, otherwise you will be charged $9.95 per month. It is a great source of information on public and private companies, market analyses and research reports on industries or competitors.

Radio Free Europe/Radio Liberty

This Web site provides news and event information for Europe. This extensive news site can be read in several European languages. You can also listen to the news with RealPlayer.

Web site: www.rferl.org

Reuters

No listing of electronic sources for business research could overlook this Web site. Reuters lists top international news and business information directly from its Web site. It also offers financial reports for a fee.

Web site: www.reuters.com/news

World News Index

This Web site contains countless links to international news sources.

Web site: www.stack.nl/~haroldkl

Yahoo! World Summary

While Yahoo! is predominantly known for its search tool, it also provides timely international news in co-operation with Reuters. Its news briefs are updated three times daily on weekdays. You can read the day's headlines or examine full stories. You can also access the previous week's news using its World News archives.

Web site: http://dailynews.yahoo.com/headlines/world

Wire services

You can also go straight to the source of much of the world's news by visiting the Web sites of the wire services. These services post media releases available for the media's consumption. In other words, many companies send their media releases directly to the wire services, which make them available for newspaper, magazine or journal editorial staff for possible inclusion in their publications.

Wire services are a great source of information about companies. They typically differ from newspapers or magazines in that they reflect the media releases of the companies who sent them in. As a result, there is often a lot of news on wire services that never gets published, yet is very valuable to the CI analyst.

The United States Securities and Exchange Commission and the National Association of Securities Dealers in the US have their own regulations, but both require that key media be sent information to achieve 'prompt disclosure to the press'. Wire services often suffice in this regard. There may be valuable information the stock exchanges send to the wire services that never actually makes it to the world of print media. Similar regulations apply in other countries.

Wire services also offer other inside information. Many people do not realize that wire services are also used to send press conference invitations and photos as well as general news. If you are following your competition using wire services, you may know in advance of media conferences, which typically indicate some significant news is being unveiled. It could take the shape of new product launches, significant advancements in the company or major restructurings. Obviously the benefits of knowing this information in advance are numerous.

There seems to be a new breed of wire service forming, which is for direct public consumption. In other words, its target market is business-people. It is sometimes difficult to know the difference. However, it really does not make much difference to the competitive analyst looking to follow the news.

There are many wire services around the world, reflecting the news of companies in their country of origin. Here are just a few of them.

American Press Wire International

Web site: www.newsday.com/ap/internet.htm

Associated Press

Beyond media releases, Associated Press offers links to some of its member sites. The newspapers are listed by geographical region.

Web site: http://wire.ap.org

Bloomberg

If your computer is equipped with Real Audio, you can listen to the news listings instead of reading it. This feature is definitely valuable to any analysts with special needs.

Web site: www.bloomberg.com/wbbr/index.html

Broadcast.com

Web site: www.broadcast.com

BusinessWire

BusinessWire contains current media releases that you can search for by geographical area or keywords. It stores the releases for up to one week only.
Web site: www.businesswire.com

Canada Newswire

This wire service is the main one used in Canada by the media.
Web site: www.newswire.ca

Drudge Report

Web site: www.drudgereport.com

Kyodo Wire

This site hosts one of the Japanese wire services.
Web site: http://home.kyodo.co.jp

News Page

Web site: www.newspage.com

PR Newswire

Beyond general news publications, PR Newswire also serves trade, technical and other speciality publications, some of which are not served by regular wire services but which can be very significant in finding information on specific companies. It offers media releases from organizations along with company and financial news. It also includes access to news photos, and audio and video news stories.
Web site: www.prnewswire.com

PR Newswire also covers international news through its international wire services and affiliates. For European news, visit www. prnewswire.co.uk. For Asian news, PR Newswire links to its affiliate newswire, AsiaNet, which can be found at http://203.63.165.107. For Latin American news, visit www.prnewswire.com/globalnews.

Universal News Services

Universal News Services is a United Kingdom-based wire service, which in addition to general news or business news includes editorial and technical services. It is available in the UK through the Press Association, but is also available through PR Newswire in North America.

US Info Wire

Web site: www.usia.gov/products/washfile/latest.shtml

US News Wire

This wire service transmits to major print and broadcast media in Washington, DC, plus the United States Senate and House press galleries. It is a valuable one for keeping an eye on US competitors or political environment.

Web site: www.usnewswire.com/topnews/current.htm

World News Index

Web site: http://7am.com/worldwires

Xinhua Wire

This is one of the Chinese wire services.

Web site: www.newspage.com/cgi-bin/np.Search?previous_module= NASearch&PreviousSearchPage=SearchResults&offerID=&Query=xin hua&NumDays=1

TechWeb

TechWeb is similar to a wire service but acts more like an umbrella for a variety of technology publications, so while you may be getting published news stories, they are hosted on a single site. At the time of this writing, their site included stories from Byte.com, CMPmetrics, Data Communications, File Mine, Information Week, Internet Week, Network Computing, Planet IT, TechWeb News, TechShopper, Tele.com, Web Tools and Winmag.com. It also hosts some affiliated sites' articles. They include Computer Telephony, Dr Dobbs, Game Developer, Imaging Magazine, Intelligent Enterprise, Network Magazine, NT Systems, Performance Computing, Software Development, Wall Street and Technology, and Web Review. The site also has 'Planet IT Tech Centers', which include E-Business, Executive Strategies, New Economy and numerous others.

Web site: www.techweb.com/

Electronic newsletters

Liszt

Don't overlook electronic newsletters, which are particularly easy to find online. These e-mail versions of standard print newsletters are available on virtually any topic or industry or industry sector and are a valuable way to follow the industry closely. Currently, there are thousands of online newsletters. Simply visit a Web site that keeps track of the many electronic newsletters, such as Liszt, which is located at www.liszt.com.

Government online

Chapter 4 indicated places to find government information, but there are a number of valuable government Web sites that are worth mentioning here. University of Michigan's Web site (see below) contains a lot of valuable international government information. It has links directly to government Web sites in Africa, Asia, Central and South America, Europe, the Middle East and North America. There are also links to international news sites, statistical information, international agencies, international laws and more.

Central Intelligence Agency (CIA)

The CIA Web site contains the popular World Factbook, which provides excellent background information on many countries.
   Web site: www.cia.gov

Europa

Europa is 'the Parliament, the Council, the Commission, the Court of Justice, the Court of Auditors, and the European Union's server' (in their own words). Information on the site is found in 11 languages. The site provides news in the form of media releases from the various EU institutions, a calendar of events and euro currency exchanges. It also details official documents of the European Union and legal texts, and provides information about the European Central Bank and other crucial European agencies. The site has a Policy section, which outlines legislative activities, loans and statistical information as well.
   Web site: www.europa.eu.int

JETRO

JETRO stands for the Japanese External Trade Organization, which is a not-for-profit Japanese government-related organization. It promotes trade between Japan and the rest of the world. This site is particularly informative and provides links to Japanese businesses, and information on exporting to Japan and investing in Japan. The site also hosts detailed information about the organization's structure, activities, history and contact information.

Web site: www.jetro.go.jp

Strategis

Industry Canada's Strategis Web site should not be overlooked if you want to get a feel for an industry or companies in Canada. Strategis provides two company directories on its main page: a database of federally incorporated companies and Canadian Company Capabilities (CCC). With over 35,000 Canadian companies listed, as well as 200,000 products and services, CCC is designed to promote Canadian businesses to the world. It also provides a great deal of valuable information, because the companies are responsible for providing the information when they register with CCC, as well as updating it. Strategis is not a bad point of departure when you are trying to gain some insight on a particular industry sector in Canada.

Web site: http://strategis.ic.gc.ca

University of Michigan

The University of Michigan houses many links to foreign government Web sites.

Web site: www.lib.umich.edu/libhome/Documents.center/foreign.htm

US Business Advisor

Researching the US government on a specialized topic and don't know where to start? Let the US Business Advisor do the work for you. This site provides access to federal government information, services and transactions. From press releases to procurement opportunities, the US Business Advisor allows you to search from a very flexible query tool. If you visit the site, you will see five methods for retrieving information: an FAQ-style section; a 'how to' section with tools and guides; the actual search feature; a categorized browse feature; and a current news section.

Web site: www.business.gov

Business meta-sites

Often overlooked as sources of competitive research, business meta-sites host sets of links to many online business resources world-wide. They make great starting places and often organize the links in a way that better enable you to find the information you are looking for. There are thousands of meta-sites. Many of them are managed by individuals, not companies, purely for the benevolence of doing so. Once you find valuable meta-sites, you may want to bookmark them for later use. Below we detail some of the most valuable ones we've come across in our research efforts.

Brint.com

Brint.com is a great truly international meta-site, which offers links in many diverse categories, including international business trade and technology, international travel and maps, international telephone and fax, international newspapers, TV and radio, international banks, currencies and markets, international languages and translation, international laws and world affairs. Brint also allows you to search by country to find the information you need.

Web site: www.brint.com/International.htm

A Business Researcher's Interests

A Business Researcher's Interests is a component of Brint.com's Web site. It houses information pertaining to many business issues including intellectual property, international trade, data mining, intellectual capital, benchmarking and more.

Web site: www.brint.com/interest.htm

CEO Express

This site links to many different resources for the researcher who may not know where to begin. It includes links to wire services, search tools, Web site locators, business magazines, SEC filing sites and major US and international news sources.

Web site: www.ceoexpress.com

Corporate Information

Corporate Information is a starting point for international industry information.

Web site: www.corporateinformation.com

Financial Data Finder

If it has to do with financial data, there is a good chance that the Financial Data Finder has a link to it from its Web site.

Web site: www.cob.ohio-state.edu/dept/fin/fdf/osudata.htm

Gonzaga University: Law Library and Computing – CEE source

This site contains links to Central and East European legal, political, business and economics World Wide Web resources. This site is a repository of news and political and legal information links for Central and Eastern Europe. Much of the information is available in English.

Web site: http://law.gonzaga.edu/library/ceeurope.htm

Virtual International Business and Economic Sources (VIBES)

VIBES is a huge meta-site for international business links. Currently it provides over 1,500 links to Internet sources of international business and economic information that are in English and free of charge. The links are broken down into full-text articles and reports, statistical information and more meta-pages.

Web site: http://libweb.uncc.edu/ref-bus/vibehome.htm

Price's List of Lists

There is also a great meta-site for finding that 'I-don't-know-where-to-start-to-find-this' information on Price's List of Lists. Gary Price lists everything from Forbes Richest Americans and the Top 500 Largest Latin American Companies to the United Kingdom's Biggest Brands and much more.

Web site: http://gwis2.circ.gwu.edu/~gprice/listof.htm

Primary research contacts

The Internet can also be a great place to find people to contact for your primary research or field data. If you are trying to find an 'expert', sift through the trade journals, newspapers and magazines online to find relevant articles on the topic of interest to you. You can then locate the people quoted in the articles, the journalists who wrote them and the editors of the publications.

You can locate the telephone numbers and addresses of the people you need to reach using some of the Internet phone books. Some of the large ones are detailed below:

Anywho

This site is a directory of US phone numbers.
   Web site: www.anywho.com

Big Yellow

Big Yellow is set up to help you find businesses or people, with a function to help you find e-mail addresses. It also offers 'global directories'.
   Web site: www.bigyellow.com

GTE's Big Book

GTE's Big Book lists business addresses and phone numbers from North American companies. You can search for the listings by company name or industry type.
   Web site: www.bigbook.com

InfoSpace

This site contains both Yellow and White Pages for locating businesses or people, as well as resources to help you locate e-mail addresses, government bodies and more. At the time of writing, it appeared that InfoSpace was only available for Canada, the United Kingdom and the United States.
   Web site: www.infospace.com

Mapquest

If you need to know where they are located once you have an address, visit Mapquest for directions or to see in relative terms where your contact person is located.
   Web site: www.mapquest.com

Industry associations and non-profit organizations

Speaking to the people at industry associations may provide valuable insight into a particular industry. If you are unsure of the associations in a particular industry, there are some Web sites that list associations and provide links to them to help you in your search. Associations on the Net and Industry.net are two examples of this type of Web site.

Associations on the Net

Part of the Internet Public Library, Associations on the Net is a database of over 1,000 trade, research and professional associations.
Web site: www.ipl.org/ref/AON

Industry.net

This site contains a database of over 440 organizations and associations.
Web site: www.industry.net/associations

There are several Web sites that list non-profit groups if you need to find them. Consider Guidestar, the National Center for Charitable Statistics, About.com, Literature of the Nonprofit Sector, the Internet Nonprofit Center and, of course, the Better Business Bureau.

About.com

About.com has numerous resources for researching non-profit groups, including a 'local connection' to help you find community groups and a 'networking center' to help you find contact information.
Web site: http://nonprofit.about.com/business/industries/nonprofit/index.htm

Better Business Bureau

The Better Business Bureau is a network of non-profit organizations that lists complaints made against companies and attempts arbitration. Its Web site offers reports aimed at consumers looking to make purchases; however, it provides valuable information to competitive analysts looking to dig up possible customer business disputes. You can also look into your organization's reputation.
Web site: www.bbb.org

Guidestar

While it is US-centric, it does provide a database of over 620,000 non-profit US groups.
Web site: www.guidestar.org/index.htm

Internet Nonprofit Center

The Internet Nonprofit Center contains a 'nonprofit locator'.
Web site: www.nonprofits.org

Consumer and industry discussion

Knowing what is being said about your organization or your competition is an invaluable resource, particularly in developing future strategies. Consider how it would be if you learnt before your main competitor that its newest product was being met with public dislike. You could ensure that the marketing department at your organization was able to create a campaign to pull in all those disgruntled customers to your products. How exactly do you learn what customers are saying? By following online newsgroups. These newsgroups or usenets are forums for discussion on a variety of topics. There are countless newsgroups available on virtually any topic. Consider the Flaming Ford group, for example. This site is hosted by the Association of Flaming Ford Owners, and was set up after a problem with ignition switches on a particular model of Ford trucks caused them to, well, ignite. On this site, Ford consumers publicly vent their misfortunes in dealing with the company. This is just one example of consumer sites that have been created to let others know about misfortunes. You can learn about weaknesses in your competitors' products, services, customer support and advertising by visiting Web sites similar to the www.flamingfords.com site to hear what consumers might be saying about your competitors. Your company can target its marketing/sales budget into campaigns that bring these consumers on to your side. Also, don't forget to find out if your company is listed on these types of sites since your competition may be able similarly to gather information about weaknesses in your company. This way, you can address the problems before they grow out of hand.

Newsgroups or usenets offer opportunities for people to post messages to a discussion group. They are not exclusively the territory of consumers, however. There are many academic, business, news and other types of group.

Deja.com

If you are trying to locate a discussion group on a particular topic, but to no avail, try Deja.com. This site allows you to search newsgroups for discussions about companies and their products.

Web site: www.deja.com

Trade shows and conferences

There is so much valuable information on an industry and its players available at trade shows and conferences, as we discussed in Chapter 3.

There are many great Web sites that post upcoming industry trade shows and conferences, including EXPOguide, Trade Show Central and Trade Show News Network.

EXPOguide

EXPOguide contains a smaller database of trade shows and conferences.
    Web site: www.expoguide.com

Trade Show Central

This site contains a database of over 50,000 trade shows and conferences around the world.
    Web site: www.tscentral.com

Trade Show News Network

Trade Show News Network enables you to locate and compare shows by industry or show name. You can also locate exhibitors or post questions you are having difficulty finding answers to.
    Web site: www.tsnn.com

Stock markets/securities exchanges online

There are many stock exchanges around the world. One of the best Web sites we have for locating stock exchanges online is the Stock Exchange Markets over the World site. It provides links to almost a hundred different stock exchanges and futures, mercantile and options markets.
    Web site: www.econofinance.com

Paid commercial databases

The Dialog Corporation

The Dialog Corporation has four information services – Dialog, DataStar, Profound and Tradstat:

1. Dialog has news, market research and financial data through a vast collection of databases, which continue to grow on an ongoing basis.
2. Dialog dubs Profound 'the world's most valuable market research database'. It includes the LiveWire service, which alerts everyone in your organization to news that fits their individual profiles.

Profound for intranets delivers information on your company, your markets and your competitors to your corporate intranet.

Web site: www.profound.com

3. DataStar provides access to over 350 databases with world-wide coverage, including business information, industry analysis and market research in various industry sectors.

4. 'Tradstat gives you statistics detailing 90% of world trade', according to The Dialog Corporation. It compiles official government trade statistics from participating countries. It can help you determine market share, monitor trade flow, identify potential trading partners and monitor price fluctuations.

Web site: www.dialog.com

Dow Jones News Retrieval

Dow Jones, the publisher of the US-based *Wall Street Journal*, brings you Newswires plus its index of 2,000 top business Web sites and 250 news and business publications. Articles at the time of this writing cost US$2.95 each.

Web site: http://dowjones.wsj.com

Hoover's Online

Hoover's provides access in depth to the largest amount of private and public company information from around the world, including a company's market position and strategy. Company profiles include full lists of officers, full lists of competitors, products/services/segment data, in-depth financial information and historical financial information. Hoover's is a paid service.

Web site: www.hoovers.com

HW Wilson

HW Wilson has two main lines of business: CD ROM and online information services. Its databases range from Business Periodicals to General Science Abstracts to Biographies.

Web site: www.hwwilson.com

ISI Emerging Markets

ISI provides news and company and financial data from emerging markets around the world, including Argentina, the Baltic states, Brazil,

Bulgaria, Central Asia/Caucasus, Chile, China, Colombia, Czech Republic, Ecuador, Hungary, India, Mexico, Peru, Poland, Romania, Russia, Slovakia, Turkey, Ukraine and Venezuela.

Web site: www.securities.co.uk

Lexis-Nexis

Lexis-Nexis houses legal, government, business and high-tech information in its more than 22,000 sources. For example, its collection of market and industry sources includes publications covering advertising, marketing, market research, consumer attitudes and behaviour, demographics and industry overviews. For this type of information, it uses sources like Clarita, American Demographics, Frost and Sullivan, Ethnic Newswatch, Euromonitor and Datamonitor, to name a few.

Web site: www.lexis-nexis.com

ProQuest from Bell+Howell (formerly DataTimes Corporation)

ProQuest includes serials and newspapers in microform, ProQuest Direct (international business databases), Sci/Tech and Medical Databases, Computing and Telecommunications and the Criminal Justice Periodicals Index. It provides summaries of articles from over 8,000 publications.

Web site: www.datatimes.com

Questel-Orbit

Questel-Orbit stresses its strength in intellectual property, scientific, technical, chemical, business and news information. It has four lines of information products – QWEB, IMAGINATION2, QPAT and NAME-WATCHER:

1. QWEB provides users with Internet-based access to 37 patent databases, 19 trade mark databases, 25 sci/tech files and over 6 million images.

2. IMAGINATION2 is advanced search software that gives you access to all the information distributed by Questel-Orbit. Using IMAGINATION2 you can turn information into various types of presentation documents.

3. QPAT offers 20 years of full-text US patents including images. QPAT has its own Web site: www.qpat.com.

4. NAMEWATCHER patrols the Web for domain names. It is a service that gives you access to a database that groups together all

the URLs registered in every country in the world. It can give you a list of new or similar domain names every week to help you keep your identity unique and protected.

Web site: www.orbit.com

SilverPlatter

Amongst its business databases, SilverPlatter includes 19 bibliographic and full-text databases covering competition, corporate trends and strategies, economics, mergers and acquisitions, new products and technologies, investment information, legal issues, information management and finance. For example, China Hand is a full-text database that explains the most common operational challenges to conducting business in China. It includes business intelligence, regulations, strategies and tactics, and operating conditions.

Web site: www.silverplatter.com

.xls

.xls is a fee-based site, which is a service of the Data Downlink Corporation. It cross-indexes and distributes often-overlooked business databases. It contains data on over 50,000 companies, in the form of demographics, economic stats and other typically numeric information. You can download the numeric data directly to Microsoft Excel and the text-based information to Microsoft Word.

Search engines and directories

Sifting through the millions of Web pages on the Internet to find exactly what you are looking for is a combination of art, science and luck. Developing skills at using search engines and directories is crucial. To start, it helps to know whether you are using an engine or a directory, because they perform differently. A directory is a database of previously selected Web pages that have been organized by subjects. Yahoo! is an example of a directory. Search engines rely on a technology known as a spider or Web crawler. It 'crawls' the Web to catalogue the links that are available. Alta Vista is an example of one of the most popular search engines.

Each tool has its strengths and weaknesses. Directories rely on human editing and categorizing and are therefore limited in size. They tend to be more organized in appropriate categories, however. Search engines, on the other hand, are typically less organized, but far more inclusive. They are many times larger than directories.

Most directories and engines recognize their limitations and have started combining the best of both worlds. Yahoo! has added spiders to become more like an engine, while Alta Vista has added directories to categorize information better. The two worlds are melding into one.

There are also metasearch engines that use several search engines at once. The concept behind them is that one site may have picked up information that another site doesn't have. Be forewarned if you opt to use a metasearch engine: you are almost guaranteed to get information overload. Here is a partial list of search engines and databases:

- Alta Vista can be found at www.altavista.com.
- Excite is located at www.excite.com.
- FAST is located at www.alltheweb.com.
- Go/InfoSeek is found at www.go.com.
- Google indexes about 1 million pages at the time of writing this book. It uses a scoring system known as PageRank to help you find sites that are actually useful. It works very well if you are looking for a corporate Web site. It can be found at www.google.com.
- Looksmart is located at www.looksmart.com.
- Northern Light can be found at www.northernlight.com.
- The Online Directory Project (ODP) is found at www.dmoz.org.
- Snap is available at www.snap.com.

Yahoo! can be found at www.yahoo.com. Yahoo! also has regional sites, which end with the particular country suffix. You can access them from the main site or, if you know the appropriate country suffix, simply enter it instead of .com, for example www.yahoo.uk or www.yahoo.jp or www.yahoo.ca.

Agents and bots

This section is not a plug for people to search on your behalf, but rather technology that will help find information for you. Bots, or agents as they are also known, can scour the Web for information on a particular topic that interests you. They can catalogue the information found based on your priorities and deliver material directly to your hard drive.

The term 'agent' has been used by computer scientists to describe high levels of artificial intelligence (AI), but it has become almost synonymous with bots (short for 'robots').

There are many valuable types of bots that can speed up the information gathering process, including stock bots, spider bots, shopping bots, news bots and others.

Stock bots can automatically send you investment alerts, market prices, market indicators or any new initial public offerings (IPOs) that hit the market. Company Sleuth or InfoBeat bot automatically sends you updates about market prices of stocks that are of interest to you.

Company Sleuth

If you are looking for information about US publicly traded companies, Company Sleuth is a valuable source. This free e-mail service will help you track new patents, SEC filings, earnings estimates, financial moves, Internet dealings, legal actions and discussion group postings. You will be alerted to changes via daily e-mail reports. While you must register to use this service, it is available free of charge. You can choose to monitor up to 10 public companies at once. Other information you can obtain includes stock quotes, analyst ratings, technical trading information, new trade marks, trades, job postings, media releases, business news and stock rumours. In addition, Company Sleuth lets you know the companies that are watching you, which is certainly valuable for your counter-intelligence function. You can register for Company Sleuth at http://www.companysleuth.com/.

InfoBeat

InfoBeat can be found at www.infobeat.com/cb/cgi/cb_merc.cgi.

Spider bots or search bots operate in the same way that the spiders behind search engines work. They scour the Web for the kind of information you need to find. If you know which Web sites you would like to track, you can deploy your own spider bot to find it for you. Simply provide the Web sites, indicate how deeply to dig through the information contained in the sites and specify the type of information you want (like sound, video, graphics or text).

Bottom Dollar

You might be thinking that shopping bots could not possibly have a role in a book on competitive intelligence. However, they are very valuable if you want to stay on top of your competitors' pricing. In today's world of 'Big Box' retailers, having the best prices may be crucial. Stores like Wal-Mart that guarantee the lowest prices can suffer dramatically if their competitor cuts prices. Shopping bots can stay on top of these changes. One example of a shopping bot is Bottom Dollar, which searches online retailers for the best prices for particular merchandise. It can be found at www.bottomdollar.com.

AdHound

Staying current in today's world of mass media seems impossible, but news bots can help. By tracking headlines or news stories of particular interest to you, your energy can be allotted elsewhere. Search through the classified ads of over a hundred newspapers using AdHound bot at http://sar.adone.com/cgi-bin/adhound?w=a.

Competitive intelligence tools and techniques online

Ciexperts.com

Ciexperts.com is Global Trade Solutions' monthly electronic newsletter delivered free via e-mail to subscribers. It details the latest tools and techniques used by competitive intelligence (CI) professionals who help businesses and organizations succeed in the competitive global marketplace. The analysts at Global Trade Solutions share their expertise with anyone looking to learn more about their competitors or their industry as a whole.

Through ciexperts.com, businesspeople are exposed to real-life examples, information sources and methodologies that they can apply to their own situation. Ciexperts is divided into six regular departments detailing the many aspects of competitive intelligence needed to compete successfully:

1. Innovative Sources – new and valuable print, electronic or lesser-known research sources from around the world.
2. Global Perspectives – considerations that are unique to conducting competitive intelligence world-wide.
3. Industry Views – insider views on diverse industries presented as mini case studies to highlight particular aspects of CI or to illustrate the value CI played in a particular industry event.
4. Expert Tools and Techniques – specific research and analysis tools to help you in your efforts to dig up effectively and analyse relevant information, turning it into intelligence.

5. Ask the CI Experts – a regular column that provides an opportunity for readers to ask the competitive analysts at Global Trade Solutions about any dilemmas their organizations are facing.

6. Technology Tidbits – news on the latest technology to improve your competitive intelligence efforts.

Free subscriptions to ciexperts.com are available at www.ciexperts.com.

Society of Competitive Intelligence Professionals (SCIP)

The Society of Competitive Intelligence Professionals is the association of choice for CI practitioners looking to stay on top of advancements in the industry. The organization's Web site offers valuable articles, databases and links. The site can be found at www.scip.org.

Miscellaneous other online sources

Library of Congress Home Page

This site provides a wealth of business, industry and market information for people looking to conduct competitive research. For example, the site contains the Global Legal Information Network, which is a great place to find information about taking a company international. There are English abstracts of laws, regulations and other legal information provided by various nations. However, the full texts of the documents are in the language of their country of origin.

Web site: www.loc.gov

Trade Compass

Trade Compass provides a range of services from its Web site, including a world information desk, international business centre, trade leads, and regulation and compliance information. It is a paid service that offers basic service free for seven days.

Web site: www.tradecompass.com

The Universal Currency Converter

Trying to analyse many currencies? Stop by the Universal Currency Converter site. It is a multilingual site that allows you to convert 180 currencies from over 250 geographic locations.

Web site: www.xe.net/currency

The Trade Secrets Home Page

With content provided by US-based lawyer R Mark Halligan, the Trade Secrets Home Page is a great online resource for anyone looking for the latest in international intellectual property developments and trade secrets cases currently in the courts.

Web site: http://execpc.com/~mhallign

Remaining anonymous online

New technologies have enabled servers to detect a large amount of information about someone who visits the sites.

Anonymous e-mail

Many companies are offering free e-mail, which is very handy to have if you are going to be visiting your competitors' Web sites frequently. Some examples are Rocketmail, Hotmail and Geocities. Their Web sites are www.rocketmail.com, www.hotmail.com and www.geocities.com respectively.

Anonymizer

If you want to do a bit of digging on your competitor's Web site, but are concerned that your e-mail address will show up on the server's visitor statistics or, alternatively, are concerned that your access will be blocked, there is a quick solution. Before visiting your competitor's Web site, stop by the Anonymizer. Instead of your rivals seeing your name as a visitor to its site, the statistics will only show anonymizer.com. This site can help you keep your personal information to yourself, ensuring your anonymity while you surf.

By using this service, you may be able to prevent a competitor from gathering the following information about you: your domain name, and perhaps your actual name; your ISP and its location; the type of browser and computer you are using; which country you are from; and the last Web page you visited.

Be prepared, however, because some sites filter out the Anonymizer domain, so you still might not be able to access them. In addition, some sites have a filter that breaks through the Anonymizer information to determine your true identity. The technology battle continues...

Web site: www.anonymizer.com

analysis:
turning **information** into **intelligence**

Do not believe in anything simply because you have heard it. Do not believe in anything simply because it is spoken and rumoured by many. Do not believe in anything simply because it is found written in your religious books. Do not believe in anything merely on the authority of your teachers and elders. Do not believe in traditions because they have been handed down for many generations. But after observation and analysis, when you find that anything agrees with reason and is conducive to the good and benefit of one and all, then accept it and live up to it.

BUDDHA

The successful (person) is the one who finds out what is the matter with his (or her) business before his (or her) competitors do.

ROY L SMITH (ADAPTED BY C COOK AND M COOK)

It is difficult to conduct business without hearing about your competitors. You should be worried if you are able to go through a week without any knowledge about what is happening in your business environment, whether it be an advertisement you see in a newspaper, a rumour from one of your salespeople or perhaps a new customer who explains why she has opted for your product or service when two of your rivals contacted her first.

While it is virtually impossible to ignore information, it is very easy to be overwhelmed by it. Information is everywhere, and attempting to know all and see all will effectively paralyse your business. How do you strike a balance? How do you learn to recognize the value in certain pieces of information, while avoiding overload?

The answer is to shift the focus away from information gathering and focus on analysis. Most business executives will tell you that, while it may be ideal to have every piece of data required for a decision, the business world is not ideal. Waiting for that level of accuracy will result in sluggish and ineffective actions, or reactions to a more nimble competitor who has recognized a window of opportunity. These executives understand that it is better to be close all the time than to be accurate occasionally. This is the value of analysis in CI.

Analysis is the key to effective business decision-making. In the intelligence age, markets are so competitive and so connected that a technological change or a new entrant in your industry can put you out of business before you know what has happened. Keeping your finger on the pulse of your business environment is crucial to avoid this fate. No business is immune. While it is common to hear about the 'category killer' stores putting local shops out of business, it is just as common today to find a new and innovative start-up introducing a cutting-edge product that renders an industry leader's wares obsolete. All businesses ignore the competition at their peril. Failure and success have as much to do with a company's ability to manage intelligence about itself, about its competitors, about the environment in which it operates and about its ability to execute strategies based on the intelligence at its disposal as it does with deep pockets and loyal customers.

The globalization of culture and commerce has brought about dizzying changes for businesses in the last decade. It is no longer a simple task to identify rivals because the competitive environment is more dynamic, expansive and unpredictable than ever before. These factors all contribute to the difficulty in anticipating what the future holds. Toss in a heaping dose of technology, a trend towards deregulation and harmonization of international standards, increasingly sophisticated and demanding consumers in markets around the world and the creation of new business channels, and the task of remaining competitive seems daunting, if not impossible. The good news is that it is possible.

How does one go about analysing the business environment? It helps first to understand the different elements of the environment as well as the different levels of analysis that can be conducted. We break the various types of competitive analysis into three main categories: market analysis; industry analysis; and company analysis. Depending on the nature of your company, industry and competitive objectives, the analysis techniques will differ. Some of the analysis techniques can be used for more than one type of analysis. For example, patent analysis is most commonly used for company analysis so we have included it in that section; however, it also has applications in industry analysis and market analysis as well.

There are many different tools to analyse industries, companies and markets. We have selected the ones we find most beneficial. There is one integral analysis tool that has not been included in this chapter. It is competitive benchmarking. We discuss benchmarking and explain how to benchmark your organization against another in the following chapter. However, a full book on benchmarking would still not cover it completely because it is such an extensive discipline on its own. Chapter 7 gives you a good overview of it and how to get started using competitive benchmarking.

We include the following analysis techniques in this chapter: event analysis, intelligence mapping, market factor analysis, company profiling, competitor profiling, merger analysis, patent analysis, personality profiling, Porter's model of five forces, ratio analysis and SWOT analysis. More analysis techniques are being developed all the time. The ones we include will enable you effectively to conduct market, industry and company analysis, thereby gaining a better competitive advantage.

Market analysis

With the global economy becoming increasingly competitive, businesses are anxious to explore new opportunities for growth in other parts of the world. Entering new markets is not a matter of duplicating your current business practices in another geographic location. There are a number of factors to analyse when you are determining the potential or opportunity within a new market, whether that market spans a region, a country or a number of countries. We include two types of analysis that can be used to analyse markets: market factor analysis and intelligence mapping.

Market factors analysis

We have identified five broad factors that need to be addressed when conducting an analysis of a market. They are political, economic, social, technological and industry-specific. This type of analysis provides you with both a historical perspective regarding market evolution and development, and an increased ability to forecast the direction in which the market is headed.

Political analysis

How would you feel if you invested heavily in a new operation overseas and, a month after you opened your doors for business, a coup breaks out in the country? The government is overthrown, the military takes over and all foreign investment, including your operation, is seized until further notice. While this example is extreme, it illustrates the potential hardship a company can face if it has not adequately analysed and assessed the political risk when it explores new markets. A bit of advance preparation can save a considerable amount of hardship later on.

One factor to consider is the type of government and legal system. Such information is available from a number of sources, such as the *CIA World Factbook*. But do not stop there. Analyse the status and personality of the present leadership, from the president or prime minister to the key decision-makers in the power departments. A historical perspective of the area's political stability, and the current political issues facing the country, are necessary ingredients for a thorough analysis. It is also important to analyse the legal system or systems within the target market as well. You should examine what laws are on the books that could affect your competitiveness in these markets, find out how effectively and fairly they have been enforced in the past and determine whether changes are pending that could also affect your ability to compete. While it is often difficult to analyse the level of corruption within a political or judicial system, any information that you gather in this regard will be extremely valuable for your decision.

Governments exercise varying degrees of control in different industries in different parts of the world. In the United States, for example, businesses are relatively free from the government telling them how to operate. As long as companies adhere to well-documented laws, they are free to go forth and prosper. On the other extreme, you have China's planned economy, in which factory output for a given business is dictated and the concepts of competition, marketing and continuous improvement are non-existent. While this is changing in China, it is difficult to describe the role of government in industry as anything but oppressive. Knowing the extent to which this occurs in your target market, and the impact that might have on your ability to succeed, is crucial.

Government control or influence is exerted in other ways that affect competitiveness as well. For example, a manufacturing company may find the environmental regulations regarding emissions too onerous to consider building a factory in a specific country. To meet all the standards required in that nation would be more costly than to ship the finished product over a longer distance into that market from a factory operating under less stringent environmental restrictions.

There are still many barriers to foreign investment in certain markets. Fortunately, they are decreasing as more countries accept open markets as a key to their growth, and international agreements and membership into international trade organizations increase the likelihood of more equitable treatment when conducting international business. Yet it is important to find out the extent to which preferential treatment is still given to domestic companies, and how such treatment creates competitive advantages for those firms.

One area in which we have advised clients concerns the impact of conducting business in a country or region in which human rights abuses are prevalent. Regardless of whether these abuses are widely publicized, there is a potential for serious backlash against the firm, which can undoubtedly affect its competitiveness. This whole situation can simply be avoided if a company sets ethical guidelines for the way in which it conducts business and respects people.

Economic analysis

An economic analysis of a target market helps you understand the historical growth or decline of a particular market, as well as its potential for greater affluence in the future. There are very few circumstances in which a company would want to invest heavily into a market that is not only economically depressed, but has been on a downward spiral for many years with no sign of hope.

On a very broad level, your company will want to feel confident that the market in question has the infrastructure in place to support whatever type of business you are in. If you need roads or railways, airline routes or office space in a particular location, this type of analysis at the outset saves time and money later in the process. If the target market does not have what you need in the way of infrastructure, you can find out if there are plans for improvements, changes or additions, and whether money has been dedicated to these efforts. Competitive advantages can be gained if you, and not your competitors, are aware of an upcoming change that will make conducting business in a previously untested market much more lucrative.

Conducting this analysis requires an examination of the strengths of the various industry sectors within the market relative to other markets, and in terms of historical growth and potential. Clearly you will be more interested in sectors of the industry that seem more relevant to your business, but you also want to feel confident in the market's economic capabilities as a whole. Your consumer-product business may have very little in common with natural resources but, if the economic strength of a particular market is in mining and forestry and these industries are declining rapidly, you will have to determine whether large-scale employee reductions in these industries in future years will hinder your efforts to sell your product or service in this market.

Many governments collect and publish economic statistics, including import and export data, from their own country as well as foreign countries. These can be valuable sources of information to forecast growth trends for certain products or services. These departments also publish demographic information, such as census results and other types of surveys. This can give you insight into a number of economic factors, including the distribution of wealth and earnings within a market.

Governments also promote economic development within their borders, and often provide incentives to attract new business. The Invest in France Programme is a prime example, where the government has tried to remove as many barriers as possible to foreign firms looking to set up shop in France. Contacting economic development agencies within your target markets to learn about incentives may result in competitive advantages that you, and perhaps your competitors, did not know existed prior to your analysis. The difference is that now you know.

Social analysis

An intelligent organization never overlooks the impact of social and cultural elements on its competitiveness. Throughout this book, we discuss a number of issues relating to competing internationally, including language challenges, belief systems and general cultural differences that organizations need to understand and respect to maximize their success in foreign markets. Some of these are obvious and well documented. Others are less obvious.

Consider Canada and the United States. These two technologically advanced and highly industrialized nations share the world's longest undefended border. They are partners in the world's richest bilateral trade, and share much of the same culture. With the exception of a percentage of the French-speaking population in Quebec, who are also exposed to all things American, the two countries share the same language. So why is it so difficult for Canadians to accept and celebrate entrepreneurial effort and success? Somehow, during the development of these relatively young nations, Canadians became risk-averse and suspicious of success while people in the US became the champions of new ideas and new challenges. While this may be a generalization, it has played itself out in the business world to the detriment of Canadian businesses. An article in a Canadian business magazine featured a very innovative Canadian entrepreneur who found success only after he left Canada to build his business in Seattle, Washington. When asked why he took this approach, he indicated that Canadian investors and potential partners loved his idea but wanted to wait until he had achieved success before backing his business. In contrast, when he approached US investors for financial backing, they wanted to know how he was going to achieve his goals and objectives. Satisfied with his vision, innovative business idea and sound strategy, they decided to get involved at the critical start-up stage.

It is not always possible to gauge the level of business sophistication in any particular market, or to understand the nuances that make different people, businesses or cultures react differently from others in certain environments. A social analysis helps give you more information on how receptive a market may be to a new product or service, and how open it may be to a new business model or an untested marketing approach.

Technology analysis

We cannot overstate the impact technology is having on the way business is conducted globally. As a result, the level of technological use and the rate of adoption are key elements of a market analysis. We have seen that the level of use of technology is directly proportional to its influence in business. We call this the law of technological influence. The technological maturity of the market you enter must be analysed. The market's rate of adoption of technology will also be a factor in any decisions you make about competing in that area. For example, a business that is a low technology user will be at a competitive disadvantage if it attempts to enter a market in which competing firms are high technology users. Conversely, a firm that has embraced technology in every aspect of its business may find it disadvantageous to enter a market in which the trappings of technology do not exist or are not readily available. It may seem obvious that a company will not expand its Internet service business to a market where 10 per cent of the population have telephones, 5 per cent have cable television and 2 per cent have computers. It is less obvious when a business that has automated all of its processes and uses computers in every department establishes an office in an area where power generation facilities are unreliable and leading-edge computer hardware is difficult to procure from local sources.

Technology plays a tremendous role in an organization's competitiveness. A thorough analysis of it will increase the value of your market analysis and, ultimately, your recommendations to decision-makers.

Industry analysis

The political, economic, social and technology analyses that you have conducted set the stage for your industry analysis. This fifth market analysis factor moves your efforts from the overall market environment to your specific industry. Some of the analysis tools that can be incorporated into this stage include Porter's five forces, competitor profiling, SWOT analysis, event analysis, merger analysis and patent analysis.

Intelligence mapping

Leonard M Fuld, author of *The New Competitor Intelligence: The Complete Resource for Finding, Analyzing, and Using Information about your Competitors*, developed a valuable competitive analysis tool called 'intelligence mapping'. It is a means to map the intelligence resources you can find in a particular country. We include it as a market analysis technique but it has value for industry analysis and company analysis as well.

Fuld suggests the following technique for creating an intelligence map:

1. Identify a business event or a company.
2. Call sources (securities analysts, Department of Commerce analysts, news reporters, banks and consulates) that follow business events for that country.
3. Ask these questions, paraphrased as necessary:
   - 'If you had to go to Country X to find information on private company Y, what sources would you go to first?'
   - 'Which sources – local newspaper, stock analyst, bank, database or government filing – would give you the most accurate and timely information on a private company?'
   - 'Which of the sources are most likely to have the information, and which are least likely? Could you rank them?'

4. Based on the answers, determine which of the sources prove to be stronger antennas and which are weaker. The stronger ones will define your intelligence map. Keep this map in mind, and you will be able to gather intelligence more quickly and more accurately (Fuld, 1995: 209).

Fuld refers to antennas as part of his intelligence antennas law, which he describes as, 'Each country or region has a set of intelligence antennas that act as information magnets and are superior in picking up and absorbing information in that country or region' (Fuld, 1995: 207). These antennas can be analysts, associations, banks, external traders, government, internal traders and publications.

Each country tends to be different in the collection and housing of information. That is the reasoning behind creating an intelligence map. By doing so at the beginning of a project, you potentially save yourself countless hours of research and frustration later. You can then refer to the map whenever you conduct research in that particular country.

Industry analysis

Having a strong understanding of the industry in which you are operating is the best way to position your organization for success. Thorough industry analysis gives you insight into industry profitability, success indicators and life cycle:

■   *Industry profitability:* What segments within the industry are getting the most attention from competitors and why? Are these the segments your company should focus on?

■   *Success indicators:* What are the areas in which your competitors excel? What are their strengths, weaknesses, strategies and relative performance in the areas in which you want to compete?

■   *Industry life cycle:* Is the industry new or mature? How will your business measure up to existing competitors? Which ones are likely to be the greatest threats to your success? Is the industry in a high-growth stage or has growth slowed as rivalry intensified? Has the increase in competition and substitute products or services made buyers and suppliers more influential? What factors are likely to be important to success in this industry in the future? How prepared is your company for that future?

Porter's five forces model

In his early works on competition within industries and competitive strategies, Professor Michael Porter of the Harvard Business School developed a model identifying five forces that act on players in a competitive environment. These forces determine an industry's attractiveness and are identified below:

- competition within the industry;
- threat of new competition;
- influence of suppliers;
- influence of customers;
- threat of alternatives or substitutes.

Competition within the industry

Competition within an industry is a way of life in most markets around the world. Rivalry in the business world is viewed as economically healthy, particularly when it is supported by a mild dose of regulatory guidance to ensure fair and equitable conditions for the business community and consumers. Most businesses, large or small, recognize the direct competition within their immediate market, whether that be at the town, city, county, provincial, state or national level. They may not recognize or consider the indirect competitors that share the territory. Consequently, they may be confused about a decline in their business because they have not broadened their scope of enquiry to consider non-traditional rivals.

International companies or multinationals may recognize the other multinational businesses or strong national competitors against which they compete in various markets; however, they may fail to consider strong rivals in smaller regional markets. These 'small fish' can quickly infiltrate the 'big pond' and change the industry environment for everyone. This is becoming more common as the international markets grow and the barriers to competition shrink. Many countries that historically controlled business through government intervention and stiff restrictions on foreign investment are embracing economic reforms and opening up to the benefits of more liberal trade.

Threat of new competition

This is a double-edged sword for any business because the creation of new markets is linked to the creation of new potential competitors, which is the second force that Porter identified. If you can entertain the idea of selling your goods or services in new markets, remember that many of your competitors are thinking the same thing. In addition, entrepreneurs in these new markets are becoming aware of the opportunities in your back yard. The threat of new competition grows every day. Many businesspeople are convinced that their product or service is so fantastic that everyone will want to buy it. This is what we call the '*Field of Dreams*' approach to business. The notion that 'if you build it, they will come (insert buy)' does not work in the business world. What such businesspeople tend to forget is that, if they are correct and their product or service is fantastic, the idea may be duplicated by many. Existing businesses that have built their reputation on specific functions of their organizations are now being analysed so that those areas of excellence can be introduced into other companies, including competitors.

The only real barriers to entering new industries, or new markets for that matter, are the decision-makers' perceptions of how difficult it is to do so. Is there a market for your company's product or service? Is it economically viable to enter the market? Is the regulatory environment supportive or overbearing? Does your company have the skills and resources to succeed in this area of business?

Influence of suppliers

It is rare to find a business today that is wholly self-sufficient. Outsourcing, contracting and partnering have all become part of everyday operation. This is particularly true in more mature industries. In the automotive industry, engines may be built in one factory, and the seats designed and constructed by another company at another location. Both components are shipped for final assembly to the factory where the automobile frame has been constructed. Of course, assembly can only occur if the tyre supplier, the exhaust supplier and the paint supplier, among others, have also shipped their key components at the same time. And the price the manufacturer charges must be competitive in its class while still leaving room to make a reasonable profit.

In most instances, your business is integrally linked to the fortunes and misfortunes of your suppliers. Their efficiency, greed, mismanagement or vision can all play a part in your success. It is crucial that you analyse the impact of their influence on your operation.

Influence of buyers

'The customer is always right.' True or not, this old adage does not adequately describe the ability of buyers to influence your business or an industry as a whole. Porter emphasized the customers' demand for greater quality or service, the bargaining power of large-volume customers and, of course, their ability to shop around for alternatives. Customers exert considerable force on an industry and have the power to make winners and losers. Businesses that are interested in success must analyse and act on the needs of customers and potential customers as part of their competitive strategy.

Threat of alternatives or substitutes

Why are there so many models of Sony's Walkman? The company took the position that it had to provide a portable audiocassette or CD player to match anything that a competitor might put on the market. Any new feature on a rival's product was seen as a threat to Sony's leadership and the Walkman's brand recognition. Why is the recording industry threatened by the Internet? Musicians now have an alternative for getting their music out to the masses, even if they do not have a recording contract. At the retail level, music stores are forced to compete with online vendors of CDs and audiotapes. Whether it be generic or 'no name' products in food stores, insurance services offered through banks, or Internet service offered by cable television companies or telecommunications giants, there is always the threat that your customers will be able to get the same thing you are offering or something similar in a way that they prefer. While Porter identified threats from alternatives or substitutes in his works in the 1980s, it would have been difficult accurately to determine the impact this competitive force would have in the business world today.

The industry level is where you see Porter's five forces being played out. Analysing the forces that Porter identified in his model of a competitive industry is an excellent point of departure.

Competitor profiling

One of the analysis techniques we use to determine a company's standing within an industry is to determine the company's main competitors and conduct a competitor profiling. On behalf of the company, we compile research covering each of the main functions of the company and each of its competitors' functions. These include company history, management information, strategy, finance, marketing, sales, products and/or services, distribution, employment, research and development, technology and image. After compiling data for each of these areas for each of the companies, we compare them.

An optional part of competitor profiling, but one that we find particularly valuable, is to assign each competitor a value for its functions. For example, out of a possible score of 10, where 1 is the least impressive and 10 is the most impressive, we might assign Competitor A a rating of 5 for its marketing efforts. We might give Competitor B a 7 and Competitor C an 8. We would continue to do this for each of the functions listed in Table 6.1 below. Afterward, we could very easily chart the results for an at-a-glance look at the strengths and weaknesses of the main companies within an industry.

While this technique has some similarities to benchmarking, it is more of an overview. Competitive benchmarking is far more exhaustive.

Table 6.1   Competitor profiling chart

	Company	Competitor A	Competitor B	Competitor C
Company History				
Management				
Company Strategy				
Financial Information				
Operational Information				
Marketing Information				
Sales Information				
Product Information				
Distribution Information				
Employee Information				
R & D/Engineering				
Technology				
Image				

To further your understanding of the competitive environment in which you operate, an analysis will be more valuable if it looks at the different levels within that environment – namely, further industry analysis and company analysis.

Company analysis

Company-level competitive analysis has several components: technical analyses, personality analyses and operational analyses. Technical analyses provide a statistical snapshot of a company that may help to explain its situation. Standard accounting reports and formulae, such as financial summaries, profitability ratios (return on sales, return on assets and return on equity), debt/equity ratios and cash flow help to create a technical perspective of the competitor.

Personality analyses give you a more qualitative type of information that may help explain how a competitor perceives itself and how it may react in a particular situation. By looking at the organizational structure, the ownership and key managers or board of directors, you can formulate an opinion on corporate culture. Combined with information on that organization's goals, marketing communications, policies and strategies, you have a useful view of the competitor's personality.

A competitive analysis at the operations level examines the key elements of operating a business. Areas such as research and development, manufacturing, marketing, sales, distribution and customer service are analysed to determine where competitive advantages exist.

General Electric, for example, has demonstrated considerable skill in this regard. It analyses its diverse core businesses to such a degree that it is able to maintain either first or second place in the markets for those businesses. If analysis illustrates that General Electric cannot achieve its goal, then that particular business is divested.

Technical, personality and operational analyses work best as analysis tools when they are considered together to create an image of a competitor. For example, imagine you are competing in a high-technology industry and are interested in the position of two rivals. You have already determined that Competitor A has a positive cash flow and very little debt. Financially, this company looks like a dangerous competitor. Competitor B has a negative cash flow and considerable debt, and does not seem to pose a competitive threat from a technical perspective. However, Company A has been in the industry for a long time. Its management team has not changed with the times and, like the board of directors, it has remained fiercely conservative in an industry that has begun to change rapidly. Marketing strategies have targeted loyal customers with discounts and incentives. New products are few and far between, and the upgrades of existing products have not introduced much in the way of innovation.

Company B has been around for less than two years and has amassed its debt by hiring and acquiring the best and brightest in the industry, and investing more heavily in research and development than you and Company A combined. The management team was hand-picked with the help of a successful industry insider and consultant. Company B has been aggressive in its pursuit of new business opportunities, and innovative in marketing its new product line, which according to rumours will set a new standard in the industry. Who is the threat? Without considering both the technical and personality components of the analysis, you are simply collecting data that may not provide you with the insights you need to analyse your competition effectively.

Business strategies are often developed in a framework that considers the financial position of the company and the corporate culture, which were discussed earlier, and the company's strengths and weaknesses in the key areas mentioned above.

The company analysis techniques that we discuss in this chapter include SWOT analysis, company profiling, ratio analysis, event analysis, patent analysis, personality profiling and merger analysis.

SWOT analysis

SWOT stands for strengths, weaknesses, opportunities and threats, and is a valuable tool that spans competitive intelligence, marketing and communications. It examines your competitors' strengths and weaknesses, and the opportunities and threats in your market.

There are many factors to consider for each variable in the SWOT analysis. The strengths are all the powerful attributes that an organization may possess. Some strengths to consider are:

- patents – quality and quantity;
- technology – owned or readily available;
- market share – current position (dominant or weak, for example) in the market;
- management expertise – who are the major decision-makers and what do they bring to the table?;
- financial position;
- customer loyalty; and
- quality of product or service – effective marketing, skilled employees, image.

Weaknesses are your competitors' liabilities or potential liabilities. They can take the form of:

- financial debt;
- unskilled workers;
- labour strife;
- poor image or visibility;
- inefficient production equipment or processes, or outdated technology;
- poor after-sales service;
- ineffective or minimal marketing;
- poor-quality products;
- lack of management experience or divisive management; and
- lack of customer loyalty.

There are as many different strengths and weaknesses as there are companies, but the above factors cover the major ones that should be considered during the analysis of a competitor. Analysis of strengths and weaknesses occurs at the corporate or business level, whereas opportunities and threats are analysed at the market or industry level, examining the favourable and unfavourable conditions that can impact on your organization's ability to compete.

Opportunity may take the shape of a new start-up in your industry that has innovative technology but lacks capital and business skills to take it to the next level. If the company's technology complements your line of business, perhaps a merger offer or a partnership would give your operation a competitive advantage. That same start-up, with a bucket of venture capital and a visionary management team, could be a threat to your position in the market. A regulatory change that impacts on your manufacturing process or licensing costs is another example of a threat that needs to be analysed, preferably before it is implemented.

Here are a few examples of opportunities that may affect your organization:

- government regulations or pending regulations that would aid a company;
- changing demographics that might assist a company in increasing its client/customer base;

- decreases in operating costs or materials costs;
- patent expirations (other companies').

These are examples of threats that may affect your organization:

- raw materials shortages;
- costly government regulations;
- increasing bank interest rates;
- new competitors.

There are many factors that need to be looked at to conduct an accurate and thorough SWOT analysis. These include: products; finances; technology; human resources; strategic alliances and partnerships; manufacturing or operations; marketing and sales; branding; and image.

When trying to predict the opportunities or threats that might arise, Larry Kahaner suggests that there are four main areas to look, as outlined in his book *Competitive Intelligence: From Black Ops to Boardrooms* (1996):

1. the company's public forecast;
2. industry experts' forecasts;
3. what the company's current or past actions indicate for the future; and
4. how the competitive environment will affect the company's future.

As part of the company's public forecast, mission statements are an excellent source of potentially valuable intelligence, which should not be overlooked. Often an organization creates mission statements at a time when it is in a shift or crisis. The resulting mission statement often reflects its perception of itself and its plans for the future. Typically you will also find information about company goals and philosophies contained in its mission statement as well. Always try to find out an organization's mission statement to determine where it is headed. These mission statements are often posted on Web sites or printed in annual reports or corporate capability brochures. If you are having trouble finding a company's mission statement, it may be under a different heading such as plans, vision and values, philosophies, goals or objectives. They come in many different lengths.

Kahaner also suggests following the industry analysts' predictions to learn about possible moves the industry as a whole might take. These may include stock market analysts, newsletter reporters, trade associations and labour unions.

Analysis of strengths, weaknesses, opportunities and threats in each of these departments of an organization is a valuable way to learn about a company or industry opportunities.

Company profiling

One of the most sought-after applications of competitive intelligence is a detailed description of a particular company. Due to the number of requests we had for this type of project, we developed a detailed technique, called 'company profiling', which we use to analyse a company's activities, operations or strategies. It entails examination of a company's background information, management, strategies, finances, operations, technology, marketing, sales, products and/or services, distribution, employees, R & D or engineering, and any other types of information we can dig up about a company. While conducting detailed research on a company is not new, analysing all the components of a company simultaneously creates an expansive picture of the company that might not otherwise have been obtained.

By researching all the functions of a company at the same time, we are often capable of analysing the company in greater detail. For example, if we learn that a company has a risk-taking management team that plans to implement some aggressive marketing and corporate strategies, but know that their finances are not in the best condition and that they are not very technologically astute, we may be able to deduce that this company could have difficulty in carrying out its grandiose plans.

Some of the best applications for this type of analysis include mergers, alliances, joint ventures and other partnership arrangements where companies need to know everything they can about the company in question.

See the accompanying box for a company profiling worksheet developed to ensure thorough research and analysis of each of the main aspects of the company being researched.

COMPANY PROFILE WORKSHEET

Company name
Address
Telephone number(s)
Toll-free number(s)
Fax number(s)
Web site address

Company background

History of the company (ie founding date, number of employees)
Key ownership of the company (ie company structure, key shareholders)
Key industry sector(s) the company is involved in
Perception of the company by media, customers, etc
Exchange on which securities are traded

Management information

Name and relevant background information of key corporate executives and advisers – there are typically six key levels of corporate executives and advisers to consider in the management of a company:

1. president, chief executive officer (CEO), chief operations officer (COO), chief financial officer (CFO), chief marketing officer (CMO) and chief information officer (CIO);
2. senior or executive vice-president;
3. vice-president of operations, vice-president of finance, vice-president of marketing, vice-president of informatics, etc;
4. board of directors;
5. legal adviser(s) – this may be a legal firm;
6. accounting adviser(s) – the person or company that audits the company's financial information.

Company strategy

Company's focus (past, present and future)
Corporate culture
New product developments
Market entry strategies/new markets
Mergers and/or alliances
Joint ventures

Financial information

Revenues
Profitability
Fixed costs
Variable costs
Debt
Capital
R & D expenditures

Operational information

Facility information
    Number of facilities
        Location
        Size
        Condition of facilities
        New/upcoming/expanding facilities
Technology used in operations
Operational output

Technology information

Types of technology used in each of the company's main functions
Server and Web site information

Marketing information

Key markets served
Market share in each market
Marketing and advertising strategies
Market entry strategies
Customers/clients served in each market

Sales information

Number of people on sales force
Key sales channels
Customer service information
Sales force compensation methods
Major customers/clients

Product and/or service information

Major product lines
Minor product lines
Sales information by key product lines
Specifications on products
Suppliers of raw materials, parts, labour or intellectual capital

Distribution information

Supply chain used
Shipping methods
Suppliers

Employee information

Number of employees
Number of employees in major employment categories (ie marketing, human resources, accounting, etc)

Salaries of major employment groups
Union information/collective bargaining agreements
Subcontracting

R & D/engineering

Types of R & D
Number of R & D staff/contractors/consultants
Types of engineering
Number of engineering staff/contractors/consultants
R & D/engineering budget

Other information

Specify

Ratio analysis

These analysis techniques are borrowed from bankers who quickly and effortlessly size up a company's financial strength and future using ratios. Some of these ratios include the current ratio, quick ratio, accounts receivable ratios, inventory turnover ratio, average days in inventory ratio, total debt to assets ratio, debt servicing ratio, debt to equity ratio and profitability ratios. Before you leave this chapter, thinking it was intended for accountants, keep reading. The ratios sound less palatable than they actually are. A general understanding of them now will be extremely valuable when you are analysing your competitors.

The current ratio indicates how liquid a company is. In other words, will it have sufficient money to pay its suppliers, contractors and other short-term debtors on time? The higher the ratio, the greater degree of liquidity a company has.

Current ratio

$$\text{Current ratio} = \frac{\text{current assets}}{\text{current liabilities}}$$

For example, if ABC Corporation has 750,000 euros in current assets and 500,000 euros in current liabilities, you would divide 750,000 euros by 500,000 euros to obtain 1.5 as the current ratio.

Quick ratio

The quick ratio (also called the acid-test ratio) is very similar to the current ratio, except that it considers that the company's inventory may be difficult to sell. It is a much stricter measure of liquidity of a company.

$$\text{Quick ratio} = \frac{\text{current assets} - \text{inventory}}{\text{current liabilities}}$$

Accounts receivable ratios

The accounts receivable ratio is an indicator of the quality of the organization's inventory – in other words, how quickly accounts receivables are collected and how quickly inventory is sold and payment received. By determining this and the average collection period a company has, you can determine how much pressure there is on the liquid position of the company and whether it will be forced to seek and rely on short-term loans.

$$\text{Accounts receivable turnover} = \frac{\text{total sales}}{\text{accounts receivable balance}}$$

$$\text{Average collection period} = \frac{365 \text{ days}}{\text{accounts receivable turnover}}$$

For example, if ABC Corporation has sales totalling 10,000,000 euros and its accounts receivable balance is currently at 1,000,000 euros, then you know that its annual sales are 10 times the amount of the outstanding receivables. This indicates that the cycle of sales and collection of receivables was repeated 10 times across the year. If you then divide 365 days in a year by 10, you can determine that it takes approximately 36.5 days to collect on each sale made by ABC Corporation, which is fairly good.

Inventory turnover ratio

Determining how quickly a company turns over its inventory is also a valuable financial indicator.

$$\text{Inventory turnover} = \frac{\text{sales}}{\text{inventory}} \quad \text{or} \quad \frac{\text{cost of goods sold}}{\text{inventory}}$$

The results of using these ratios can be very different based on the type of data you are using. Cost of goods sold is typically a more accurate representation of inventory turnover. If you further divide 365 days in a year by the inventory turnover, you can determine how many days on average inventory sits in a warehouse or store.

$$\text{Average days in inventory} = \frac{365 \text{ days}}{\text{inventory turnover}}$$

A competitor may be considering a huge inventory amongst its assets, yet if you can determine its inventory turnover to be extremely slow, then you can more realistically gauge its strength.

Total debt to assets ratio and debt servicing ratio

To determine a company's level of indebtedness, there are two main ratios to consider: total debt to assets ratio and the debt servicing ratio.

$$\text{Total debt to assets ratio} = \frac{\text{total debt}}{\text{total assets}}$$

$$\text{Debt servicing ratio} = \frac{\text{EBIT} + \text{depreciation}}{\text{Interest} + (\text{principal payments}/(1-t))}$$

where EBIT stands for earnings before interest and taxes and t stands for the marginal tax rate.

Debt to equity ratio

$$\text{Debt to equity ratio} = \frac{\text{long-term debt}}{\text{shareholders' equity}}$$

The best use for the debt to equity ratio is to get an understanding of a company's ability to generate new funds for financing its growth strategies. The larger the resulting number from the equation, the worse off the company is. The acceptable debt load to equity ratio differs between industries.

Profitability ratios

A competitor's profitability is an extremely important factor to understand to enable your organization to be more competitive. There are two main ratios used to determine profitability of a company. They are return on assets and return on equity.

$$\text{Return on assets} = \frac{\text{net income}}{\text{total assets}}$$

$$\text{Return on equity} = \frac{\text{net income}}{\text{total stockholders' equity}}$$

A healthy return on equity is approximately 20 per cent. However, these ratios vary from industry to industry, so be sure to determine the industry average before deciding if a company is reasonably profitable.

Event analysis

Monitoring the movements of a company and looking for competitively significant moves or events is an immensely valuable analysis tool, which we label 'event analysis'. It entails analysing past and current events within a company or marketplace to detect possible future events that may result in changes to your competitive position. For example, if a company signs a licensing agreement or memorandum of understanding with a foreign company, this is a 'red flag' that the company has expansion plans, either to a new market or for new technology or products. If a company purchases land, at some point in the near future it will probably build some facility or office on that property. If it acquires a company whose processes are outside the realm of its usual products or services, obviously it has plans to expand into other areas.

When a company books a significant block of advertisement space in trade or consumer publications, it might indicate a new product or service launch, or a new marketing strategy. If it advertises many new job listings, it may be embarking on expansion in a particular area of the company. For example, if a company advertises many new job listings in engineering, it probably has plans to design a new product or significantly change an existing one. If it plans to hire many new marketing people, the chances are it has a new or improved product or service already well under way and is about to promote it.

Event analysis from a historical perspective is often useful for illustrating why certain industries or industry players struggle with the changing nature of competition. Electrical utilities are a prime example. For decades, the electricity business was a relatively risk-free, stable and profitable industry. All this has changed in the last few years with concerted efforts by governments to deregulate energy markets. Competition, not surprisingly, has now become critical in developing a company's strategy. Strange as it sounds, thinking about competition was not always a vital aspect of conducting business in the electricity industry.

Deregulation is an event that creates opportunities and threats. In the case of the utilities, long-standing monopolies are being forced to compete by new rules. Strategies and motives, mergers and alliances, national and international competitors, and more demanding customers are all now key elements in business strategies. Players in the electricity industry are looking to diversify – whether it is in the form of selling off volatile power-generation operations to companies better able to manage the risk, or merging with natural gas companies. Utilities and other electricity businesses cannot ignore the increasingly competitive environment.

When analysing industries through event analysis, keep the historical perspective in mind when you conduct your competitive analysis. Where a company has come from may give you valuable insight, not only into where it is going, but how successful it may be in getting there.

Patent analysis

If you are trying to measure innovation and potential in a company, follow its patents and trademarks. Patents and trademarks can tell you which companies are assuming leadership roles or will take future leadership roles and which countries are at the cutting edge of technology. They can also tell you about strategic alliances between companies and the relationships between subsidiaries of the same parent corporation, maturity of technologies and the duration needed to exploit different types of technologies or innovations fully, where research and development funds are being spent, and individuals within organizations that are particularly innovative.

Personality profiling

Personality profiling is one of the most interesting ways to analyse a company and predict its future moves. It entails creating a profile of the key decision-makers to help predict the direction in which they will take the company. For example, it is very common to see a shift in corporate culture and priorities when a new CEO steps into the shoes of a previous leader, and is clearly looking to put his or her mark on the company.

People tend to have patterns in their attitudes and behaviours, which you can see if you look at their history and background. For example, a corporate executive who has a history of relying heavily on financial information and, more importantly, the bottom line will probably guide the company in the direction of its most profitable business units. Efforts will be directed to those units. An executive with a marketing background will continue to focus a lot of attention on the marketing of the company's products and services. Whatever has proved successful for a person will be a pattern that he or she continues. Conversely, whatever strategies failed probably will not be repeated again.

When trying to put together a personality profile of an executive, start by looking at the community newspapers of the towns or cities the person has lived in. Typically these papers include articles about their more successful residents. Each article on its own might not tell much about the personality of the person in question; however, when pieced together, they start to paint a picture and may expose some very apparent traits. Another way to start when creating a personality profile is to examine articles about the company as a whole to create a profile of its CEO or other very senior executives. Often these people make the decisions for the company, so their actions are reflected in the strategies and direction of the overall corporation.

You can gain valuable insight into someone's identity by examining his or her:

- childhood history (where the person was born, whether he or she was poor and what traits the parents might have imparted);
- education (where he or she studied, for how long and what the person has learnt outside of school);
- work history (how the person handled situations that arose in his or her previous job, what types of organizations he or she has worked for and whether it was in the private or public sector);
- current lifestyle (how the person spends his or her time and money);
- goals and objectives (what drives the person and whether he or she appears to be conservative in approach to reaching goals or whether he or she is driven by instinct).

Also consider body language and gestures when analysing a personality. These may be evident during speeches or television interviews. Some analysts also examine the handwriting of a person, using graphology to determine a person's identity.

Merger analysis

What if your organization is looking to acquire or merge with another one? What would you do? Take a few tips from the king of acquisitions, also known as John Chambers, the President and CEO of Cisco Systems. He cites five things that he looks for when analysing the prospects of acquiring a particular company, according to a recent interview in *Business 2.0*:

1. shared vision of where the industry is heading and similar or complementary roles each company wants to play in it;
2. short-term gains for acquired employees who may be uncomfortable during times of merger or acquisition;
3. long-term strategy wins for the shareholders, employees, customers and business partners;
4. similar cultures and chemistry; and
5. geographic proximity, particularly for large acquisitions.

If a deal does not meet at least three of the above criteria, Cisco will not touch it. If it even has four, there is some scepticism. For Chambers, meeting all five of the above criteria makes for a successful acquisition candidate.

Daimler's Jurgen Schrempp and Chrysler's Robert Eaton might disagree with the necessity for similar cultures and geographic proximity. Their merger to form Daimler Chrysler was an atypical union. Considered by some to be competitors and unlikely candidates to join forces, their merger has been highly successful, despite the Atlantic Ocean between them and the differing cultures between Germany and the United States, both at a social and corporate level. This merger is discussed in greater detail in Chapter 14.

The best and most successful forms of analysis incorporate more than one technique before drawing conclusions. For example, if you consider the strengths and weaknesses together with the capabilities of a competitor, you will have a picture of what that company is capable of doing. If, at the same time, you analyse the corporate culture and management personalities of the competitor, you will have an understanding of the ways the competitor will act within the industry. Not only will you know what it can do, you will know what it will do. One without the other would create an incomplete picture.

Consider the case of Pointcast, the 'push technology' that allows online subscribers to indicate the news they would like to receive from numerous sources. Users simply launch Pointcast on their computers and the application brings the news to their desks. Soon after push technology appeared in the marketplace, it was 'all the rage'. Yet the technology never took off the way 'experts' anticipated. In fact, very early in its existence Pointcast turned down a multi-million dollar offer and assistance from a much larger and wealthier firm to market the technology itself. Years later, Pointcast was bought for a fraction of the earlier bid. If you had been competing with Pointcast, it would have been critical to have examined the company's aggressive 'I'll do it alone' management style, as well as its capacity to turn the technology into the phenomenon it could have been. If you had analysed both concurrently, you would have recognized that, while Pointcast was aggressive in its approach, it lacked sufficient human and financial resources and business savvy to make push technology the household (and business) name it could have been. Your conclusion would have been not to worry about Pointcast as a threat.

Analysis is the lifeblood of competitive intelligence. Without it, there is only information or knowledge; with it, data, information and knowledge are miraculously transformed into intelligence. Companies that conduct strong analysis will see the fruits of their labours in the form of competitive advantage. In the intelligence age, strong analysis skills will be instrumental to an intelligent organization's success. Analysts who master these skills will become the intelligence innovators of this age.

analysing your company
through benchmarking

If you know your enemy and know yourself, you need not fear the result of a hundred battles.

SUN TZU, 500 BC

If you know your competitors and your organization, you need not fear the result of competition.

MICHELLE COOK AND CURTIS COOK, AD 2000

An intelligent organization has a clear understanding of its strengths and weaknesses, as well as those of its competitors. As a result, it stands a much better chance at success in a competitive environment. There are both fewer surprises and greater confidence that the various elements comprising its business operations are functioning as effectively as possible. This confidence is rarely generated by simple introspection alone. It is both arrogant and groundless to claim you are the best at something when you have very little evidence against which to compare. This is the reason so many companies have been quick to adopt the process of competitive benchmarking.

Benchmarking is the ongoing process of finding, researching and analysing best-in-class organizations, products, services or practices, which will lead to improvement within one's own organization. Books have been devoted entirely to the topic due to its relevance in today's business environment. Benchmarking had its genesis in the efforts made by Japanese companies during the early days of their ascent to dominance in the production and manufacture of so many consumer goods. These firms recognized that it was inadequate simply to duplicate efforts made by current manufacturing leaders like the United States. Rather, they had to combine the best techniques, the most efficient processes and the most effective methods found in diverse industries. The Japanese realized that they could learn from both the good and bad ideas of others who had covered the territory before, and build on those ideas to create something better. This practice, which has slowly found its way into North American and European businesses over the last decade, has become known as 'benchmarking'. Put simply, benchmarking means learning from other people's mistakes and, even better, their successes.

Competitive benchmarking means using the lessons learnt by other companies to implement changes that will increase your company's competitive advantage. Effective use of competitive benchmarking techniques helps companies leap over the competition, avoid costly mistakes and learn from the experiences of other organizations. All of these benefits lead to a better competitive position in the global marketplace.

There is a significant amount of confusion surrounding benchmarking in the marketplace. Before we explain how to use competitive benchmarking effectively in your organization, it is important to have a clear understanding of exactly what competitive benchmarking is and what it is not. In our consulting practice, we routinely come across the same misunderstandings of what constitutes benchmarking. We have identified five main misconceptions, which we continually try to dispel.

Myths about benchmarking

You must benchmark your company or organization against your competitors

The first (and most common) myth is that you must benchmark your company against your competitors. This is not necessarily true. You should know what your competitors are doing and how they are doing things better (or worse) than your organization. This knowledge allows you to differentiate your organization, capitalize on your competitors' weaknesses and confront their strengths in a competitive and strategically advantageous manner. However, looking outside your industry to organizations that have demonstrated best-in-class performance in some area of their operations is often more effective in assisting your organization with becoming better at what you do.

Benchmarking is used to cut costs and eliminate people

The second myth we have identified is that benchmarking is solely a means to reduce costs or human resources. This has indeed been the result of some benchmarking efforts within certain organizations; however, it is not necessarily the case. In many instances, there may be a reallocation, reduction or increase in resources as a result of benchmarking efforts. For example, a benchmarking exercise in the area of expenditures on research and development may reveal that successful companies in various research-and-development-intensive industries have been sustaining success despite outsourcing much of their research efforts to private laboratories or universities. Further analysis of this option for your company may uncover a particular firm that has significant expertise and complementary objectives in the area of your research. You can now explore the feasibility of outsourcing some or all of the work, or establishing some type of strategic partnership. Maybe you will want to buy the firm.

Benchmarking is a finite activity

Thirdly, many people believe that all benchmarking activities have a beginning and an end. While some benchmarking efforts are project-based and therefore have a conclusion, benchmarking also works well as an ongoing process. This is true because industry methods continually change. There is not a single industry or industry sector that does not change. Change is the one constant in the universe, in nature or in business. This is especially true in the intelligence age, for example, as the rate of innovation in technology continues to increase. If you want to keep your organization innovative and visionary, track and evaluate the advances in technology and adopt those that are worth while. If your company had stopped looking beyond its own operations when electric typewriters, interoffice memos in triplicate and regular postal service were the standard, how long would it last in the age of mobile computing, the Internet and e-mail?

'Continuous improvement' is a well-worn phrase, but it remains relevant in the world of benchmarking. It does not matter whether it is a change in the way documents are managed within your organization, the methods used by your sales force to gather and act on sales leads or the criteria you use to identify potential partners or acquisitions. You can always improve your competitiveness by analysing the efforts of others.

Benchmarking means copying the best-in-class organizations

The fourth myth that we have come across is that benchmarking is simply a matter of determining what best-in-class organizations are doing and implementing them to improve success. This is a goal, but it is not always an achievable one. For example, your organization may simply not have the budget to implement some of the best-in-class processes. There are many factors that determine the likelihood of being able to apply best-in-class processes or advancements to an organization successfully. Just because you know how Bill Gates developed and marketed Windows products does not mean that your company has the capacity to become a multi-billion dollar organization like Microsoft. Consider the case of Federal Express, the company that revolutionized long-distance shipping. Just because you benchmark your company against FedEx's excellence in shipping operations does not mean that you will be able to organize your company's shipping efforts or distribution methods more effectively. Handling a huge quantity of packages does not necessarily make you a shipping expert.

Benchmarking is only relevant to businesses

We have encountered many government departments that claim benchmarking efforts are really inappropriate to the public sector. This is myth number five: that benchmarking is only applicable to the private sector. Government organizations and associations can and do benefit just as much from benchmarking as the private sector does. Some departments, which did not previously see the value of benchmarking, now sing its praises. One government department regulating the health industry found a process that was being utilized in a private company within the aerospace industry and was able to implement it to improve its own organization.

Benchmarking can enhance your ability to understand how to improve your organization and change your corporate culture to one that is less inward-focused. Over time, most organizations, whether they are private or public sector, small or large, can start to become myopic, that is they can only see what is taking place within their own walls. By shifting that focus outward, the organization has a better opportunity to become more innovative, to see things in new and different ways, and to break out of barriers that may be limiting the company's competitive position or overall effectiveness and efficiency within the industry. If an organization knows where it stands *vis-à-vis* its competitors, it will be in a better position to improve. If your organization, on the other hand, operates within a vacuum, your strategies and processes may have little bearing on the world outside your company's doors. If you set goals to improve your operations as a result of benchmarking, you will be in a better position not only to meet those goals, but also to improve on them. Improvement rarely takes place without goals and an effort to improve.

Types of competitive benchmarking

There are two types of competitive benchmarking: operational and strategic. Operational benchmarking involves benchmarking specific operations or functions of an organization in an attempt to improve performance in those areas. Strategic benchmarking entails benchmarking corporate or organizational strategy based on contrasting a best-in-class organization's strategies against your company's strategies.

Ideally, it is best to perform both types of benchmarking simultaneously to determine why a company is succeeding both at the strategic and operational levels. It is important to note that, typically, operational benchmarking tends to take longer than strategic benchmarking and is more intense both in the data-gathering and analysis processes.

Operational and strategic benchmarking in action

Consider the case of Xerox Corporation. The company is well known for its competitive benchmarking efforts and the resulting successes, but this was not always the case. Xerox was an overconfident industry leader in the early days of photocopy technology. As international competition grew, Xerox rested on its laurels, confident in its supremacy. Unprepared for Japanese competition in the early 1980s, Xerox finally recognized that it was competitively disadvantaged, and it turned to its Japanese affiliate, Fuji Xerox, to benchmark the Japanese quality processes. Upon completion of the benchmarking process in Japan, Xerox implemented a similar process in the US with tremendous success. Some experts cite this move as the strategy that put Xerox back on the photocopier map. Using operational benchmarking, Xerox regained its market share and leadership role in the industry.

Xerox also used strategic benchmarking to address serious customer satisfaction concerns. Initially, the company had decided to incorporate a money-back guarantee into its sales of photocopiers; however, Xerox later discovered that its customers did not really want a money-back guarantee. They wanted a strong replacement guarantee. People who purchased Xerox copiers simply wanted to know they would work properly and, if something went wrong, that Xerox would stand behind its equipment. Before implementing their replacement guarantee, Xerox identified a leader in customer satisfaction and benchmarked against it. In this case, the company was in a completely different industry, but the value Xerox received from the benchmarking exercise was proven. It implemented a guarantee that essentially assured customers that, if during the three years after purchase of Xerox equipment a customer was dissatisfied, then Xerox would replace it at no charge. The successful implementation of such an impressive guarantee restored customers' faith in the company and helped Xerox re-establish its name as an industry leader. Xerox's use of strategic competitive benchmarking helped the company reclaim its competitive position.

The process of benchmarking

Benchmarking works best when the parties involved consider themselves partners and recognize that there are mutual benefits as a result of participating in the exercise. Accomplishing this is easier in an environment of non-competition, where there is little likelihood that a competitive advantage gained by one participant will harm the other participant. Benchmarking can become more difficult if you have determined that you need to implement the process to measure aspects of your rivals' competitiveness. The concept of recognizing your competitors' strengths and working with them to benefit from those strengths may seem ludicrous, but it does occur. Competitors have become great allies in the benchmarking process. Consider the case of Dell Computers, one of the most successful computer retailers in the world. Instead of trying to develop a new service to provide support for business clients, the company found a best-in-class organization that had a proven record in the area of business customer support. Coincidentally, the company they found was also familiar with computers and Dell recognized that this company could actually provide this service on their behalf. Who did Dell turn to? None other than the company's direct competitor, IBM. The two companies partnered to offer IBM's expertise in service and support to purchasers of Dell hardware. As an intelligent organization, Dell recognized that there was no place in its competitive strategy for the 'business as war' mentality and, instead, looked to its competition for strategic partnership.

Competitive benchmarking can be accomplished without the active participation of the target organization, and this is often the case when a competitor is involved. These benchmarking efforts require the tools and techniques that we have identified in this book for gathering information, analysing it to create intelligence and acting on it to improve the function, operation or strategic approach you have identified. This is a more complex and often less rewarding process, because you do not have the full and active participation of the other company. It is an excellent test of the competitive intelligence process and worth pursuing to help improve your company's competitive position.

The eight stages of competitive benchmarking

Following these eight stages will help you implement and successfully complete a benchmarking effort in your organization.

1. Determine the functions and/or strategies of your company you wish to benchmark. It is important to remember that you can benchmark virtually any aspect of your business. Your goal is to improve what you do and the way you do it, improve your firm's competitiveness and increase your success. Part of this process will be to determine if your organization should conduct functional or strategic benchmarking, or both. This decision will largely depend on your needs. Some of the functional areas that could be benchmarked include customer requirements for products or services, products or parts manufactured, services provided, distribution or delivery methods, products purchased, or the many processes within an organization such as account collection practices, customer service resolution and virtually any other process within your company or organization.

2. Identify factors and variables to measure cost and quality for the functions you have chosen in step 1. This is also known as identifying benchmarks. Establishing benchmarks may be difficult if you have decided to examine your corporate strategies. These are often more difficult to quantify or measure in some type of unit. However, it is critical to your overall benchmarking process that you create benchmarks that will help you gauge success.

3. Determine the best-in-class companies for each factor to be benchmarked – companies that are low-cost operators for the above functions or whose quality or customer satisfaction is high. In the case of strategic benchmarking, determine those companies whose strategies you can learn from. These companies or organizations can be domestic or foreign competitors or they can be from a different industry altogether. Try to be creative and flexible in your pursuit of a best-in-class or best-of-breed organization. Robert C Camp has compiled a set of guidelines to follow when you are working with a benchmark partner in his book, *Benchmarking: The Search for Industry Best Practices that Lead to Superior Performance* (1989). It includes the following suggestions:

- Determine the most appropriate person to contact at the benchmarking partner's firm.
- Have a clear statement of the purpose and objectives for the visit prepared.
- It has been found most productive to stress the interest in uncovering industry best practices. If this is done on a professional-to-professional basis it should create initial interest in sharing information.
- Prepare an outline of the topic areas of interest to act as a guide for the visit.
- Obtain and review all available, relevant data on the company in advance.
- If the company is a customer or a supplier, contact the sales rep or account manager and request assistance in:
  - identifying the appropriate organization and individuals to contact; and
  - acting as an intermediary to set up the visit.
- Ensure that the equivalent internal operation is documented and understood from the point of view of the practices involved as well as the applicable performance metrics.
- The best team size is two or three individuals. Roles should be agreed to in advance such as who the leader will be, and who will ask the questions.
- Prepare a list of questions for which answers are desired in two major areas:
  - best practices – practices currently in use or planned; and
  - metrics – output ratios that support the justification for the best practices.
- Conduct the site visit and gather all relevant data and information.
- During the tour it may not be possible to take notes. Retain key points to be documented as soon after the tour as possible.
- Use time after the tour to obtain clarification of observations and information.
- Be prepared to discuss the equivalent internal data and information.
- Clarify data and information understanding before leaving or provide for follow-up methods to validate information interpretation.
- Offer a reciprocal visit and tour if appropriate.

    — Debrief the tour among the team members as quickly as possible following the tour. A productive way to accomplish this and prepare a trip report is to have a recorder present during debriefing to capture the discussion. The discussion should cover observations as well as the information received.

    — Thank the benchmarking partner for their time and cooperation both informally and formally by letter.

    — Document the tour in a written report.

4. Measure your performance for each factor or variable. This step entails delving much deeper than merely compiling industry statistics or data for competing firms and determining where you stand in contrast. In addition, it requires some serious honesty. Organizations often have a tendency to overestimate their strengths and underestimate their weaknesses, rather than looking at the 'cold hard facts'.

5. Measure the performance of the best-in-class companies identified in step 3. You should be assessing the factors and variables you identified in step 2 to learn how your target company or target companies measure up. For example, if you identified the cost and speed of producing widgets as key variables to examine, in this stage you would attempt to learn what the target company's cost of producing widgets is and how quickly it is able to produce them.

6. Evaluate the gap between your organization and the best-in-class organization. Once you have filled in all the key data for various factors and variables on your organization and the best-in-class organization, you can assess any variation between the two. In this stage, you compare or contrast the two companies very closely to learn more about possible areas of improvement within your organization. The better the analysis in this stage, the better can the overall results of the competitive benchmarking process be applied to your company to enhance its capacity to improve.

7. Determine ways to improve your organization and close the gap. This is a stage that is often overlooked by many organizations that conduct benchmarking efforts. However, it is important to fulfil this stage from a business development perspective. Just because you know the key areas where your organization differs from your best-in-class target does not mean that your company can improve if it simply implements those changes. There are often many barriers to organizational change that need to be closely examined in relation to your company. Perhaps your organization does not have the exhaustive budget or human resources available that the

best-in-class company does. Perhaps you have determined that the corporate culture in the target company is so different from that in your own business, that it would require nothing short of brain-washing to implement comparable strategic approaches to sales and marketing. That does not mean that the overall benchmarking process was useless, but rather that your company needs to devise an effective strategy to be able to implement what you have learnt from your competitive benchmarking efforts. Step 7 is about creating that strategy.

8. Develop improvement targets for the implementation of the programmes determined in step 7. Step 8 is closely paired with step 7. In fact, it is often most effective if the two steps are conducted simultaneously. This process entails determining the areas in which your organization could improve and adding that information to your corporate strategy.

The process of benchmarking is most effective when a partnership effort is constructed from the outset. It is mutually beneficial for these partners to share information and discuss practices. Both parties will derive far greater benefit from the whole exercise if they view each other as partners. Communication is also important and very necessary if benchmarking is going to work well. In his book, *Benchmarking: The Search for Industry Best Practices that Lead to Superior Performance* (1989), Robert C Camp provides his insight into the factors that make benchmarking a success. He cites the following success indicators:

- an active commitment to benchmarking from management;
- a clear and comprehensive understanding of how one's own work is conducted as a basis for comparison to industry best practices;
- a willingness to change and adapt based on benchmark findings;
- a realization that competition is constantly changing and there is a need to 'shoot ahead of the duck';
- a willingness to share information with benchmark partners;
- a focus on benchmarking, first on industry best practices and second on performance metrics;
- the concentration of leading companies in the industry or other functionally best operations that are recognized leaders;
- adherence to the benchmarking process;
- an openness to new ideas and creativity and innovativeness in their application to existing processes;
- a continuous benchmarking effort; and
- the institutionalization of benchmarking.

In the intelligence age, we anticipate that competitive benchmarking partnerships will flourish as more and more companies recognize the competitive advantages of working together to ensure continuous improvement within their respective industries. Intelligent organizations are recognizing that the 'business as war' approach is ineffective. The results of strategic partnership through benchmarking can lead companies to a better competitive position that they could not have achieved alone.

presenting and using your findings

Life happens too fast for you ever to think about it. If you could just persuade people of this, but they insist on amassing information.

KURT VONNEGUT, JUN

Now that you have analysed your information and turned it into intelligence, you have to find the most effective means to communicate it to the decision-makers in your company or organization. Or perhaps you are a decision-maker within your organization, and must be prepared not only to stand behind your competitive intelligence team but also to act on their findings. In Chapter 12, we discuss the role of an ongoing CI function within your intelligent organization, where intelligence that is gathered on a daily basis is shared throughout the company or department for use by everyone. However, truly to be an intelligent organization, you must recognize the value of competitive intelligence and implement both types of CI to be effective in dealing with marketplace shifts. You should set up a regular competitive intelligence function that gathers and analyses data on an ongoing basis as well as dealing with 'special projects' as they arise. This chapter focuses more on a 'special projects' basis, where a competitive intelligence task has been undertaken to address a specific need and the presentation of findings is for a select audience.

In a small company or organization, you may be the information-gatherer, analyst and decision-maker, which makes the presentation of the findings very easy. In larger organizations, these roles may be filled by numerous people, all of whom feel they have a stake in the outcome. It is also possible that the final decisions relating to the CI project will be made by a person or people who have not had a significant role in any aspect of the project and its progress. This makes the presentation all the more important. A competitive intelligence project is as likely to fail at this late stage as it is at any other point in the effort.

In Chapter 2, we discussed the importance of the executives being 'on side' with the competitive-intelligence team. It is critical to the success of any CI project and is essential to the competitiveness of your organization. If you have been following the competitive intelligence model, you might recall that, ideally, executives get involved and 'buy into' the process in Phase 1, prior to the 'needs assessment'. This chapter is essentially about Phases 8 and 9 of the model, 'disseminating intelligence to decision-makers' and 'acting on intelligence' respectively.

There are many ways in which important intelligence can be shared – written reports, verbal presentations and videos to name a few – and the effectiveness depends as much on the audience as the nature of the intelligence itself. The timing of the delivery is also a crucial determinant of the value of the intelligence. This chapter looks at some of the more reliable methods for intelligence delivery and examines related issues such as measuring success and promoting feedback.

Information, and especially intelligence for that matter, does not come in a can. The following examples illustrate two approaches to presenting findings that are very different yet equally effective. A sales representative may be speaking to a potential client who happens to know that a rival company has just decreased the prices of all its products. How does that sales representative deliver such key information to the people who can initiate action? A lengthy report and presentation is probably not the best option, nor is it likely given the sales representative's schedule; rather, a telephone call to the vice-president of marketing or the equivalent individual in the company with the details and suggestions for verification and action will maximize the value of the information provided the executive makes him or herself available and respects and understands the value and implications of the information presented by the sales representative. Such unplanned and immediate intelligence needs are not uncommon. In fact, verifying and acting on rumours, gossip and innuendo constitutes a significant part of CI work, and is generally a 'rush job'. This is likely to continue since there is no sign of the pace of business slowing in the intelligence age.

Financial analysis of a competitor may require a different approach. Usually, this is a planned project that, if successful, requires more formal presentation of the findings. Financial analysis and recommendations are often best presented in person using visual aids such as charts and graphs to represent the outcomes of financial analyses and forecasts. Ratios and numerical statistics that are incorporated into a lengthy written report may be glossed over or ignored because they do not lend themselves to the format.

The following suggestions will help you make the most of your competitive intelligence findings.

Work with decision-makers, not against them

This is not always as simple as it sounds, for two main reasons: 1) the decision-makers do not always know what they want; or 2) the decision-makers know what they want but fail to communicate it effectively to their employees. A colleague shared his experience at a mid-sized product manufacturing company that was consistently losing sales to a couple of competitors. The owner of the company rallied the troops in marketing (there was no competitive intelligence function) and demanded that they find out everything they could about the competitors. Over the next couple of months, experienced marketing employees became inexperienced information-gatherers, neglecting the duties at which they were proficient to conduct an exhaustive and directionless search for 'everything' about the rival companies. After compiling mountains of data, the CI novices were confronted with another dilemma: what to do with the stuff. When it was brought to the busy owner's attention, he demanded a report of their findings. Of course, all they had found was a disparate heap of facts, statistics and general information. The report was massive, completely useless and apparently never read. The company continues to lose ground to its competitors.

The role and participation of the decision-makers in a competitive intelligence function are critical to its success. For any CI project or process to succeed, it must have the backing of the bosses, and they must clearly communicate their needs if they expect them to be fulfilled. Conversely, you need to be responsive to those needs once they are known. The best place to start when determining what method of presentation is desired is with the decision-makers. If they advise you of their preferences and receive the intelligence as requested, the chances of it being absorbed and acted upon are far greater.

Some people are more visually oriented and prefer a short slide show or graphics outlining the findings in charts or graphs. Other people respond better to the written word, and should receive findings in one- or two-page intelligence summaries, which provide the recommendations to be acted upon and how they were derived. Other executives are more interpersonal in nature and may just want an informal and brief presentation of your findings in person. Since people absorb intelligence differently, consider the possible delivery options. It might make the chances of the intelligence being understood and acted upon by the decision-makers far better.

Timing is everything

One of the basic strengths of CI is that it allows you to act rather than react to events that can impact on your company or organization. The process is designed to address strategic needs before they arise or, if necessary, to foster the ability to counter changes in your competitive environment quickly. A strong recommendation for action based on rock-solid analysis of wholly verifiable information is worthless if the recommendation is made too late. This is why CI projects must be balanced with expectations, and 'being close' is better than 'being accurate' in most cases. In other words, financial findings may not be to the decimal point, but neither is that necessary. You can take as much time as you want to determine if your competitor is developing a new product. You may have the answer by the time the advertising campaign begins, at which time you can watch helplessly as your rival establishes the new product in the market. Conversely, you can set a time line for a focused CI project to determine where the new product is in the developmental stage, leaving your company enough time to prepare a strategy to compete, by either pre-empting the other product launch with your own product campaign or countering the product launch in another fashion. Perhaps you do not have the time or resources to launch a new product, but you may be able to design a new marketing and promotional campaign to deflect some of the attention away from the competitor. You may be able to find pricing information that allows you to make changes to remain competitive until your new product is available.

Timing is crucial. Business leaders will tell you that there is little time for navel-gazing, and CI professionals will tell you that information-gathering overkill is the greatest threat to success. Provide your decision-makers with intelligent and timely recommendations based on sound analysis.

So what exactly are you saying?

The end of the CI project is nearing and it is time to deliver your findings and recommendations. You know that management has asked for a one-page summary and a brief presentation in person. You hand out the summary and you talk about the findings and the recommendations. 'Based on the expressed objectives of management, the research and development strengths, and the successful and innovative launches of complementary products, Private Company A is a prime candidate for acquisition,' you begin, 'but they are carrying a substantial amount of debt and employee morale is rumoured to be very poor.' You had been asked to determine if Private Company A could be acquired. The decision-makers in your company still have no clue. How significant is the debt? What is the concern with employee morale? How do these elements figure in the grand scheme of things? The analysis is incomplete and the analyst is hedging his or her bets.

This type of fence-sitting serves to minimize the effectiveness of the whole CI effort. If the CI analyst is uncomfortable making a recommendation and backing it up with analysed information, it is quite possible that the CI process was flawed or the analyst simply does not have the backbone to stand behind the findings. The results must be clear and focused rather than general. CI analysts must be prepared to deliver good news and bad news equally, if they believe it is in the best interest of their company or client. They are being asked for a recommendation for action based on a process they have followed. All of this information is available to the decision-makers, and the analyst can explain the recommendations by referring to the findings and the background information. The presentation must identify the opportunities as well as the threats, and clearly indicate if certain elements of the project or the question remain uncertain. The presentation will be more valuable and the flow will be improved if the presenter has prepared in advance for questions or possible objections to the intelligence report by anticipating the concerns of the decision-makers. Not only is this more efficient, it adds credibility to the findings.

Ultimately, a decision must be made, but it is not up to the CI analyst. Whether or not a company acts on the recommendations that come out of a CI project is the responsibility of that company's decision-makers. The CI team or the analyst should not take this personally, particularly if the job has been done with skill and integrity to give the company or the client the best intelligence available. Leadership at this stage is the responsibility of the decision-makers. Jurgen Schrempp, co-chairman of

Daimler Chrysler was quoted as stating, 'I'll listen to any rank, it's the arguments that count. However, leadership means at some stage you have to summarize the arguments and make a decision. Decision is not a matter of committee; you have to take responsibility. Debate is not forever. Speed is a competitive factor. It's better to have 80 per cent than to wait for 100 per cent' (1999). This is never truer than with competitive intelligence.

Why should I believe you?

The trust factor is one of the greatest obstacles that a CI practitioner faces, whether that individual is a consultant or employed by a business or organization conducting CI. As a consultant, you may be preceded by your reputation or you may be grilled with questions about your expertise to conduct research and analysis, and make recommendations for a particular company or in a particular industry. As an employee, you may also be dealing with colleagues or supervisors who are less than convinced of your capabilities or suspicious about the CI process. In some instances, we have observed that executives or managers do not personally know the individuals within their company who are involved in CI and use this unfamiliarity as an opportunity to question their abilities. In these situations, building trust may take some time, but it is invaluable. Conversely, you may be the Chief Executive Officer, the chief information officer or other senior executive at a company, who may need to substantiate your decision with solid evidence and build trust from your shareholders. Use the logical, credible CI process to help explain the systematic approach that led to your findings or decision.

In a perfect world, the people who make the decisions participate in the competitive intelligence process throughout, providing leadership and direction as intelligence is used to develop business strategies. It becomes an integral component of all the moves a company makes to improve its competitive situation. However, it is often not possible for the executives to keep their fingers in the pot throughout the whole process.

What happens after the presentation has been made, the questions have been answered and the decision-makers are satisfied with the recommendations? If you are a consultant or a CI analyst for the company, your primary role is complete until the next project is identified. You simply need to make yourself available to assist with any questions or concerns that arise while the decisions are being made. However, if you are one of the decision-makers, it is your turn to take the lead. This is the point at which so many competitive intelligence efforts fail. If you have been a champion of the CI process, you will understand how critical this juncture is in any project. If you have not been a champion and you reach this stage, it is quite likely that luck or superhuman determination from your employees or consultant has made it possible. Either way, it is time to act.

Plan your strategy

If the CI process has been effective to this point, the intelligent organization will have a clear mandate to proceed with a strategy to act on the concern that led to the CI project. Depending on the nature of the intelligence delivered, the strategy could be as simple as continuing business as usual, or as complicated as redesigning a product and initiating an international marketing campaign under severe time constraints to beat a competitor to the punch. Regardless of the nature, the strategy must take the form of a plan, so that everyone in the organization is reading from the same page.

Communicate your strategy

It is a wonderful feeling to know that the executive board in a company, the president and CEO, the various vice-presidents of finance, marketing, business development and engineering, and other executives are all informed that a strategic change is taking place as a result of a competitive analysis. Yet these people do not actually perform a number of the tasks that are required to turn the new strategy into a reality. The intelligent organization ensures that channels are created to disseminate new strategic directions to the front line – the operational people responsible for making an organization profitable and successful. To borrow from the world of technology, these channels must be high-speed and secure. Chapter 12 delves more deeply into the communications issues when a company or organization establishes a competitive intelligence function. Critical advantages are lost if sales representatives, public relations people, design engineers or accountants are not informed about changes that impact on the way they are currently fulfilling their tasks. Critical advantages may also be lost if communications are too widespread. If it is necessary for a distributor to know that your company is taking a different approach because it will affect the relationship and change the way in which you conduct business, the distributor will need to know. If it is a change that has nothing to do with distribution channels and that particular relationship, why create a source of information for your competition? Take the time to establish 'need-to-know' communications within your intelligent organization. Consider also your options when it comes to incorporating non-disclosure agreements, as this may be a necessary evil for these types of circumstances. (Chapter 13 discusses the means to protect your organization's intellectual property.)

Implement your strategy

If the planning and communication stages discussed above are carried out effectively, the implementation phase of the strategy will be relatively painless. The decision-makers have reached the necessary people with a clear message for action. Communications channels are two-way, so that feedback and questions can be received and addressed. The marketing group understands that it has five months to develop and launch a campaign around the new safety feature that is now the high-priority project within the engineering group, which has been given nine months to perfect it. An information presentation, sales literature and pricing information are being prepared for the sales force and will be made available to all the sales representatives closer to the launch. In the interim, they have been asked to identify existing and potential clients who may be making a product purchase in the next few months. Enquiries from the sales force indicate that they want to know the details of the new feature so they can start to sell it. They are told that the details will be made available once the company is convinced that the time frame is too small for another company to duplicate the feature, were that other company to find out the specifications. At this point, it is a question of everyone simply doing his or her job. There are no surprises, yet there are clear and measurable objectives and goals.

Tracking results and measuring success

It can be quite challenging to track the results of a strategy, because the impact is not always apparent immediately, or even over a considerable amount of time. Of course, certain strategies elicit immediate results, both positive and negative. You can only hope that your strategic moves do not result in threats of legal action, or draw the attention of the competition authorities, for example. The chances are that you have made a strategic blunder if either of these outcomes proves to be warranted. The nature of your competitive move will determine what type of results you will experience. A targeted strategy to take market share from a leader in your industry will seem to be working if you start gaining new customers, including former customers from the industry leader. Yet that result might be tempered if the leading rival reacts to your strategy and takes steps to maintain its position, through more competitive prices, increased advertising, incentives or other means. Sometimes a smaller company escapes the wrath of a big player that considers itself invincible. Sometimes the strategy just ends up drawing unwanted attention, which negates the objective of the competitive move.

Measuring the success of a competitive action also presents challenges, particularly if the objective was not something quantifiable, like a percentage increase in sales or market share, or a set reduction in operating costs as a result of implementing new practices from a competitive benchmarking effort.

Presenting your findings in an effective way, using the recommendations to create and implement the plan, measuring the outcome to determine your success and evaluating the areas in which the whole process could have been improved (which is Phase 10 of the competitive intelligence model) bring you full circle. You are now in a position to formulate your next competitive intelligence need. It is important to remember that every action you take, every strategy that you develop and every plan that you implement creates a new set of needs. One competitive intelligence cycle is complete but your job is far from over. For example, Mannesmann AG, Germany's biggest mobile-phone company, played an instrumental role in Olivetti's successful acquisition of Telecom Italia (discussed in Chapter 11); however, it had only a brief moment to savour its number two position in the wireless industry in Italy following the Telecom Italia deal before it offered to buy the UK's third-largest mobile operator, Orange plc. With all of these rival companies vying for an increased share of the hyper-competitive European cellular market, which is set to double in the next two years, it was only a matter of weeks before Mannesmann was plunged into a hostile takeover bid by Vodaphone AirTouch plc, the world's largest wireless services provider. While no hostile take-over has ever succeeded in Germany, Vodafone's strategy caused Mannesmann to react immediately, not only to an unattractive bid, but to conduct damage control on joint ventures it was pursuing in other European countries.

At its best, competitive intelligence can successfully enable your organization to act rather than react to marketplace pressures. Indeed, when the whole competitive intelligence model is implemented effectively, success despite these external pressures is greatly enhanced.

nine

Technology tools and techniques

> However much intelligence computers may attain, now or in the future, theirs must always be an intelligence alien to genuine human problems and concerns.
>
> JOSEPH WEIZENBAUM

Just as technology has revolutionized every aspect of our lives, technological advancements are changing the rules of the competitive intelligence game. In the intelligence age, technology will play an ever-increasing role in all aspects of business, including competitive intelligence. Innovative applications for analysing competitive factors and forecasting the outcomes of strategic decisions may seem like the unrealistic dreams of CEOs and CIOs alike; however, the reality is that we will probably see such competitiveness enhancing software in the not-too-distant future.

Technology has also increased the confusion as to what constitutes competitive intelligence. For example, many software developers claim they have created intelligence products that can do any and everything, just short of running entire organizations. Over the last decade, there have been incredible advances in the use of technology in business planning, particularly in enterprise applications known as business intelligence. Interestingly, the processes, tools, techniques and model we have described as competitive intelligence in this book are often referred to as business intelligence as well. In reality, it lives up to the name far better than its computer-based counterpart, despite the claims of many of the software vendors. Still, there is a role for business intelligence software and many other technology tools in the world of CI. These tools include the Internet, business intelligence software such as data warehouses and data mining tools, databases, and online services, to name a few.

Realistic expectations of what technology can do for your organization's competitiveness, coupled with an understanding of competitive intelligence as a management discipline, will improve your ability to integrate both in your business. This chapter discusses the role of these technology tools in an overall CI function. It also explains what they can (and cannot) do to help a company compete more successfully.

The Internet

Widespread use of the Internet has contributed to the growth of CI around the world. Exhaustive secondary or library research was not an option for organizations with modest budgets and scarce human resources. The Internet has pulled information collection and research from the realm of large corporations and placed it in the hands of any individual with an Internet service provider. With the Internet at its disposal, a business can reduce its cost and time in gathering information, making the information-gathering component of competitive intelligence more feasible. However, many people have mistakenly started equating Internet searching and Internet tools like Web crawling with competitive intelligence. Internet searching is Internet searching, plain and simple. Web crawlers 'crawl' the World Wide Web to retrieve data you specify that you need. They can crawl the Web sites of competing companies, customers, suppliers or others and retrieve data, if it is readily available. Web crawlers were discussed in greater detail in Chapter 5.

Business intelligence software

If you attend technology trade shows or scan the advertisements in technology publications, you are probably quite familiar with the surge of business intelligence software offered by numerous companies. These products are generally built around two concepts: data warehousing and/or data mining. On their own, data warehouses or data mining software cannot produce business intelligence for your operation. No software can do that. However, when used with good old-fashioned intuition and analysis, as only human intervention can supply, these software tools are valuable additions to your organization's intelligence function.

Data warehouses

Building a storage place for the data your organization collects and needs to use later is a valuable adjunct to an overall CI programme. One way of doing this is to use a data warehouse. Data warehousing provides access to logical, structured data that is buried within databases and electronic files. The concept of data warehousing is not new. Decision-makers have always required access to logical, structured data buried within departmental databases and electronic files to assist them in monitoring different aspects of their operations. The foundation for effective data warehousing is still a well-designed, user-friendly, accurate and consistent set of data. This is not easy to achieve when you have reams of data and multiple users with diverse needs. The expression 'GIGO' – garbage in, garbage out – is especially true of data warehousing software. It is only as good as its contents. Valuable data is often time-sensitive and can become dated very easily. Keep that in mind if your organization implements a data warehouse. Developing a data warehouse to meet your department's needs will take a lot of teamwork, project-management skills and an investment in time. Do not expect the perfect solution overnight.

One major misperception about data warehousing is that the value is primarily linked to how much data you can get into the warehouse; in fact, the value rests with how easily decision-makers can get the information out for analysis. In many cases, all you are getting out is data too, unless you have business intelligence applications that facilitate the users' ability to access, analyse and create reports using data in the warehouse. These applications generally require two types of data to maximize the functions they are capable of providing. The first type is relational data, which is ideal for very detailed or specific information, such as individual customer transactions or inventory statistics. The second type of data is often referred to as online analytical processing, or OLAP data. This data is summarized or aggregate information, which helps measure aspects of business performance and other trends that can impact on the bottom line. These applications help you transform data into potentially interesting associations – what you could define as information – and you may even be able to use your software to build and test your hypotheses further. Granted, you still have to do all the 'intelligent' work, the real analysis, to make that information actionable – in other words turn it into intelligence to help you make decisions. In addition, any data that is not numerical, which is a considerable amount in most CI projects, cannot be stored, retrieved or analysed using this type of business intelligence software. We are still waiting for a computer application that can automate the competitor profiling analysis for us.

The real value of data warehousing is the software's ability to organize quantitative data in specific streamlined packets, store it for relatively easy access and reporting, and call it up for assessment. Departments with overlapping needs may consider more than one warehouse, or smaller stores of related data in 'datamarts'. Having a datamart for financial information, another for human-resource information and another for client profiles, for example, may be the most efficient method for your department; however, if there is the slightest chance that data in one datamart could be combined with data in another to produce useful information, the design must allow for that type of integration.

A data warehouse, or database, or accounting ledger for that matter, is useless unless you can harness its full potential. And it is only as good as its contents. Dirty data or incomplete data is going to have an impact on your queries and modelling. Because data warehouses are typically storage depots for corporate information, you may be able to pinpoint key successes and failures based on your own operational data, but you will not be able to measure quantitative elements of your operations against the 'best-in-class' departments or external organizations, unless you actively collect data about these external organizations and use it in your querying and modelling. This type of benchmarking is a crucial element in human-driven business intelligence.

One company that specializes in business intelligence software claims that its analysis tools will give you global views of your operation. However, a truly global view of your operation looks beyond your database. Because some of the most valuable data you need may not reside within your organization, you may have to rely on public or proprietary databases to supplement your existing data. You may be faced with inconsistencies in data definitions and values as you try to combine data from more than one source.

If the data is only about the internal functions of your organization, it will be difficult to generate meaningful information to analyse the external environment in which you operate. Before implementing a system, it is important to evaluate departmental reporting needs, as well as the requirements of the various users. A data warehouse with an onerous reporting tool and questionable content will be a data graveyard. A warehouse with current, well-defined and organized data, combined with powerful querying and modelling tools, can yield rich information for your department. However, the output of these systems is *never* 'intelligence'. It is information. In competitive intelligence, there is a well-established flow from data to information to intelligence. Data becomes information with some associations and analysis. Information can only become intelligence after the information is skilfully analysed and directly applied to a specific problem. So keep your expectations in check when building a data warehouse. Real intelligence only comes from skilled human intervention.

Data mining

Data mining is the process of finding, exploring and modelling data to reveal potential patterns or associations. With the growth of database software use and the warehousing of data in quantities most humans could not comprehend, let alone access, data mining tools are becoming increasingly common as a way to extract interesting patterns or relationships between data. By using sophisticated statistical analysis, data mining software uncovers relationships between data that would be missed using more traditional methods. Data mining finds these relationships using various modelling techniques, some of which are designed on the neural networks of the brain. These models serve as guides for further analysis. Sound complicated? It can be.

Data-mining tools create classifications, associations, sequences, clusters and forecasts by manipulating your data and creating models. These are not the kinds of models you create in your spare time – these processes can be time-intensive if you are not a real fan of all things statistical. Just preparing the data for the mining process can require significant time and effort, so it is crucial to know in advance what you are trying to achieve with your queries and modelling efforts. The best way to ensure this is to define a specific objective that focuses on solving a particular operational problem in a manner that can be measured. It is the measurable results that you will analyse to identify ways to improve your operation.

The models you create with this information are only valuable if they can help you make better decisions in your department. Of course, the human intervention is still required to analyse all this information and actually make the decision. And while your model may be accurate, it may not reflect reality. The proof lies in testing it in the real world. In 1999, Fuld and Company, Inc released a study on business intelligence applications it had conducted a year earlier. The study surveyed intelligence department managers, market researchers, librarians and senior management, primarily from Fortune 1000 corporations. The results of the study indicated that 'intelligence software designed to create intelligence for corporations does not deliver'. It also concluded, 'At their best, these applications, ranging from tailored intranet applications and Lotus Notes to specialized knowledge management packages, such as Wincite, deliver or organize information. They do not analyse and hence do not create intelligence.' Twenty different software packages, including Wincite, Access, Lotus Notes, Exchange, Business Insight, Oracle's ConText and others were studied over time, not only to rate product characteristics, but also to analyse the customers' experiences in using them.

James T King, Systems Section Manager for the State of Maine's Bureau of Information Services, has reached similar conclusions. The Bureau deployed a business intelligence application to users across 42 state agencies throughout Maine. According to King, the software is used to retrieve information from the Bureau's data warehouse to analyse financial, budgetary and payroll/personnel information. It provided immediate access to valuable information for decision-makers such as financial and administrative managers, as well as their staff, allowing them to satisfy their own information needs without the involvement of the Information Services. One disadvantage, according to King, was the considerable human resources required to distribute the software and models to the numerous client locations across the state. When asked what suggestions he would give to other organizations looking to purchase, set up or use business-intelligence software, King recommends involving the intended users in the evaluation of the software and in defining their reporting needs to ensure the software will do what they need it to do.

If your CI needs include the ability to access your corporate databases and the information they contain, business intelligence software may provide the solution you need. A well-structured data warehouse, clean data and easy-to-use query tools and reporting functions will help keep you on top of the internal functions of your organization. You may even be able to incorporate data from other sources, even other warehouses. But true business intelligence still resides in human intervention, through analysis, forecasting and, ultimately, strategic decision-making.

Databases

In Chapter 4, we identified the Japan External Trade Organization (JETRO) as a valuable source of information. JETRO is a sophisticated organization maintained by the Japanese government to dispense valuable commercial information to domestic companies looking for foreign market intelligence. It is also a prime example of the effective use of technology to organize and disseminate intelligence. More recently, JETRO has provided similar information services to foreign companies looking at opportunities in Japan. Much of JETRO's information is accessible on its computerized database service. A database is a collection of information that is organized and indexed, and housed on computers or computer networks, found online or captured on CD ROM. It can be as simple as contact information, such as company names and addresses, or as complex as medical research from around the globe.

Databases do have their drawbacks. They are not always current, which means the information you access could be months or even years old. It is important to remember that, in these cases, database information may only be useful to create a historical profile or to point you to potential leads for additional information. Databases may also be selective in terms of content, especially those that compile information from journals or magazines. You may not even have access to complete articles, let alone valuable information that may have been available in advertising or other content within the original publication. Sometimes it is worth the extra effort to find the original version, if the information is critical. You should determine how comprehensive a database is before you buy the CD ROM or subscribe to a pay service. Paid commercial databases were discussed in greater detail in Chapter 5.

Databases can make very specialized information collection efforts much simpler. Earlier in the book, we discussed searching for patents electronically. Industry Canada, the federal government organization responsible for promoting commerce in Canada, has implemented a technology solution that combines a massive database with business intelligence software to make regular patent searching easier. Known as Tech Source, it is a tool used by the Canadian Intellectual Property Office (CIPO) for researching patents. IBM developed Tech Source as a research tool and integrated it with an enormous database, complete with both domestic and international patent information, to enable patent inspectors to go through the process of verifying whether or not a patent application represents original art.

Industry Canada's next move is to make some parts of Tech Source public, so that not only can patent inspectors at CIPO mine the data, but Canadians can take advantage of the information online as well. The trademarks database is already available on Strategis, Industry Canada's Web site (www.strategis.ic.gc.ca).

Understanding the competitive intelligence model and the process of turning raw data into intelligence will give an individual or organization a better understanding of the role technology can play in strategic decision-making that is supported by competitive intelligence. Human-created and human-inspired competitive intelligence is an organized, methodical approach to gathering data and making associations to turn it into information, and then analysing it further to create knowledge, which is further analysed and applied to particular situations or problems to create intelligence. It is this intelligence that allows strategic decisions to be made with confidence.

In contrast, much of the software claiming to create business intelligence is really little more than sophisticated database software that gathers quantitative data and draws some loose connections. Put simply, it takes raw data and turns it into information, not intelligence. True competitive intelligence, or business intelligence for that matter, must add value to all the stages of the strategic process, from data gathering straight through to strategic planning and action.

If you provide company, industry or market analysis reports, a reliance on technology alone could be detrimental to the people you advise.

Consider a fictionalized example. You are employed by a company that makes specialized measuring equipment for commercial applications. Your CI efforts consist of following your main competitors in different markets around the world. You are able to obtain or estimate their sales and product pricing in various markets and analyse them using business intelligence software. You have one key competitor in a foreign country that has always had greater market share, and you have had difficulties making headway against this leader in the market. Yet over the last two sales quarters you have noticed a decrease in the prices of their products. You do not understand what has prompted this, but you report it to your manager. She asks you to find out more and determine if your company will need to take action, whether it be an equal price reduction or some other strategy.

You continue your information gathering on the Internet by conducting a scan of different online news sources, particularly those from the country in question. While there is little of consequence in the way of industry news, there is a story that mentions your competitor. The story is a couple of months old, and indicates that your rival is laying off 20 per cent of its workforce in a production facility that you believe produces the equipment sold in this market. You make a note of this and conduct a Web crawl of the competitor's Web site. You are well aware that the site contains product and pricing information by region, but you want to see if any changes have taken place. As you suspected, the products have been reduced in price, but you are surprised to see that some of the products are not even available any more. That must be significant, and you are anxious to report your findings.

You tell your manager that the rival has cut prices, laid off workers and eliminated some competing product lines. You suggest that they could be in financial difficulty, leading them to these desperate moves. Your manager pounces on this information, and decides an increased marketing campaign in this market, including focused efforts on the competitor's known clients, is likely to increase sales for the company. She believes it might be worth matching or beating their prices just to push the rival over the edge. Your company decides to pursue this strategy.

In reality, a completely different scenario has occurred, but business intelligence software, the Internet and Web crawling tools were unable to help you uncover it. A regulatory change took place in the country six months ago. It was the result of an international agreement harmonizing technical standards. Consequently, the commercial applications in which your products and equipment, and those of your rival, are used must be able to measure in metric units. Users of this equipment had been given two years to comply with the change. While you were unaware of this event, your competitor had cut prices to sell off inventory that could still be used over the next two years. It had also reallocated resources from manufacturing to research and development and engineering, in an effort to design and develop new products to meet the metric requirements. The rival had also updated its Web site so that potential customers would not be misled about products that were no longer available.

Your company found this out in the midst of your plans for the marketing campaign. One of your sales agents in the country, whom you never used as a source of information, asked why you were planning to promote old products when he was inundated with questions about the new metric products. Since communications from your office to the sales agent had never been strategic in nature before, he just assumed you knew about the regulatory change and was waiting for new product information. You assumed technology was giving you intelligence. In this case, a telephone was the only technology necessary to address the dilemma.

Assumptions based on business intelligence garnered from software or other technology tools always need to be verified. Such information needs further analysis to draw truly accurate and useful conclusions. There is plenty of value in these tools. As far as housing and organizing vast amounts of data and extricating it in a format that shows associations and provides some useful information, the business intelligence software is an excellent addition to an overall competitive intelligence function. We have already explained how the Internet has revolutionized the flow of information, and our capacity to access and use it. While Aristotle used less sophisticated technology when pondering, analysing and philosophizing, he said it best. 'It is the mark of the trained mind never to expect more precision in the treatment of any subject than the nature of the subject permits.' Something to keep in mind when introducing technology into the competitive intelligence process.

ten

Legal and ethical considerations

In the arena of human life the honours and rewards fall to those who show their good qualities in action.

ARISTOTLE, NICOMACHEAN ETHICS

Consider the following scenario. You walk into your office and are greeted by an assistant in a panic. By the time he has calmed down and told you what has happened, you feel sick to your stomach. One of your highest-level executives and a number of key managers and employees have left your company, the second leading company in your market, defecting to the number one company in the market. Not only did they take all the knowledge and experience residing in their memory, they took over 20 boxes of stolen documents. Your main competitor will be able to use this information for any number of purposes – cutting its own costs, understanding your company's long-term strategies, increasing its market share, effectively debilitating your operations and your ability to compete.

Is it against the law to hire employees away from the competition? That may be difficult to argue in legal terms. Is it against the law to steal a company's secret and confidential files? Of course it is and, if it can be proven, it should be punished accordingly. The case above is a moderately fictionalized version of one of the most prominent trade secrets cases in recent years involving General Motors Corporation and a former General Motors executive who held covert discussions with Volkswagen during his tenure with GM and eventually accepted an offer to join the company. Additionally, he agreed to bring confidential business plans and worked in collaboration with other GM employees to collect trade-secret information for VW. This group then joined VW for more lucrative salaries, bringing the GM information with them.

Would you hire a former employee of your rival simply to find out everything she knows? Would you eavesdrop on a conversation of executives of a competing firm and take notes? Would you dig through the garbage outside the headquarters of the leading company in your industry looking for discarded yet potentially valuable memos, plans and reports? Is it possible that desperation and fear might lead you to hire someone to hack into a computer, break into an office or blackmail an executive working for your competitor? It may seem simply distasteful, or it may conjure up images of a Hollywood thriller, but it happens all the time. Individuals, businesses and governments frequently engage in activities that push the boundaries of ethical and legal behaviour in the pursuit of competitive advantage. These actions are either unethical or illegal, and they have no place in the practice of competitive intelligence. Intelligent organizations never have to resort to these tactics to compete effectively in the marketplace.

Competitive intelligence professionals are quick to remind clients, doubters and anyone who will listen that CI is not spying or espionage and that it relies on legal and ethical means to gather information, analyse it and disseminate intelligence. They may point to the Society of Competitive Intelligence Professionals (SCIP) Code of Ethics or their own version of a company ethics policy to give you an idea of their approach to competitive intelligence.

SCIP CODE OF ETHICS

- To continually strive to increase respect and recognition for the profession.
- To pursue one's duties with zeal and diligence while maintaining the highest degree of professionalism and avoiding all unethical practices.
- To faithfully adhere to and abide by one's company policies, objectives and guidelines.
- To comply with all applicable laws.
- To accurately disclose all relevant information, including one's identity and organization, prior to all interviews.

- To fully respect all requests for confidentiality of information.
- To promote and encourage full compliance with these ethical standards within one's company, with third party contractors, and within the entire profession.

Source: Society of Competitive Intelligence Professionals

SCIP's efforts to establish a standard of ethics within the profession are admirable and they do provide guidelines to provoke further thought in a profession that has been unfairly associated with unscrupulous practices. Outside of the SCIP community, the good news is that companies committed to ethical behaviour have a clear competitive edge. According to a study conducted in 1997 by DePaul University in the United States (*Human Resource Management News*, 9 January 1999), firms with a defined commitment to ethical principles and practices had a stronger bottom line. The study indicated that a commitment to ethics increased both customer loyalty and employee retention.

We stumbled upon a quotation attributed to Valdemar W Setzer, a professor of computer science at the Institute of Mathematics and Statistics at the University of São Paulo in Brazil. Setzer stated, 'Ethics is not definable, is not implementable, because it is not conscious; it involves not only our thinking, but also our feeling.' This dilemma is complicated by the diverse national and corporate cultures that comprise the international business world. Competitive intelligence practices considered acceptable in France, for example, may be very questionable to a businessperson in the United Kingdom. The methods and approach with which a German CI practitioner feels comfortable may seem conservative and ineffective to an Italian professional. Within cultures and corporations, there is also the issue of personality and experience. Are you a 'win at any cost' individual? Would you hire competitive analysts simply because they have a CIA or security service background? Is it possible that, in conducting CI for you, they may resort to past methods that were authorized for covert intelligence efforts on behalf of a government or paramilitary organization? What are the implications for you if they break the law?

Intellectual property and trade secrets

Much of the concern about legal and ethical information gathering is focused on intellectual property rights and trade secrets. The definitions for these two terms differ around the world, as does the protection a company or individual can expect from national laws.

Intellectual property

The World Intellectual Property Organization (WIPO), an agency of the United Nations, offers the following definition for intellectual property:

> The rights relating to literary, artistic and scientific works; performances or performing artists, phonograms, and broadcasts; inventions in all fields of human endeavour; scientific discoveries; industrial designs; trademarks, service marks and commercial names and designations; protection against unfair competition; and all other rights resulting from intellectual activity in the industrial, scientific, literary, or artistic fields.

Many national definitions or definitions found in bilateral or multilateral agreements are less broad. For example, the North American Free Trade Agreement refers to 'copyright and related rights, trademark rights, patent rights, rights in layout designs or semiconductor integrated circuits, trade secret rights, plant breeders' rights, rights in geographical indications and industrial design rights'.

Typically, intellectual property is protected in the following way:

- patents – for inventions;
- registration – for trademarks and industrial designs;
- copyright – for literary and artistic works;
- integrated circuit topographies – for integrated circuits (computer chips, for example);
- plant breeders' rights – for crossbreeding to create new plant types.

Protecting intellectual property serves many purposes beyond protecting the developers or creators. It promotes creative activity within a country and promotes economic growth through increased innovation and technological change. It also makes it easier to access valuable information in many fields of achievement through official documents filed with government agencies. This was discussed in detail in Chapters 4 and 5.

Intellectual property issues are integral to conducting competitive intelligence, or business in general, in international markets. A company cannot be assured that it will receive the same legal protection in some countries that it receives at home. As a result, the competitive advantage of opening a new foreign operation, or of partnering with a foreign firm or individual, can be greatly decreased if the company is not confident that its intellectual assets are protected. And if a company does pursue a business relationship in a domain with questionable protection, it may transfer older technology or pursue investments in sales and distribution rather than more knowledge-intensive operations such as research and development or production.

While the short-term impact of strengthening and enforcing intellectual property regulations may have a negative impact on economies that abuse the intellectual property of businesses and individuals for profit, the long-term benefits of creating a stable environment for sharing and transferring knowledge are far greater, and will only enhance the economic development of those countries. Additionally, such strengthening and enforcing of intellectual property regulations may contribute to a global standard for ethical business practices, as the intelligence age will demand greater respect for intellectual property.

Trade secrets

Even in countries with stringent intellectual property laws, the protection of trade secrets is less distinct. In Canada, for example, information is considered a trade secret if it is specific in nature, treated by the owner as confidential at all times and regarded by the owner as a secret. While it must be information that is not generally known to the public, it may be information that is available to the public if enough time and effort were devoted to uncovering it. This seems extremely vague.

Mark Halligan is a Chicago lawyer and a frequent lecturer on the law of trade secrets. He has been retained as an expert witness in trade secret cases in the United States. Halligan has developed (and trade marked) *The Trade Secrets Home Page* (http://execpc.com/~mhallign), a vast online resource dedicated to intellectual property law and trade secret cases around the world. Halligan's site contains valuable information about many of the countries we are examining in this book. For example, you can learn that in the United Kingdom there is effective protection for trade secrets, including the issuance of search and seizure orders to protect trade secrets and preserve evidence. UK law includes injunctive relief, damages and third-party liability to address breaches of confidence. The French Criminal Code has had provisions relating to the theft of trade secrets since 1844. French law distinguishes between manufacturing trade secrets, know-how and confidential business information. Information on the laws governing industrial, literary and artistic property in France can be obtained from French embassies or consulates. A document of particular interest is the *Code de la Propriété Intellectuelle*, an official gazette of the French Republic, printed by the Commission Supérieure de Codification.

The Trade Secrets Home Page will also inform you that trade-secret theft is a crime in Italy, and that Japan enacted a national trade secrets law in 1991, which covers any 'technical or business' information that has commercial value, is not in the public domain and which has been 'administered' as a trade secret. The site provides information on the status of the law in China as well. China adopted its first trade secrets law in 1993. It defines a 'business secret' as information that has commercial value, is not in the public domain and which is subject to reasonable steps to maintain its secrecy. While the law suggests that full protection is available, there is concern whether the new law will be effectively enforced. Halligan's site does not yet address Brazil, but this Latin American power shares some of the same issues China is facing. Brazil has been strengthening its laws on intellectual property and trade secrets, but the same concern remains – will the laws be enforced in a country with a long history of abuse of intellectual property? Brazil is a signatory to some of the significant international agreements protecting intellectual property; however, many companies are wary about the true measure of protection they can expect if they are competing in the Brazilian marketplace. Even Brazilian scientists, for example, are hesitant to submit their findings for patents due to the poor domestic protection. Despite calls for changes in the regulatory regime, the country still holds a reputation for both trademark and software piracy. Restrictive technology transfer laws have provided little motivation to outside investors looking to enter the market. The result, as with many other developing economies, is an uncompetitive economy that will continue to struggle with old technology until laws become more supportive of innovation and less bureaucratic for companies looking to compete on a level playing field.

Halligan's site also looks at Germany, which provides strong protection for trade secrets, with unfair competition law dating back to the early 1900s. The modern law on trade secrets recognizes information that is commercially valuable, not in the public domain and which its owner has shown an 'objective intent' to keep secret. The German history is quite interesting, as we discovered from Dr Mauri G Gronroos, a corporate adviser for large enterprises, author of a book on knowledge management and a leading authority on the protection of trade secrets. Gronroos states that the norms protecting trade secrecy in German civil law had their roots in France, but have evolved in Germany since the end of the 19th century, as Halligan also noted. The doctrine became an important element of legislation against unfair business practices. German legislation has in turn served as a model for many other countries, such as Switzerland and Austria. Gronroos notes that, as the 19th century came to a close, trade in Germany grew, and freedom of competition was a leading business concept. As time passed, however, it became apparent that unscrupulous practices were jeopardizing the reputation of German industry. In 1896, Germany enacted a law to prevent unfair competition, modified it in 1909 and continues to enforce it.

A hundred years after Germany's first legal efforts regarding unfair competition, the United States implemented a very solid and very public law regarding economic espionage and the theft of trade secrets. It is worth examining it in greater detail.

In October 1996, the Economic Espionage Act (EEA) came into existence in the United States. This federal law enables US federal authorities to investigate and prosecute individuals or companies engaged in economic espionage, such as stealing or obtaining trade secrets fraudulently. It also gives the authorities power to investigate and prosecute any individual or company that buys or receives trade secrets obtained fraudulently by a third party. Previous law in this regard resided at the state level and was governed by common law; however, the US bumped the law to the federal level to deal with the increasing numbers of cases of economic espionage conducted by foreign governments and businesses. The result is a law with heavy penalties for anyone who steals a trade secret, for their personal business, or on behalf of anyone else.

The EEA uses the following definition for 'trade secret':

All forms and types of financial, business, scientific, technical, economic, or engineering information, including patterns, plans, compilations, program devices, formulas, designs, prototypes, methods, techniques, processes, procedures, programs, or codes, whether tangible or intangible, and whether or how stored, compiled, or memorized physically, electronically, graphically, photographically, or in writing if –

(A) the owner thereof has taken reasonable measures to keep such information secret; and

(B) the information derives independent economic value, actual or potential, from not being generally known to, and not being readily ascertainable through proper means by, the public.

When the EEA was first implemented, many CI professionals were concerned (and some rightly so) that the new law would encompass some of their intelligence-gathering activities, putting them or their company at risk of legal action. Three years after its introduction, it has become apparent that the EEA was not designed to limit the effectiveness of law-abiding, ethical CI professionals. The rules had not really changed, but the consequences of violating them had.

Individuals who violate the section that addresses domestic misappropriation of trade secrets face penalties of up to 10 years in prison. While the fines for such a violation are unspecified, the maximum fine for felonies in the United States is US$250,000. If a corporation or any other organization is found guilty under the EEA of domestic spying or theft of trade secrets, it faces fines up to US$5 million. The penalties for foreign economic espionage are more severe: the maximum fine for an organization is US$10 million and the maximum prison term increases to 15 years.

Halligan believes the passing of the EEA was, at least in theory, an effort to balance the playing field for US companies, which do not have the benefit of government intelligence agencies to help them dig up information and compete against foreign firms. In the US, according to Halligan, 'I cannot call up the FBI and CIA on behalf of one of my clients and say, "Give me the information on this French company making aircraft", where the French company can get the assistance from the French government and French intelligence agencies to collect that information about American aircraft manufacturers.' He suggests that the EEA was designed to criminalize that kind of conduct. The reality, according to Halligan, is that the definite separation that exists between the private corporation and the government in the United States does not exist in many foreign nations. As a result, in such nations the national interest and the corporate interest coincide, creating anti-competitive business environments.

While a stringent law like the EEA serves a purpose as a deterrent and sends a message to anyone spying on US businesses, many grey areas do remain in the world of CI, including situations that do not violate the law but do call into question the integrity of the individual or business engaged in certain practices. The fact that laws around the world vary in the treatment of trade secrets compounds these situations.

According to Dr Gronroos, there were approximately 20 countries world-wide with effective and explicit legislation to protect business trade secrets by 1995. Some of these were common law countries, while the rest implemented European civil law. Presently, an annex to the

WTO Agreement, the Agreement on Trade-Related Aspects of Intellectual Property Rights (TRIPS), obliges all member states to enact effective legislation to protect trade secrets. However, the protection is not uniform in all countries and, in many cases, the legislation guarantees only a minimum protection. As mentioned earlier, the extent of the protection depends heavily on the action taken by the owner of a trade secret, and inadequate measures will lead to the loss of trade secret status.

Dr Gronroos is an advocate of the new theory of growth, which emphasizes that the speed of economic growth depends on a company's success in the new global market, as well as the ability of a company to compete using new ideas and innovations. According to Gronroos, the traditional factors of production – capital and labour – become less important as ideas and innovations become more important. The value of the latter, however, rests upon the company's ability to keep the ideas and innovations out of reach of the competitors. Gronroos advocates the protection of ideas and innovations as a form of property, and has developed the following checklist for protecting trade secrets:

1. It is unimportant what the secret is. It can be a formula, pattern, method, process, piece of information or object. What is critical, however, is that a trade secret is economically important as long as it is kept secret. This means that if the trade secret becomes commonly known, the owner (usually a company or an entrepreneur) loses its competitiveness against the competitors.

2. Inform all employees about the nature of your business. Emphasize the fact that the success of your operations depends on certain confidential information, such as trade secrets. Tell them what things are secret, for example 'our price calculations'. Ensure that everybody has understood this. Do not rely on spoken information but give this statement in print, in the internal rules or the quality manual. Consider a signed document that confirms all employees are familiar with the rules or the manual. Stress the fact that an unauthorized disclosure will lead to a prosecution.

3. Ensure that the trade secret is only shared with those employees who need it to fulfil their work tasks.

4. Mark clearly all documents that contain confidential (secret) material.

5. Keep confidential material apart from all other documents in your plant or office.

6. Restrict the access of unauthorized people to the space where you keep your confidential material.

7. Make a non-disclosure agreement with the employees who are exposed to confidential material. Without such an agreement, a former employee is free to disclose or use all your confidential information. Thus former employees (or employees about to quit) are the biggest hazard to your secrets. Be sure that the scope of the agreement is not too broad. The agreement should only cover the actual secrets by name, for example the moulding method, profitability calculations, future strategies, upcoming products, etc. Do not forget to make non-disclosure agreements with everybody outside the company who might get in touch with your confidential material, such as suppliers or customers. The latter group is very crucial because many buyers have a tendency to rotate your quotations around in order to squeeze the price.

8. Always prosecute any violator immediately. Be prepared to give full evidence that the disclosure of your trade secret has financially harmed you and that you had taken all possible measures to protect your secrets. The World Trade Organization's TRIPS agreement speaks about 'reasonable steps' to keep one's information secret. The term is, however, very vague and it is strongly recommended that you go beyond this.

9. Last but not least, remember that the defence of the offender usually, if not always, argues with two claims: first, 'your secret was not secret at all but already widely known'; secondly, 'you never told or acted as if the information should be kept secret'. Be prepared to answer these arguments.

Theft of trade secrets and intellectual property will remain a global business concern as long as businesses want to compete in foreign markets and as long as no harmonized international law and enforcement body exists to regulate in this area. For example, Halligan envisions a World Court in the future, an international body well beyond anything in existence today, where trade secret theft or the threat of misappropriation of trade secrets is addressed. Member countries would consent to this court and a company would be able to seek immediate injunctive relief. Until such time, he believes that the international enforcement issue will remain unaddressed. Halligan does offer the following recommendations for businesses that still want to compete with the rest of the world on foreign turf:

- Assume you are going to lose your intellectual property rights when you compete outside your own jurisdiction.

- Get some kind of guarantee or compensation up front if you are sharing intellectual property. Put a present value on whatever it is and make sure you get that up front, or a guarantee of that up front so that, if you lose it, you still have compensation for it.

- Set up effective enforcement mechanisms through private agreements and private arbitration, binding arbitration or submission to the jurisdiction of your national court, for purposes of litigating a dispute (assuming your legal system offers you adequate protection).

- Never give away all the pieces of the puzzle. Give a little bit here, and a little bit there. If you lose one piece of the puzzle, no one else will get the full value of it because they do not have the other pieces of the puzzle.

National laws and anti-competitive business practices

An additional concern for companies looking for competitive advantages in foreign markets is the impact of national laws governing anti-competitive business practices. Governments are constantly changing regulations in ways that affect the marketplace, as well as a company's ability to compete. While they do this under the guise of creating a fair and equitable business environment, the regulators are not above singling out a particular industry or industry player (usually a 'big shot') for extra special scrutiny. Just ask everyone's favourite software giant, Microsoft. Anti-competitive behaviour is just one of the many areas in which a regulatory regime can impact on a business strategy. This is no different in foreign markets, and a company that relies solely on its past experiences to implement a strategy in a foreign market risks drawing attention to itself. An effective strategy in one market can quickly put you at a competitive disadvantage in another country. An interesting example in this area occurred in 1999 in Italy, where the cola war strategies long known in North America were publicized and became the target of regulatory authorities. Both of these examples are discussed below.

For these reasons, legal considerations are also a prominent issue once the information gathering is complete, the analysis has been conducted and a competitive strategy is prepared. Anti-trust laws and accusations of anti-competitive behaviour often decide how effective a strategy is going to be before it even gets off the ground. In the case of Microsoft discussed below, a long-term strategy that challenged the definition of fair competition drew the attention of consumers, rivals and, ultimately, anti-trust regulators. Clearly, anti-trust laws affect competitive strategy. These strategies can become the subject of investigations and lawsuits by government authorities, effectively bogging down the strategy and eliminating whatever competitive advantage a company may have forecast by choosing the action in the first place. This happens for a number of reasons, but we offer four broad ones here.

Firstly, the anti-trust regulations may actually be restricting competitive strategies that are, by all appearances, legal. This seems to be the case in many attempted mergers and acquisitions, where government interference or regulatory interpretations simply complicate the process. Government intervention can be the most unpredictable factor when it comes to competing in an industry. For example, in August 1999 the Canadian government suspended competition rules to allow the private sector to find a solution for the country's troubled airline industry, namely the incessant and myopic competitive struggles between Canadian Airlines and Air Canada. Less than two weeks after the announcement, Onex Corporation, a Canadian-based conglomerate, had launched its bid for the healthier of the two national carriers, Air Canada. Some insiders suggested that Onex had been tipped off that the government would be lifting legislative constraints on the airlines. While this seemed like a simple domestic merger, it actually had significant international impact. AMR Corporation, the parent company of American Airlines, was funding most of Onex's C\$2.2 billion plan to buy Air Canada and Canadian Airlines to merge them. On the other side, Air Canada was relying on C\$730 million worth of assistance from alliance partners, like Deutsche Lufthansa AG and UAL Corporation, the parent company of United Airlines, the world's largest carrier.

Instead of a simple merger to clean up an ugly and unprofitable domestic industry, the takeover attempt became a battle between the two largest global aviation code-sharing groups in the world. The Star Alliance, number one, was determined to keep Air Canada within its alliance while the Oneworld group, which included American Airlines and British Airways, saw the advantages of getting Air Canada out of Star. Because code-sharing allows airlines to generate additional revenues by using a partner's routes to provide customers with relatively pain-free travel to international destinations, the cross-border routes between

Canada and the United States, as well as the key gateways to Europe and Asia, looked very lucrative.

Over a period of 10 weeks, accusations, insults, bids and counterbids flew back and forth, culminating in Onex's final bid of C$2.2 billion for both the airlines. It was all for naught, however, when a Quebec court ruled that the Onex bid contravened a law limiting ownership in the airline. Apparently, a 1988 Canadian law limits voting ownership in Montreal-based Air Canada by a single shareholder or group of associates to 10 per cent. Air Canada was previously owned by the government of Canada, which seemed to retain a vested interest in keeping a 'Canadian' airline industry competitive. Who is to blame for the time and money wasted on this failed merger? Who is responsible for the personal turmoil resulting from the uncertainty created for thousands of employees? The Canadian government should have recognized if the bids contravened the law they created and communicated this to the parties involved. Onex should have analysed the legal implications affecting their strategic move prior to proceeding. Hindsight is a wonderful thing, but the bottom line is that a protectionist law prevented a rescue attempt in a very troubled international industry that the Canadian government still believes is a national entity. While they suspended competition laws to find a solution, they closed the doors on those who wanted to offer one. This is just one example illustrating how important it is to analyse your strategic plans from a regulatory point of view. The better prepared you are at understanding the regulatory environment, the less likely you will be of running foul of laws that you did not know existed.

Secondly, a strategy that is effective in one country or jurisdiction may not have been modified to account for changes in the regulatory environment elsewhere or adapted to consider differences in cultural or ethical standards. Coke and Pepsi are well known in North America for their leading soft drinks as well as the 'cola wars', which have included strong-arm tactics with retailers, restaurants and distributors. These battles for shelf space and market share have been accepted as the way to win this particular competition. Yet Coke tried to take the same aggressive strategies to Italy and found itself facing an investigation. The ensuing report drew the attention of the Italian authorities, as well as those of other European Union countries and Latin American and Asian authorities. Coke was accused of implementing a business strategy that was more focused on removing the competition than it was on increasing sales of its products. Perhaps the soft-drink giants' legendary reputations and relatively equal competitive positions in the United States and Canada foster a 'blind eye' approach from the authorities, but the Italian government does not seem to have this bias. Much to its dismay, Coke may face similar scrutiny of its competitive strategy in a number of markets in the European Union and Asia, at a time when its reputation has already been sullied by a poorly managed product recall. To add insult to injury, France rejected Coca-Cola's bid for Pernod Ricard SA's Orangina soft drink in the autumn of 1999, claiming the purchase would give the world's largest soft-drink maker too much control of the French market. Coca-Cola had been pursuing Orangina for over two years but could not allay the French authorities' concern that a sale would hurt competition.

Thirdly, success draws both attention and suspicion. While this book was being written, a US District Court judge determined that Microsoft held a monopoly power in personal computer operating systems and that the company has used its power position to punish competitors and harm consumers. Despite Microsoft's arguments to the contrary, the judge found three main facts to support this decision:

1. Microsoft's share of the market for Intel-compatible PC operating systems is extremely large and stable.
2. Microsoft's dominant market share is protected by a high barrier to entry.
3. As a result of this barrier, customers lack a commercially viable alternative to Windows.

In summary, the judge concluded, 'Some innovations that would truly benefit consumers never occur for the sole reason that they do not coincide with Microsoft's self-interest.' At the time of publishing, the actual decision on whether Microsoft broke anti-trust laws had not yet been made. The US court must decide if Microsoft has liability for breaking the law and, if it does, it could apply sanctions ranging from restrictions on the way Microsoft conducts business to breaking up the company. How did this happen? Well, it depends on whether you believe Microsoft's argument that it has used fair and legal tactics to build its business and compete in the marketplace. Many people believe that success draws both attention and suspicion, and each time a company reaches the pinnacle of success, like Microsoft, a herd of politicians, regulators and less successful competitors try to knock it down.

The other camp believes that Microsoft's current competitive advantage and sheer dominance are the result of abusive strategies that have stifled competition. Regardless of its success, it must make amends for the measures it took to achieve that success.

Fourthly, the strategy may be poorly conceived and the research and analysis that lead to its implementation may be weak or flawed. One may argue that the three examples above fit into this category. Why did Onex and the Canadian government not consider the ownership law? Why did Coca-Cola overlook cultural differences and the regulatory climate in Italy? Why did Microsoft continue to push the boundaries of fair competition when the Justice Department was watching its every move? Rather than debating the merits and faults of the strategies of corporate giants around the world, this fourth point is much more valuable to remember for your business. Anti-trust issues and the potential for anti-competitive actions must be evaluated in the early stages of strategy development, well before the strategy is implemented. It actually works to a company's advantage on some occasions. If a company believes a competitor's upcoming strategy is anti-competitive, it may raise enforcement issues for anti-trust authorities and potentially deter the competitor from following through with its plan. This is the strategy GTE Corp has adopted to deal with AT&T in the cable Internet market.

Intelligent organizations will always incorporate the legal and ethical considerations of their strategy into their analysis efforts. They will look at the effects of their strategies to determine if they can be accused of anti-competitive behaviour. They will also ensure that if they proceed, they are prepared for the impact any challenges to their strategy will have on its implementation. They will be secure in their knowledge that they can address anti-competitive problems later or that they are in a position to weather the storm. And they will maintain their position on firm ethical grounds.

Regulators may never be a businessperson's best friends, and they can certainly be your worst enemies. This is particularly true when you choose not to consider their role in your business strategy. To compete in any market, you must understand the impact your strategy has from every angle, and the response it will draw from other players. Include the regulatory regimes of a country or market when preparing your strategies for competing. Every country has its rules, and you ignore them at your own risk.

When it comes to competitive intelligence, it is crucial that you establish legal and ethical ground rules for your company, your associates and outside professionals acting on your behalf. You cannot be assured that they automatically operate under the same rules as you. The price for playing a different game, with different rules, can be very high indeed. After reading all of this, why not test yourself with the series of actions below? This 'ethics test' originated with the Society of Competitive Intelligence Professionals to give CI practitioners some food for thought. You can rank the following practices on a scale: 1 is very ethical; 5 is very unethical.

1. picking the brains of a competitor's engineer or technician at a trade show or conference;

2. interviewing competitors' employees for a job that does not exist to gather information indirectly;

3. hiring key executives for what they know;

4. hiring the same consultants as the competition;

5. debriefing competitors' former employees;

6. talking to your regular customers who may provide information about competitors;

7. asking your loyal customers to put out phoney bids that may provide technical details about competitors' products;

8. infiltrating customers' operations with missionary salespeople or engineers to learn about competitors' new product designs;

9. prodding buyers about competitors' sales under the pretext of a need for information about level of sales to help provide the buyer with a special package such as two-for-one promotional offers;

10. asking suppliers for capacity plans to deduce competitors' manu-facturing plans;

11. analysing want ads to determine the type of project competitors are contemplating;

12. obtaining negotiated contracts to find information on labour costs of competitors;

13. obtaining aerial photographs of competitors' plants that have been filed with government agencies;

14. obtaining information through Freedom of Information Act or Access to Information filings;

15. studying public documents filed with agencies to draw inferences about competitors' borrowing and financing practices;

16. observing competitors' loading areas to determine shipping levels;

17. taking tours of competitors' plants and facilities to observe manu-facturing processes;

18. buying competitors' products to study components and evaluate costs and manufacturing techniques;

19. buying competitors' rubbish from waste-disposal contractors.

eleven

Competing around the **world**

Nothing average ever stood as a monument to progress. When progress is looking for a partner it doesn't turn to those who believe they are only average. It turns instead to those who are forever searching and striving to become the best they possibly can. If we seek the average level we cannot hope to achieve a high level of success. Our only hope is to avoid being a failure.

A LOU VICKERY

At this point, you have probably realized that regardless of whether your business operates domestically or internationally, you need to monitor the competition. A couple of decades ago, the competition used to operate on the other side of town. Now, it operates around the world. When you expand to new markets, keeping an eye on the other players is essential.

We have discovered that many businesses are quite adept at conducting research on their very large and public global competitors (companies that, like themselves, are operating in international markets); however, their weakness is in understanding the local competition in new markets. Many opportunities are surfacing in countries that have begun to develop their market economies. These nations have made huge gains in the use of technology and are rapidly developing products and services for both the domestic market and exporting. Huge multinational life sciences firms may not understand the intricacies of the Chinese pharmaceutical industry and market, for example, as well as a Chinese pharmaceutical company with a fraction of their resources. Such local companies may be filling a void, which may have been previously addressed in part by foreign firms or not addressed at all.

By focusing CI research and analysis on the international players you already know, you risk the success of your venture into new markets. A good method to make sure you do not forget the local competition is to enlist the assistance of an 'expert' in the market you wish to access. Often this expert will be a local businessperson or someone who has worked extensively in the region and industry in which you are interested.

There are many obstacles to conducting competitive intelligence in the international arena. The more obvious ones include language, culture, and the political and legal environment. While many sources for information gathering may be the same, actually extracting the intelligence may present you with greater challenges because of these barriers.

Culture

You are going to encounter difficulties in collecting information as a result of the culture. For example, conducting a telephone survey using the methodologies familiar to Western cultures may not be effective in other cultures. In some parts of Asia, for example, they are completely unacceptable. Additionally, the concept of providing a rank or rating as an answer to a survey question may be alien to many people.

It is crucial to approach any competitive intelligence project that involves data collection and contact with international sources with a sensitivity to the culture you are entering. A small investment in understanding the business environment and respecting diversity may pay dividends in the end. People are more likely to co-operate with someone who has not offended them. In Chapter 3, we discussed a number of methods for improving your ability to communicate cross-culturally and these serve as a great point of departure for improving your international intelligence-gathering efforts.

Language

Many people state that the language of international business is English. More often than not, this statement can be attributed to individuals who speak English, and believe the only information that is valuable is information they can read or hear and immediately understand. The intelligence you require may come from any number of sources, including interviews, government documents and company reports. Conducting any of this research in China or France, for example, may not yield much data you will understand if you are from the United Kingdom, the United States or Canada and speak only English.

There are a number of ways to address data collection in languages in which you are not proficient. Translation services are very common, as are language consultants and interpreters, who can be hired on a contract basis. There are even software and online translation applications, which can usually help you ascertain the meaning of the text, even if they do not perform precise translations. Additionally, it is becoming more common in this increasingly globalized workforce to find employees who speak, read and write two or more languages, in addition to other valuable skills. Perhaps the engineer you hired speaks Spanish, or the receptionist in your office was raised in Germany. An intelligence audit in your company reveals these often overlooked assets, which can save an intelligent organization time and money, and increase its effectiveness in using data and information collected. If you will be collecting information on the Internet, search engines like Alta Vista incorporate translation technologies to enable you to translate Web pages into the language of your choice.

Political and legal environment

Understanding the political environment of the country in which you are conducting competitive intelligence is vital. Research will reveal very different levels of government involvement in business and industry, whether through state control of companies or corruption. Understanding the intricacies of the government–industry relationship will help you focus your CI efforts better and prevent you from running into barriers. One point of departure in understanding this aspect of global competitive intelligence is to look at the laws and policies relating to competition. Laws protecting and promoting competition can be found in all the industrialized countries belonging to the Organization for Economic Co-operation and Development (OECD). Some of these laws are quite old, such as the United States' Sherman Act, dating back to 1890 – the very first piece of legislation prohibiting agreements restricting competition and attempts to create monopolies. This law forms the basis for the US government's 1999 case against Microsoft. Over the last decade, anti-trust laws and anti-competition rules have developed and improved in Latin America, parts of Asia, and Central and Eastern Europe. The European Union has made harmonization efforts to create a more competitive market, and similar efforts are also occurring on a greater international level among industrialized nations. It will be some time, however, before a company will feel comfortable with the level of protection international agreements offer when it comes to competition in the global market. Bilateral agreements on competition between major trading partners, such as those between the United States and Japan, and the US and the European Union, which offer co-operation on investigations and research, are much more likely. It is important to understand the implications of these international influences on competition. When conducting intelligence work in Europe, for example, competitive intelligence professionals might want to familiarize themselves with the European Commission policies on competition before proceeding to the national level for a Member State.

The European Commission

The European Commission has taken the position that there would be little relevance in a single market if competition between companies from different Member States can be limited by anti-competitive actions and agreements. Member States continue to have their own authorities to enforce national competition laws, but it is the Commission that monitors the single market to keep it fair and equitable. Consequently, EU competition law takes precedence over national law and is directly applicable in Member States. The Commission's powers are extensive, ranging from investigations of possible breaches of the competition laws to blocking mega-mergers. The targets of its competition policy include cartels, firms abusing 'dominant positions' and even state aids. This last example would seem to be completely within the national interest, yet the Commission looks at public subsidies that potentially threaten competition in trade between Member States. The Commission's powers of investigation border on frightening. Its staff can visit companies without warning to demand access to documents. If, following its investigation and any subsequent hearings with the alleged offender, the Commission establishes that anti-competitive actions have taken place, it can impose fines of up to 10 per cent of annual turnover. Companies may appeal the Commission's decisions to the Court of Justice, which sometimes reduces the fines.

Chapter 4 lists contact information for the national competition authorities in France, Germany, Italy and the United Kingdom.

Competition law beyond Europe – selected countries

In the United States, anti-trust laws fall under the jurisdiction of the Bureau of Competition, which is part of the Federal Trade Commission. The Bureau has a mandate to prevent business practices that restrain competition. It investigates alleged law violations and, when appropriate, recommends that the Commission take formal enforcement action. Antitrust laws in the US are enforced by both the Bureau of Competition and the Antitrust Division of the Department of Justice.

In Japan, the Fair Trade Commission is both a quasi-legislative and quasi-judicial organization that implements the Anti-monopoly Act and competition policy. As such, the Commission can establish the process for handling cases and hearing procedures, and it can deliver a decision after a hearing. It is considered an 'extraministerial body' of the Prime Minister's Office, which means it independently exercises its authority without being directed or supervised by anyone else.

In Canada, the Competition Bureau examines issues relating to business practices in Canada. The Bureau is an agency of Industry Canada, the federal government department responsible for promoting both economic growth and a fair and efficient marketplace for Canadian businesses and foreign businesses investing in Canada.

Brazil's Administrative Council for Economic Defence is the country's competition agency. It comprises six commissioners and a president appointed by the president of the republic. The Council serves a two-year term and exercises considerable power in its investigations and decision-making functions. We discuss Brazil's efforts to clean up its business environment in more detail below.

Competing internationally not only has repercussions in the foreign market, but it also affects the competitive landscape within a country. You cannot rely on national loyalty or patriotism to protect you from competitive strategies. In one of the most talked-about and analysed business battles and mergers in Europe in 1999, Olivetti managed to outbid Deutsche Telekom for Telecom Italia. Olivetti's purchase of a 51 per cent stake in the much larger telecommunications company shocked powerhouse Deutsche Telekom and threw a wrench into its plans to create a pan-European telecom giant able to compete with the likes of US-based AT&T. In all the excitement of the chase, the German giant failed to analyse the role of the other players in the game, including those in its own back yard. If it had looked for an answer to one question – 'Who will be at a competitive disadvantage if we merge with Telecom Italia?' – it might have analysed the potential role of Mannesmann AG, Deutsche Telekom's main rival in Germany.

When the merger dust began to settle, it became apparent that Olivetti had partially financed the deal for Telecom Italia by selling its stake in two Italian telecom subsidiaries, Omnitel and Infostrada, to Mannesmann AG. This sale also prevented Olivetti from being a target for any anti-trust action, and turned Mannesmann into the biggest wireless company in Germany and the second largest in Italy. Later in the year, Mannesmann offered to buy UK cellular operator Orange plc, the UK's third-largest mobile operator, in an effort to increase its share of the European cellular market, which is expected to double in the next two years.

Conversely, national rivals may co-operate if they feel they can benefit on a greater scale. With a 'whole is greater than the sum of its parts' philosophy, and a visionary strategy regarding the future of the European energy markets, VEBA AG and VIAG AG, the second- and third-largest German energy and speciality chemicals companies merged to form a powerful industrial group with a streamlined corporate structure, a clearer international strategy and more muscle to make it a reality. Ulrich Hartmann, the CEO of VEBA, was quoted as stating that the merger put the new company 'in the vanguard of Europe's rapidly changing and increasingly competitive energy market. We're leading the consolidation process. By merging VEBA and VIAG we're creating a powerful and energetic company of European dimensions. And in chemicals we'll now concentrate even more forcefully on the specialty segment.' The merger allowed the two companies, already low-cost electricity generators, to manipulate their competitive advantage further and to capitalize on opportunities in gas and water distribution. In the chemicals segment, the merger created the world's largest speciality chemicals group

Time will tell, but in the manic merger world of the late 1990s, bigger seems to be better to many companies. The marriage of these two German firms was probably more the result of a strategic business analysis than of nationalistic fervour.

Competing in selected countries

The rest of this chapter is devoted to an overview of each of the countries we have been discussing throughout the book – Brazil, Canada, China, France, Germany, Italy, Japan, the United Kingdom and the United

States. We look at the countries' current standing in the global market-place, as well as the development and status of competitive intelligence in the nation. Additionally, we highlight some special concerns relating to competing in these diverse nations, and take a closer look at China, which is experiencing phenomenal changes. It serves as a valuable case study to highlight many of the issues discussed in this book, from setting up a CI function to overcoming cultural barriers and government interference.

Brazil

Brazil possesses the largest economy in Latin America, as well as the largest population. Despite recent economic slumps, the country has made progress in international markets. The government has also made headway in reducing restrictions on foreign investment and decreasing the complexity and corruption that has plagued the business environment in the past. Coupled with privatization efforts and deregulation, the Brazilian market is becoming more competitive and more attractive to firms, but it still has a long way to go to clean up its tarnished reputation.

At a presentation delivered at the 1999 Antitrust Conference: Antitrust Issues in Today's Economy, in New York, Lucia Helena Salgado of Brazil's Administrative Council for Economic Defence (CADE) spoke about competition in Brazil in the 1990s, and the changes the country has implemented to create a more favourable environment for fair competition. As mentioned above, CADE is the agency that regulates competition in Brazil and, like many government institutions in the country, has made considerable efforts to reduce both bureaucracy and corruption, and to improve competition laws. Examples of this include the agency's concern with harmonizing rules and procedures with other jurisdictions, and both its approval of a new set of procedures for reviewing mergers review and its adoption of the OECD proposal for merger review notifications.

While it is encouraging that intellectual property protection for trade secrets is improving in Brazil, the actual legal process remains onerous. If you are involved in a trade secret case against a Brazilian citizen, you are likely to experience an elaborate and unrewarding procedure through the Brazilian Supreme Court.

Competitive intelligence, and all the tools, techniques, and ethical and legal practices, is really in its infancy in Brazil. As the country becomes more receptive to the expectations of foreign investors and international business grows within its borders, so too will the use of legal and ethical CI practices grow. Outside influence will be critical to the evolution of CI in Brazil, and all of Latin America.

Canada

Canada is blessed with abundant natural resources, which form the basis of an economy that is also strong in technology, manufacturing and service industries. The United Nations consistently picks Canada as 'the best place on earth', or some equally grand title. Canada is a wealthy society that closely resembles the United States in its market-oriented economic system; however, Canadian business has been harshly criticized for lacking the drive and competitiveness possessed by its US neighbours. This is one of the main differences between Canadian and US businesses. It is also not surprising that the two nations are great trading partners, considering the geographic proximity, the similar cultures and the similar demands for products and services. It is interesting to note that, while competition is relatively fair in Canada, a non-US foreign firm evaluating the competition in Canada will probably be analysing as many US companies as it will Canadian businesses. Such is the nature of Canada's business environment, particularly with the backing of the North American Free Trade Agreement (NAFTA).

Canada has also lagged behind the United States in embracing and adopting competitive intelligence processes into the strategic functions of business. While Canada has enjoyed enviable growth in membership of the Society of Competitive Intelligence Professionals (SCIP), the number of new members has yet to translate into strong CI functions in many businesses. It is still much more likely to see CI in action in a Canadian-based foreign firm than in a Canadian company or government department. That is not to say that Canadians have not heard of the term. Rather, they borrow it to describe something that they may already be doing, such as market research or corporate library research, rather than grasping the full value of the competitive intelligence process and challenging themselves to try something new and valuable. We have chalked this up to Canadians' innate, seemingly hereditary, fear of new and potentially successful ideas.

With its enviable data and information-collection capabilities, within both the government and the private sector, and its early adoption of leading-edge technology, Canada is in a position to take advantage of all that CI has to offer. Canadian businesses and organizations simply need to familiarize themselves more with the CI process, recognize the value of analyses, learn the techniques and become more assertive in the international marketplace.

China

The economic growth and political changes that have occurred in China over the past two decades have created seemingly unlimited opportunities for both domestic and foreign firms. The country needs just about everything, from infrastructure to consumer goods, and foreign capital and skills will play a huge role in ongoing development. Yet businesses seeking to profit from the enormous potential of this market face formidable barriers. The economy still suffers from considerable central planning and government management of growth. State-owned operations remain protected from competition in many instances, whether by law or because it has always been that way. The legal system is also complex, although a number of efforts have been made to improve civil, administrative, criminal and commercial law. In the international legal and economic sphere, China has been making strides to improve its competitive position in the global economy. As we completed the writing of this book, the United States and China agreed on terms for Chinese entry into the World Trade Organization. This brought to an end 13 years of negotiations and will give motivated businesses additional access to this incredible market.

With one of the world's oldest histories for the use of military intelligence, China has only grasped the potential of competitive intelligence for business in the last 10 to 15 years. This is not surprising considering the strict, centrally planned economy and government control, which negated the need for strategic planning, marketing and other business functions that a competitive market takes for granted. According to Qingjiu (Tom) Tao, China used two distinct intelligence systems under the planned economy: the scientific and technical intelligence system (S&T IS) and the economic intelligence system (EI IS). These systems were used to collect, analyse and distribute intelligence to decision-makers at all levels of various government agencies to fulfil the information needed for planning. Tao, a former industry analyst at China Aero-Information Center, researches competitive intelligence at the University of Pittsburgh and has conducted a large-scale survey on CI practices in China with Professor John Prescott of the University of Pittsburgh. State-owned enterprises and companies did not have intelligence functions, according to Tao, unless you count library and translation services as intelligence functions.

The 1990s saw greater decentralization of power in China and more active participation in the global economy. This increase in competitive activity opened the door to CI practices in China. In 1995, the Society of Competitive Intelligence in China (SCIC) was formed in Beijing, and many major academic institutions introduced or are planning to introduce CI into their study programmes. SCIC is also playing a leading role in CI training programmes in China, holding an annual conference that includes training sessions on various aspects of CI. Outside expertise, from Japan and other sources, has also helped China further its CI development. Tao has seen many Chinese firms setting up their own competitive intelligence programmes or converting their existing scientific and technical intelligence programmes into CI functions. However, the shortage of well-trained CI professionals remains one of the greatest obstacles for these companies. Therefore markets for CI skills training and CI consulting are clearly emerging. On the government side, Tao believes there has been active promotion of CI in some state-owned enterprises, such as in Beijing and Shanghai; yet he has uncovered no evidence that suggests the central government is trying to get involved in CI at this stage. Consequently, private firms, international joint ventures and wholly owned foreign enterprises are most active in using competitive intelligence.

Conducting CI on domestic companies in China, as in many other nations moving to a free-market economy, requires a unique understanding of cultural, historical and business environment issues. There are so many types of ownership models for business in China, and the government's involvement in these varies. Additionally, the location of the company within China can greatly influence the regulations and taxes that apply to the business, much more than one would expect within a single nation. Foreign firms looking to take advantage of the immense commercial opportunities that the Chinese markets present should balance their excitement with the realization that stronger intellectual property protection, among other things, is still required to support the significant outside investment that will promote long-term growth and development in China.

Joe Chao, founder of the JCI Group Inc in Chicago and a former Chinese government official, concurs that CI is relatively new in China and believes the government still creates obstacles for growth in the field. One way in which they have done this, according to Chao, is to require all foreign firms to seek government approval prior to starting any competitive intelligence or market research project. CI is still not accepted as a legitimate and professional business endeavour; rather, CI researchers in China are considered industrial spies in many cases.

Chao points out that the greatest strength of CI practitioners in China is their knowledge and experience with conducting business locally. Tao refers to their understanding of the complexity of business dynamics in

China's market and their established personal 'guanxi' network – personal business networks are channels of vital intelligence. As we pointed out earlier in the book, local professionals lend strength to a project simply because of their familiarity with the language, and a familiarity with the domestic industries in many cases. Chao stresses the importance of working with an individual or a firm that will be sensitive to suspected issues and skilled at analysing and converting the information received from Chinese sources into intelligence. In an earlier chapter, we discussed how communications methods differ from culture to culture. Knowing how to read between the lines in each culture is almost as difficult as learning each foreign language.

In terms of information, print and electronic sources are not as widespread in China as they are in some other countries, and the political and economic state of the nation makes CI professionals a little wary of the mainstream data and statistics produced. But these secondary sources are not the key to reliable information gathering and, ultimately, intelligence. Chao advocates face-to-face interviews in particular as the key to effective and reliable competitive intelligence research in Asian countries, including China.

For CI practitioners in China, there are additional obstacles beyond the infant state of CI in their country and government interference. When Chinese CI professionals are looking to develop intelligence on foreign or international firms, they too must contend with cultural and language differences, and economic and political systems very different from their own, as well as the diverse ways in which business is conducted in other parts of the world. With respect to information sources, Tao points to the lack of a national-level information infrastructure, such as publicly available databases.

Chao believes that there is a future for CI in China. Both increased competition and a free market system will make CI more acceptable and popular. Business planners and managers will have to learn how to use intelligence-gathering and analysis methods if they want to compete in the global economy. Chao stresses that supportive regulations will also improve China's ability to be competitive. This thought was echoed by none other than the Visiting Chief Economist of the World Bank, Joseph Stiglitz, who during a visit to the Chinese Academy of Social Sciences in July 1999 cited competition as the key to the huge success in China's reform policies over the past two decades. Stiglitz also stated that the creation of effective regulatory structures and the development and enforcement of strong competition policies would lead to long-term sustainable and equitable growth.

France

France is a leading economic player, with the fourth-largest industrial economy in the world. Although the government still retains considerable control over key industry sectors, it has also implemented considerable tax incentives and financial subsidies at all levels of government to attract more investment in the country. France is one of the most equitable countries, in many regards, when it comes to offering foreign firms the same treatment as domestic companies, yet its reputation for less than fair play still prevails.

France is no stranger to competitive intelligence, whether in the private sector or the government. For example, the government actually sponsors CI training to increase awareness in French businesses and make them more aware of, and receptive to, the concepts of intelligence gathering and competitive strategy. France has also publicly acknowledged that it has conducted economic espionage, so concerns are raised about the length to which some French companies will go to get intelligence from other sources as well as to protect their own business interests. As a result, France has a reputation for comprehensive, yet dirty, intelligence gathering.

The close relationship between government and industry is still a concern for foreign businesses competing against French companies. In Chapter 10, the impact of such a relationship was discussed in relation to trade secrets. In that chapter, it was suggested that the Economic Espionage Act might have been an effort by the US government to send a message to foreign governments that involve themselves in gathering 'intelligence' on behalf of domestic businesses.

Germany

With the third most powerful economy in the world, and Europe's largest market, Germany is an attractive market. It is even more attractive as a result of the European Union, allowing foreign firms a base within the heart of Europe, complete with a skilled workforce known for its high productivity – the downside being high wages and taxes. Like those of many countries, the German regulatory system and other government operations seem complex, bureaucratic and slightly protectionist of domestic firms, but the market is open and competitive.

Germany has a very organized and advanced CI community. As with most areas in which it has been since the Second World War, Germany has been very cautious and methodical in its approach to international business, including CI. Coupled with the fact that German industry prides itself on technological innovation and quality products, it is less interested in stealing the ideas of others. Although its competition laws date back a couple of centuries, Germany has examined the US Economic Espionage Act with interest. Unlike France or China, Germany is not on the US target list of known economic espionage offenders.

Italy

Italy possesses the world's fifth-largest industrial economy. The country has been undergoing a political and economic rehabilitation, to address widespread corruption and numerous scandals brought to light in the late 1990s. The government is taking a smaller role in controlling the economy, by continuing with its privatization efforts and maintaining a relatively controlled budget. Because of the historically close relationship and co-operation between government and Italian industry, the same caution that is taken with France can be taken with Italy. Mark Halligan points to Fiat's very aggressive approach in the US and the fact that the company is closely aligned with the government. This type of corporate allegiance to government raises red flags.

It is safe to say that Italy is well schooled in the concept of competitive intelligence.

Japan

Japan's economy ranks as the second strongest in the world, behind the United States. This incredible rise to power following the devastation of the Second World War has been attributed to a number of factors, including a history of co-operation between government and industry, expertise in the area of high technology, and a skilled and motivated workforce.

Japan is a highly regulated country and this creates additional burdens for both domestic and foreign firms. This over-regulation affects the ability of companies to compete in a number of industry sectors. In recent years, the government has implemented changes to lighten the regulatory burden to entice new businesses and foreign direct investment.

Competitive intelligence is not new to Japan. Many CI veterans attribute the birth and growth of CI to Japanese business practices. Japan has been a leader in competitive intelligence practices and implementation for a couple of decades. CI is a staple for most Japanese firms. They are also known for their expertise in the area of competitive bench-marking, which has its genesis in quality-control processes embraced by Japanese companies following the Second World War.

Information sources on Japanese companies and industries are readily available and quite reliable. However, the most valuable research method is field research, particularly face-to-face interviews with industry insiders.

United Kingdom

The UK has long been one of the great trading nations and financial centres in the world. For many decades, it has been politically and economically stable and has possessed a fair regulatory environment. The UK remains attractive to exporters and investors for these reasons, as well as for its relatively low rates of taxation and inflation. Foreign ownership is relatively pain-free in the UK.

Competing in business in the UK is also relatively pain-free, as a result of effective laws and enforcement mechanisms. A relatively conservative approach to business dealings is also reflected in the competitive intelligence efforts of UK businesses and consultants. Typically, they are very restrained in terms of what they will do to get information, sticking to conventional methods and ethical practices. Businesses in the UK, like those in many other leading economies, are beginning to grasp the value of competitive intelligence in their organizations.

United States

The US economy leads the world, in terms of power, influence, diversity and technological advances. It is arguably the most market-driven economy in the world, with little government interference in decisions made by companies to develop their businesses at home and abroad. US businesses believe that they face much more difficult barriers to entry in other nations than foreign-owned firms face when they want to set up shop in the US. It does not seem to deter them though, and this may simply be chalked up to the healthy attitude many US businesspeople possess regarding the challenge of competition.

The United States has been catching up to some of the more advanced CI nations and, although competitive intelligence is a relatively recent phenomenon there, some of the most efficient practitioners are US-based companies like Microsoft and Motorola. The Futures Group, a US-based consulting firm, conducted a survey in October 1997 that found that 60 per cent of the US corporations surveyed had an organized 'business intelligence' system, while all of the respondents claimed to be gathering intelligence in various areas of their businesses. The 60 per cent figure was a modest 2 per cent increase from a survey conducted in the previous year. As is the case with many other nations, the larger the US company, the more inclined it is to gather information for competitive intelligence purposes.

As in most other areas of business, US companies will continue to adopt competitive intelligence and excel at it. As a result, they will continue to dominate many sectors of the global economy in the intelligence age.

twelve

Setting up a competitive intelligence function

An empowered organization is one in which individuals have the knowledge, skill, desire, and opportunity to personally succeed in a way that leads to collective organizational success.

STEPHEN R COVEY, *PRINCIPLE-CENTERED LEADERSHIP*

Whether your business operates in many countries and earns billion-dollar revenues or is a small but growing local operation looking to expand, you can implement competitive-intelligence practices to improve your strategic capabilities. Throughout this book, we have explained the power of competitive intelligence as a management tool and how it helps businesses and organizations better understand their competitive environment and make sound business decisions. We have illustrated its value in tracking all the factors that could impact on an intelligent organization's ability to compete, such as regulators, customers, suppliers, distributors and, obviously, competitors and potential competitors. We have also used examples to demonstrate how CI has been used by some of the most successful corporations to maintain their leadership position in markets or to improve their competitiveness. While the concepts and practices that have come to be defined as CI have been implemented in larger corporations for over two decades (particularly in Japan and Europe), small and medium-sized enterprises are also beginning to recognize the value of implementing a competitive intelligence function in their daily operations.

In this chapter, we examine the issues relating to the planning and implementation of a competitive intelligence function in any business or organization. Using existing resources, including people and technology, you can create an intelligent organization with improved competitiveness. We suggest ways in which you can identify and harness the skills, knowledge and expertise within your company and use them in the competitive intelligence process. Additionally, we examine the ways in which these skills can be blended with technology to enhance the CI function.

A colleague working at a mid-sized electronics firm, where she is responsible for developing new business, recently shared her frustrations regarding her employer's approach to competitive intelligence. She had gained a considerable amount of knowledge regarding CI from employment in another industry and was keen to share her expertise with the senior management team at her new company. Shortly after her arrival, she delivered a presentation to the decision-makers to illustrate the potential value of a competitive intelligence function in the company. She focused on both the costs and the benefits and made several recommendations on how the function could be integrated into existing operations with minimal expense and training. Following a few questions, she was convinced that the organizational leaders had bought into the idea. They made it clear to her that the firm needed this kind of strategic process to help with future decisions and that they wanted her to continue pursuing it, starting with the various functional managers. This is the point at which her dream became a nightmare.

Effectively, what happened was that the key people who needed to champion this effort passed the buck to individuals who:

1. were not familiar with the concept of CI, necessitating a time-consuming and onerous education process;
2. were wary of the possibility of additional work or additional drains on their dedicated resources;
3. with the exception of sales and marketing, were focused primarily on internal aspects of the operation and not particularly visionary; and
4. most importantly, did not have a powerful message from their bosses that CI was a fundamental and critical change to the way the company conducted business.

The management team at this firm never did 'champion' the cause of CI. Although they threw a little money at the effort, the lack of cohesiveness among the functional managers negated any impact the funds may have had, leading the decision-makers to conclude that the CI function was not particularly useful. They were never prepared to back the good ideas this woman brought to them, nor were they prepared to back her efforts. The company is still in business, but it has not experienced any growth within its market. Our colleague continues to use the tools and techniques of CI in her daily functions, but has given up wasting her efforts to change the corporate culture.

The moral of the story is simple. You can lead your company or organization to CI, but it does not guarantee the implementation of a CI function. Obviously, if management does not understand why it should embrace CI within its operations, it will not be in a position to support a CI function in a company. The reasons why such leaders choose not to embrace CI when the value of it has been made apparent are less obvious. Some CI professionals conclude that arrogance, hubris and even a sense of immunity to competitive factors play a part in this ignorance. Yet Microsoft, Motorola, IBM, Kodak and GE are just some of the companies that have recognized, from the top executive down, that CI delivers value to their operations. These companies are demonstrated leaders in their business lines today because of the efforts they have made to understand the competitive environment in which they operate. Without a champion at the executive level, many business processes fail.

If you are fortunate enough to be the decision-maker, then your job is to communicate the importance of CI to your company, and how it is going to become an integral part of corporate strategy. Getting 'buy-in' from your employees is your first challenge. It is up to you to determine the best way to motivate your employees and provide them with real incentives to be proactive and diligent. There are a number of books available on motivational theories for business owners and managers. This is not one of them. It is important to remember that this challenge will involve an education process.

In the intelligence age, setting up a CI function in your business becomes a management project, an operational project and an information technology project. The key to success is not letting the initial task of building the CI function consume all of your time and resources. As overused as the idea may be, you should probably consider a team approach for this early stage. There are also many books about organizing teams. Again, this is not one of them. Competitive intelligence is so valuable to an organization because it transcends any one department or function in the company. It can be used for virtually any business requirement. For example, the information-gathering and analysis techniques described throughout this book can be used for strategic, financial, marketing, research and development, technology and product development issues. There are very few businesses in which one manager, salesperson, engineer or IT specialist will be able to address adequately all of the intelligence requirements of an organization. A team approach serves two purposes: it increases the likelihood that the organization as a whole will embrace the concept of competitive intelligence; and the actual CI function will be more valuable and usable as a result of the input from the team members representing diverse strategic needs within the organization.

If you do not have the resources to approach your CI function in the manner described above, your challenges are greater, but not insurmountable. Traditionally, the competitive intelligence function is organized and structured to support the stages of the CI process identified in the competitive intelligence model illustrated in Chapter 2. For example, the CEO of your company might want to know whether acquiring a new and innovative competitor, which seems to be struggling financially, is a good move. According to the model, the question has been formulated, and you are aware that the next steps require an organization of the process followed by some reliable background research and information gathering. In businesses with resources for specialized positions, this background research and information-gathering step might be carried out by a corporate librarian or researcher. Once the information has been gathered from various sources, such as government filings, online searches and field research, the project might shift to an analyst. It is the analyst's role to examine what may be seemingly unrelated pieces of information and, using various methods, depending on the nature of the analysis, to develop answers for the original questions. The analyst may enrol the assistance of other analysts with specialized skills, such as a financial analyst who may be better able to interpret various financial reports on a target company. These analysts may be employed by the company or they may be retained by the company on a contract basis. Following a presentation of the analyst's findings, the decision-makers within the company have the intelligence they require to develop a new strategy or plan, which can be implemented to improve the company's competitive situation.

Not all businesses and organizations can afford a corporate librarian and dedicated CI analysts on the payroll. In smaller companies, or less affluent businesses, these roles may be fulfilled by the same individual, who serves as a one-person CI function. Clearly, this is not the best situation, but it is better than forsaking CI completely. Fortunately, technology can reduce some of the strain in such a situation, particularly if the individual is an intelligence innovator with strong analysis skills.

The next step for the individual or individuals who will actually be involved in the planning and implementation of the CI function is to conduct a needs analysis, similar to the concept discussed in Chapter 2, but not focused on a project. This analysis looks at broader organizational needs. Such an analysis is essential to ensure that the goals of the business or organization can be obtained from a CI function. For example, do you want to gather valuable information on competitors, analyse it and disseminate it to all the people who need it? Do you have a need to analyse your customers' and potential customers' buying habits? Or are you looking to benchmark different functions within your business against other companies known for excellence in those areas? A competitive intelligence function must be able to address two key strategic needs: the need for ongoing intelligence; and the need for 'special projects' intelligence – the case-by-case situations that can arise at any time. Addressing these needs in advance will save you time and agony further along in the process. The critical element in this step is to define your current needs while at the same time ensuring flexibility in the system to expand the functionality of CI. It is quite possible that your organizational needs will change, and having built-in flexibility will make such adjustments much easier in the future. Needs analyses produce the greatest results when they are developed with the input of the people who will ultimately use and act on the intelligence you create. Find the other possible intelligence innovators inhabiting your marketing, engineering, financial and other departments, and listen to their ideas and views. You may be surprised to find that your needs are far different from what you may have come up with on your own.

We have mentioned the value of creating a detailed record of where information and knowledge reside within the company or organization. This idea is not new, and has been referred to as an 'intelligence audit' or a knowledge inventory. This inventory can save you countless hours of searching over a number of different projects by documenting where all the information within your company resides. A thorough inventory will include both the various types of information and skills residing within the human minds in your company, and the various databases, publications, contacts and secondary sources of information that do not have widespread use within the company but add value to a specific function. For example, your inventory shows you that Michael, the manager of the marketing department, speaks and writes three languages fluently and worked in Germany for three years in the telecommunications industry.

You are looking for contacts in the telecommunications industry in Europe. The business development group has been using an online database to track developments within your industry but they have neglected to mention this tool to the other functional groups. Having a current inventory of in-house information at your fingertips maximizes the effectiveness of any project you may want to pursue. It also gives employees a chance to contribute to your company's success in ways that may fall outside their traditional roles in the organization.

It is crucial to establish where the competitive intelligence function will reside within your intelligent organization. There are a few schools of thought on this, but they all seem to share a common principle: the CI function must support the flow of intelligence throughout the organization, from the bottom up, and from the top down.

The following four sections discuss some structures that can be effective when they maintain this principle.

The dedicated competitive intelligence team

This option is typically reserved for the wealthier and larger corporations that recognize that CI can be instrumental in maintaining their wealth and size. The CI team comprises individuals who handle information retrieval and management tasks for the organization, as well as strategic analysts with specific areas of expertise. These individuals support the strategic decision-making function within the organization and act as the intelligence link between the decision-makers in the organization, and the front-line and operational employees who are typically responsible for implementing strategic plans.

Competitive intelligence function resides in a specific business unit

This structure is quite common for a few reasons. A company may feel compelled to stick CI within its existing corporate framework, or it may be using CI in a limited manner that supports its placement within a particular business function. Our experience has shown that, typically, the marketing function within an organization is either blessed or cursed with the responsibility for CI. It is a blessing if they use it to their advantage, and we look at an example of this in Chapter 14. It is a curse if the department is not familiar with the tools and techniques required to benefit from CI or, worse, is expected to perform strategic, competitiveness-enhancing miracles on behalf of the whole company, including finance, engineering and management. While a company may be able to isolate the CI function within one department or group, it is counter-productive to isolate the rest of the organization from CI. Go ahead and stick the CI function in the marketing department, but train the people properly, educate the rest of the organization as well, and create the necessary communications channels that open up the whole company to the intelligence flow.

Competitive **intelligence responsibilities reside in each business unit**

This structure can be very effective if the whole organization believes in the value of competitive intelligence. By assigning an intelligence innovator or innovators from each of your business units (sales, marketing, finance, engineering and management, for example), you increase the potential intelligence you can extract from the information you have collected. This structure operates like a permanent version of the trade show CI team we described in Chapter 3. The Corel Corporation example in Chapter 14 touches on the benefits of this type of arrangement. As in the other structures, open and effective communication channels are crucial to make this arrangement deliver the type of intelligence an organization needs. This often requires both scheduled and timely information exchanges in the form of meetings, and the flexibility to disseminate crucial knowledge at a moment's notice to the other business units, and to key decision-makers. Later in this chapter, we examine how technology can assist the competitive intelligence function in this regard. A well-trained and motivated CI function, which incorporates intelligence innovators from various business units in the organization, will become one of your greatest strategic tools.

Competitive **intelligence function performed by external competitive analysts completely or in combination with one of the other options**

Some CI projects yield greater returns for an organization when they are performed by a third party, such as a competitive analyst or a CI consultant. Benchmarking, for example, is often influenced by the biases an employee or executive may have about his or her company. The individual may feel ownership for a particular process that is being analysed and introduce this bias into the analysis. Additionally, information gathering is often easier for a professional who is not affiliated with the company conducting the project. It reduces concerns about exposing the project or the company's intentions.

CI professionals and competitive analysts may also have more experience in a particular industry or market, and a wider variety of skills and contacts at their disposal than someone within a company. These skills and contacts become a part of the company's knowledge inventory, or intelligence audit, for the purpose of its intelligence requirements.

The power of competitive intelligence can also be maximized by combining expertise from outside the company to work with the CI experts within the company. This makes sense when specialized research and/or analysis skills not currently found in the organization are required, or when a company is embarking on a CI project that is distinctly different from anything it has experienced before. Seeking this kind of partnership will increase the potential for success.

If you decide to seek external assistance with your competitive intelligence needs, whether it be for training, consulting, project management or any aspect of the CI project model, do your homework. If you have read most of this book, you will have a good idea of the skills and abilities you are seeking from an individual or firm. Many of these skills are identified in Chapter 2. While it is sometimes difficult to get references from CI professionals because they are respecting the confidentiality of clients (maybe you simply want to know who is using CI services), ask many questions regarding the techniques they use (legal and ethical) and the skills they have relevant to your needs.

Technological considerations

In the intelligence age, the role of technology in all aspects of a business continues to grow, and its future value to an organization will grow primarily out of the exposure to technology of intelligence innovators throughout an organization. These individuals will recognize unique and profitable applications for technology, in areas that may previously not have been altered by technological innovation. There are countless technology-related tools that can assist a CI function, and that number continues to grow. It would be cost-prohibitive to implement them all. Fortunately, this is unnecessary.

Technology needs are best addressed early in the establishment of a CI function. Planning is crucial to avoid blowing the budget on attractive yet unnecessary software applications, equipment or paid services. During the needs analysis, you should identify the sources of information readily available to your business. For example, if you have sales representatives across the country, you have a fantastic information supply at your disposal. These employees are in contact with customers (and potential or former customers), suppliers, distributors and even the competition on a daily basis. All you need to determine is the best way to draw upon this source of information. It may be as simple as purchasing cellular telephones and setting up a toll-free CI hotline. After consulting with the sales force, you may discover that mobile computing with e-mail and a CI section on an intranet will be more effective. If your budget is more modest, you may be able to convince your sales force to fill out a quick form and fax it back to the individual involved in the CI function.

Here are some ways in which technology can be incorporated into the CI function, without bankrupting the company. Additionally, we have tried to identify the pitfalls you should avoid.

Telephones and e-mail systems

As mentioned in the example above, common communications technologies like telephones and e-mail can be effective in establishing a dedicated competitive intelligence hotline. This hotline can be used by anyone within the company who might come across valuable information that can help your company make better decisions. Setting up a system and designating an employee to take telephone calls and e-mail is cost-efficient and the benefits can be numerous. This type of system works best when the individual assigned to the task is aware of the significance of CI and understands the channels to which information should be routed. Any information that comes in that has immediate value can easily be forwarded to executives in a timely manner. Advice for salespeople who need to know the best way to approach particular customers, suppliers or even competitors is only a phone call or e-mail away. This type of system is easy and inexpensive to establish and can be used by small or large companies.

Keep in mind, however, that the telephone number and e-mail address should be kept confidential so that it does not get into the hands of unscrupulous competitors who might be inclined to send misinformation your way. A CI hotline should not be a full-time job; rather, it can be incorporated into an employee's job function or rotated throughout a group of individuals familiar with the importance of CI to your organization.

Competitive intelligence and the Internet

We have discussed the value of the Internet to the CI process throughout this book. It has revolutionized the way information is collected and the speed at which business is conducted. However, if the Internet is a company's main source of information, it may want to consider some alternatives. In Chapter 5, we examined the usefulness of the Web, and the fact that there is no greater volume of information available from any other single source. We also raised the point that much of the information on the Web is dubious. Since it has been edited, regurgitated and reproduced from alleged 'original sources', the accuracy of the information should be questioned and, whenever possible, verified by a more reliable source.

The Internet is a great point of departure, but only if the information requirement is clear, search skills are strong and the individual conducting the search knows when to stop. Information overload is the death of any CI project. If you spend all your project time gathering information on the Internet or anywhere else, the reason for needing it will pass. Use the tools and information sources listed in Chapter 5 to develop effective Internet capabilities. It can be one of the least expensive and most valuable technology tools for your CI function.

The company intranet

In this book, we echo the sentiments of many knowledge management theorists, who believe that most of the information a company needs to succeed resides within the company. Our experiences have reinforced the notion that the real difficulty with this situation is extracting that knowledge and sharing it throughout the organization. It is a challenge to get valuable intelligence to the people who need it. For example, an employee who works in research and development may attend a trade show on behalf of her company. She may hear a very detailed description of a competitor's upcoming marketing campaign for a new product. A number of questions come immediately to mind: will the engineer recognize the value of marketing information? If so, will she be aware of the other people in the organization who may benefit from this information? Will she have tools at her disposal to get this information to key people? This type of situation illustrates the advantages of a well-planned company intranet.

Many firms have discovered that intranets, which function like a limited-access Internet within a company, are excellent additions to a CI function. Intranets are typically dedicated to employees only. In some cases, access to company intranets is granted to customers or suppliers as well. Proponents of intranets claim they increase the accessibility to knowledge residing in the company, cut down on decision-making time, and save both time and money when it comes to communicating key strategic information throughout the company. The usefulness of a company intranet is further enhanced by linking it to information databases within a company and providing the appropriate software tools to access even more of an organization's information. An intranet can open up new and valuable communications channels that were previously ignored. In this way, the employee who overheard the marketing strategy would have the capability of sharing the information, not only with the marketing unit, but also with anyone else in the organization. If a sales representative then heard a conflicting report, from a customer for example, that too could be communicated back to the marketing unit and a decision made on how to confirm which strategy the competitor was actually preparing to implement.

An intranet only serves a CI function, and an organization for that matter, if the employees find it easy to use and want to use it. It must enhance the access to information within a company and it must make communication easy and timely, whether employees are in the same office, or located around the world. As is the case with the introduction of any new technology, education and involvement are the keys to getting full participation at every level. If all employees understand the strategic benefits of using the intranet for creating and sharing intelligence, and are rewarded for their efforts, it can become the powerful core technology in the CI function.

Business intelligence applications

Chapter 9 discussed the advantages and disadvantages of business intelligence applications in the world of competitive intelligence. There are a number of drawbacks when it comes to business intelligence applications, because they do not actually deliver intelligence. They organize data, store it and provide tools for its extraction. These packages offer analysis tools as well, some of which are very complex, but in all cases they require quantitative data for analysis. It is highly unlikely that your CI function will only be used to analyse questions involving numerical statistics.

No software can actually produce all of the 'business intelligence' an organization needs, but these products do contribute valuable statistical and data modelling functions to the CI function.

A truly effective CI function uses these types of technology to enhance the capabilities of the most valuable resource within the organization: the people. Unfortunately, many businesses forget that some of the best sources of valuable intelligence rest within their own office. Consider the example of the sales force we used earlier in the chapter. Enlisting your sales force into the competitive intelligence function will help your company maximize the effectiveness of its resources and get the edge on the competition. Your sales force may be one of the best assets your company has for finding 'intelligence' and keeping the competition at bay.

Here are some pointers for gathering information from your salespeople:

1. Educate your sales team about competitive intelligence and what it is.

2. Educate them about the things they should *not* say. They are in constant communication with customers, and often with suppliers, distributors and maybe even the competition. Make sure they know what information your company needs to keep under its hat.

3. Put an efficient system into place that promotes feedback. Because the salespeople are regularly in touch with so many people, they often come across valuable information that can help executives make more strategic decisions. Make sure they communicate with key people in a timely manner.

4. Make them aware of your strategic needs so they can better assist. If your sales team regularly knows what kind of information you need to make better decisions, they can ask the right questions of the people they are in contact with.

5. Train them in effective interviewing skills so they can glean more valuable information from every contact.

6. Let them know who the best sources of valuable intelligence are likely to be and the best ways to approach information gathering with each. Distributors, competitors and customers need to be approached in different ways.

7. Do not overburden them with long reports to fill out, because they are likely to stop doing it. Their first job is to sell; information gathering is secondary.

8. To promote buy-in, increase awareness of the importance of everyone's participation in information gathering.

9. Ensure that they receive some value back from the overall efforts as a means to reward them. Note: we heard some horror stories of

companies who rewarded their salespeople through financial incentives – leading them to use illegal or unethical means to obtain the information.

10. Make them comfortable in providing feedback and suggestions. Give them an avenue to let executives know what they have learnt. If executives treat salespeople as though their time has been wasted, salespeople's information gathering will quickly come to a standstill.

When implemented correctly, a CI function that draws on the experience and knowledge of the company's sales force can be one of its greatest assets.

Developing a competitive intelligence function within your organization requires focused planning and preparation. It also requires the backing of management and a commitment of resources for effective implementation. Following the steps in this chapter will help you increase your potential for success. Ultimately, the success of competitive intelligence within your company depends on the people within the organization. All the best intentions, money and leading-edge technology in the world will not guarantee success if the employees do not recognize or understand the benefits of using competitive intelligence to help their company gain or maintain a competitive edge. In the intelligence age, CI will be one of the most powerful strategic tools at a company's disposal, and intelligence innovators will lead organizations to growth and profitability. Technology will help them do it. This is the winning combination that levels the playing field in the business world, allowing small firms to compete on more equal footing with corporate giants. Regardless of company size, market or industry, organizations that invest in a CI function are investing in their future success.

thirteen

Counter-**intelligence:** **protecting** your **company** from **competitors**

Integrity without knowledge is weak and useless, and knowledge without integrity is dangerous and dreadful.

SAMUEL JOHNSON

Now that you have read this book, you probably realize that you will have to contend with all your competitors who have read the book as well. This is the chapter that helps you deal with this dilemma. There are a number of ways in which you can protect your company, ranging from employee education to legal activities to technology. Implementing any or all of these techniques could save your company money and agony. In fact, they could save your company. The field of counter-intelligence is a rather large one so we will focus on some of the techniques that are most crucial.

The cost of lost intelligence is high. Whether it is the intellectual capital that resides in the heads of former employees who end up working for competing firms, or the electronic file of the business plan that gets intercepted by a hacker, intelligence flows out of a business at an alarming rate. The objective is to stem the flow and preserve your competitive advantage. Clearly, it is impossible to keep everything about your business a secret, and why would you want to? This would border on paranoia. However, it is in your best interest to protect certain aspects of your business.

Education is probably the single most effective thing you can do to protect all of your assets. The American Society for Industrial Security (ASIS) published a study indicating that 75 per cent of all competitive intelligence is gathered from human sources, as opposed to hacking into computers or using other electronic sources. It really is not surprising when you reflect on the overwhelming amount of contact and communication that happens in the course of a day, both directly related to the conduct of business, and after the office doors are closed for the day. An intelligent organization helps its employees at all levels of the organization understand the risks of giving away too much information, as discussed in the following sections.

Conversations and telephone calls

Consider the example given in Chapter 1. Simple as it may sound, your competitor could call your office and speak with the receptionist to find out some information about your company. The receptionist may not have known that the new product or upcoming announcement was confidential information because he or she was not informed. Often employees at this level are overlooked in training and education programmes to ensure people understand the implications of any information they divulge. For some reason, people often assume that such employees are not a threat to a company and its confidential information. Yet they are the front-line workers who come into regular contact with people outside your organization. Nothing prevents your competitors from calling a number of people in your organization, each of whom may provide a piece to the puzzle. Can an operator or an automated telephone system help? Possibly, but consider this story about losing more than just valuable information.

A small company in British Columbia, Canada, installed an automated telephone answering system that provided a single access number coupled with extensions for each employee. A rival company in the United States figured out the names and extensions for each employee by methodically going through the automated system. The US company then called each employee and offered every individual a lucrative job at a substantially higher salary. The Canadian company was left with two employees, wiped out by its competitor. And what happened to the employees who jumped at the chance to work in the US for a big competitor? Within a matter of months, most of them were let go after the company was satisfied it had gained the intelligence they had to offer. There are no guarantees that competitors strive for the same ethical standards that your company advocates. This sounds a bit far-fetched, yet in today's business environment, some companies will go well beyond ethical boundaries into the realm of desperation in an effort to stay competitive. Ethical companies must still compete with firms that 'play dirty', so it is important to be aware of the possible tactics they may use.

Leaving internal business files and confidential documents in public view

If your business uses hotels or conference facilities for strategic meetings, it is worth securing these facilities because it is very easy for competitors to find out what types of events are taking place from the staff at these locations. If you have booked a room, find out who has booked the room next to yours if you can. Hotel staff can be very co-operative. If you leave a meeting room for breaks or meals, consider some kind of security to prevent others from gaining access to documents or other valuable information. This advice applies to your own office as well. We are always amazed by the number of strangers we encounter wandering through the offices of clients. Generally, the individual looks confused and mutters something about being a courier, maintenance person or visitor without actually ever being confronted by an employee of the company. At the end of the day, you realize that your vacationing colleague's notebook computer has disappeared, along with all of her files. She just happened to be working on the business plan for next year. It is important to ensure that any guests or visitors to your office, including couriers or maintenance people, are observed and in the company of employees of your office. While it does not prevent all possible theft or foul play, this simple step can greatly reduce the frequency of these types of incidents.

Creating information for public consumption that provides more detail than is necessary

This can include speeches, conference presentations, government filings or, as in the case of a UK biotechnology firm, media releases. Biotechnology is an industry of the future. Many national governments are banking on their ability to make biotech a bread-and-butter (albeit a genetically modified bread-and-butter) sector of their economies. On the corporate level, the competition is fierce.

So why would a biotechnology firm in the UK 'give away the farm' in a company media release? The company in question shared with the world, and all of its competitors:

1. its strategic and operational objectives, including the areas of its research focus, as well as the programmes it was going to discontinue;
2. its plans for reductions in employment levels by almost 18 per cent by mid-2000, described as a 'restructuring';
3. the appointment of new executives in key positions, with considerable background information; and
4. its estimated annual savings from all of the changes the company was making.

This information was provided to the media and the public over a year in advance of the company's plan to start its 'restructuring'. From a competitive-intelligence perspective, all of this information could have been obtained or, through analysis, could have been estimated with a fair amount of confidence. But it would have taken some time and effort. This company revealed the information freely and prematurely, which is certainly a real asset to its competitors.

Businesses need to be acutely aware of the quantity and type of information they divulge in media releases, speeches, Web sites and all other communications vehicles. Even if it is not a corporate secret, think twice about the impact the release of information may have on your business, particularly to an astute analyst. When it comes to government documents, err on the side of caution. If there is some information that you do not want to divulge, confirm the actual information requirements with the department in question. If you have not provided enough detail to comply with their requirements, let them tell you. Always err on the side of caution when it comes to revealing information about your organization.

Classified advertisements for employment opportunities

It is often surprising how much information a company gives away when it is looking for new employees if it uses newspaper advertising or other mass communication means for publicizing its hiring needs. Often, businesses not only describe what they are looking for (specialized engineers, marketing or sales professionals, etc) but outline the reasons why, as well as the pay and benefits information. This is all valuable information for a competitor, who can also dial the convenient human resources telephone number that is provided in the advertisement to ask a few more pointed questions about why the hiring is taking place and obtain more detailed information about your organization's hiring practices.

Gossip and out-of-office relationships

It is up to you to ensure that employees know what aspects of the business they should not share with spouses, neighbours, friends and even competitors. It is not unusual for individuals from competing firms to come into contact and discuss business or the industry in general. This occurs at conferences, trade shows and even on sales calls to clients or potential clients. It is common for a person who has had a particularly hectic or exciting day at work to return home and impart the news of the day to his or her wife or husband. While this may be a common occurrence, it is not necessarily a safe situation for your company's confidential information or strategic plans. The confidential nature of the news may not be obvious to the person on the receiving end of it, who may, in turn, share the news with others.

Disgruntled employees

If there are people in your organization who are unhappy with their current work situation, they can be loose cannons as well, letting everyone who will listen know about morale in your company, hirings and firings, failures and problems throughout the operation or wages they feel are inadequate. They may feel they have a need for revenge for being passed over for a promotion perhaps. They may simply feel hostility toward their manager or co-workers, or speaking freely about the circumstances may make them feel more important or give them a sense of exhilaration through doing something they know is unethical. Companies and organizations that implement and promote discreet assistance or counselling programmes for troubled employees may have an advantage in reducing the potential for this type of behaviour. In addition, open lines of communication between employees and their managers can help prevent this type of volatility. Conversely, proud and enthusiastic employees can be liabilities as well, bragging about the new product they are working on, or the expansion plans the company will be announcing to overtake its main competitor. You cannot prevent people from speaking and you cannot prevent them from having friends and acquaintances; however, you can make it very clear to your employees that they are not to discuss certain aspects of your business outside the office. (The use of non-disclosure agreements to protect trade secrets or confidential information was discussed in Chapter 10.)

Lawsuits

This one should be easier if you have read Chapter 10. Stay out of court and you minimize the amount of information about your company that becomes public. That could be any type of information: financial, operational, technical or virtually any form of information you could imagine, depending on the reason why you are in court in the first place. If you stay on the right side of the law, you eliminate another source of information for your competitors.

Trade shows

All year long, companies try to keep their plans under wraps, only to go overboard at the key trade shows for their industry. As we mentioned earlier in this book, a two- or three-day trade show often yields as much competitive intelligence as year-long information-gathering efforts. In this microcosm of your industry, all the same rules apply. You must educate all your trade-show personnel prior to the show on what information is not for public consumption. Additionally, all of the printed materials such as brochures, media releases and presentation notes should be scanned for sensitive information by a skilled competitive analyst who can spot 'red flags' or potential problem areas before they are printed and distributed. With a little effort, your staff can also ensure they can identify key personnel from rival companies, putting them in a better position to discourage enquiries from these people.

A powerful and paranoid technology company took this last protective measure to the extreme at one of the largest technology trade shows in the world, when it retrieved photographs of competitors' employees, as well as of individuals suspected of being employees or somehow affiliated with competing businesses. It installed security cameras and communications technology around its booth to monitor the traffic. Whenever it was suspected that someone approaching the booth matched a photograph in the collection, company employees radioed down to the personal security team, provided a physical description of the offending individual and had the security team escort the individual away from the booth. Perhaps if it had prepared more thoroughly in advance for the show, the company in question would not have taken such extreme measures to protect its booth from competitors. It really is a ridiculous power trip when you consider that anyone else could simply walk up to the booth and take it all in. So do not worry if your company lacks the resources for trade show surveillance equipment and a security team. Some of the less expensive methods outlined above will give you more than adequate protection at the show and far less paranoia.

Businesses that employ a sales force can focus not only on how to improve their ability to gather intelligence from customers, distributors, suppliers – even that friendly sales representative from the rival company – but also on the skills required for not giving information away. Front-line employees who receive telephone calls can be taught to screen unknown callers politely and informally, especially after they have been advised of the type of company information that is not to be disclosed to the public.

Although it is not foolproof, a non-disclosure or confidentiality agreement with any subcontractor or other service provider, such as printers, graphic designers, consultants, etc, will at the very least give these individuals a warning to remain silent about your business. It is a terribly common occurrence for us to hear about companies whose confidential information is shared by unscrupulous printers, designers or consultants who may or may not understand the implications of their actions. If you use non-disclosure agreements with these third-party suppliers, if necessary the agreements can provide you with some legal options if they are broken.

So how do you keep track of all of these protective measures? A great point of departure is a security or counter-intelligence policy for your intelligent organization. This is the 'operator's manual' for protecting the company and its intelligence. Make it part of your company's orientation for new employees and conduct periodic reviews of the policy to keep it fresh in your employees' minds, as well as to improve upon its contents. It is a small investment in time, and it can be formulated with the input of employees to reinforce it and to give them ownership of the policy.

Counter-intelligence extends beyond the actions and behaviours of the people within an organization. Technology has given companies numerous tools to protect the valuable intelligence that resides in their factories, filing cabinets and computers. We are not just talking about complex security systems and alarms. Technology has advanced far beyond the simple task of protecting hard assets. Consider your computer network for a moment. Your company may rely on a firewall to restrict traffic between your network and the 'outside world'. It may also employ various technologies to protect data, identify who is trying to access the network (authentication) and limit access to specific individuals (authorization). These types of tools, combined with user education and threat of legal action, still do not protect companies against motivated and skilled hackers.

One of the more recent and interesting additions to the world of counter-intelligence technology is SHADOW, or Secondary Heuristic Analysis System for Defensive Online Warfare. Considering the ominous-sounding name and the fact that it was developed by the US Navy, you might think that SHADOW is a complex technology designed for military applications. As of 1998, it has been freely distributed online as an intrusion-detection tool to help companies spot and analyse possible attempts by outsiders to break into computer networks.

In Chapter 10, we looked at legal issues that might arise during the competitive intelligence process, as well as those issues that could arise as a result of implementing a competitive strategy following the CI process. Counter-intelligence also comprises these two elements: protecting your company from the competitive intelligence or illegal intelligence-gathering efforts of rivals; and protecting your company from responses or retaliation to the competitive strategies you have implemented.

Occasionally, a company ends up having to defend itself against the reaction of other companies to its competitive objectives. Many strategic moves have a considerable impact, not only on the company that implements them, but also on their customers, suppliers and competitors. Often, the company's response to the outcome of a strategy is that, if it had known that outcome in advance, it would never have implemented the move in the first place.

For example, Yamaha implemented a very aggressive and very public marketing strategy against Honda many years ago. Honda felt both threatened and insulted by the Yamaha campaign and responded with an intense and pointed strategy that included a complete overhaul of its motor-cycle line. This resulted in newer, less expensive and more attractive bikes, all in the name of burying Yamaha for its hubris. Yamaha was stunned, almost into submission, and actually issued a formal apology to Honda.

A company must consider in advance whether what it is proposing will be perceived as a threat, what type of retaliation might be taken and how it may be forced to protect itself. Here are some questions to consider:

1. Who will be affected by this strategy? Remember that competitive strategies affect competitors, suppliers, distributors, partners, customers and regulators. It is important to look at all the players.

2. How will they be affected? A company's position within the industry plays a significant role in forecasting how it might be

affected by your competitive move. Would Monsanto be concerned if your 20-person biotechnology start-up merged with another small biotechnology company? Maybe, but probably not. Would they be concerned if your 20-person company entered into a strategic alliance with Bayer AG for many millions of euros? They might want to find out what you had been up to. An industry leader is going to get a different response to its strategic moves from competing businesses than is a company with significantly less clout and market share. It is vital that you look at where you are positioned in the grand scheme of things, as well as where your competitors are positioned. It is also vital that you analyse the potential impact of your moves on your supply chain and your customers so as to prepare yourself better for any changes, resistance or backlash that you may encounter, or to ensure you take full advantage of the positive outcome of your strategies with these key business partners. One of our clients was considering a change at the distribution level of its business as a cost-cutting measure. What the company had overlooked was that the new distribution channel it was considering was not capable of covering the territories into which it planned to expand. Its initial competitive intelligence question was focused on cost-saving options, which it had pinpointed to distribution expenses. Yet it had spent a significant amount of time and resources identifying a new and lucrative market to pursue and was ready to move ahead. It was not until the analysis of the impact of this expansion on the distribution component of the business that the company realized the conflict with the cost-saving measures.

3. Is it likely that they will retaliate? There are many reasons why a company might or might not retaliate. By knowing more about the company you are competing with, you can gain a better understanding of what it might do. One factor to consider is the nature of the company. Does it have a reputation for retaliation or has it been a very conservative company that is shy of conflict or aggressive approaches?

4. Do they have the resources/skills/motivation to retaliate effectively? Retaliation will largely depend on the resources available to the company, both human and financial. By examining the company's existing resources, you can infer the likelihood of whether it will retaliate. If it does, you will be better able to determine if the outcome will be successful for the company.

5. What type of retaliation is likely? Consider whether the company has a reputation for aggressive advertising campaigns, legal action or other form of retaliation.

6. What can we do to minimize retaliation or the impact of retaliation? This will vary greatly from company to company and will depend on your organization's resources, corporate culture, reputation and many other factors.

It is important to develop answers for questions like these for all possible 'retaliators' because your competitors are all different, and they all view your position vis-à-vis their business as unique.

Recently, it seems that one of the most popular methods to protect your company is to buy your competitors. Unfortunately, not all of us are in the position to do it and, in reality, it may not always be the most effective way to maintain a competitive advantage. Historically, mergers have resulted in more failures than successes and, in some cases, have brought on the decline or demise of the players involved. In his book, *The Synergy Trap* (1997), New York University professor Mark Sirower looked at the merger phenomenon and found that two-thirds of all mergers fail. Of the thousands of mergers he tracked, he determined that many of the failures could be attributed to a lack of strategy and poor vision. Competitive intelligence provides the framework for developing sound strategies and 'correcting' the poor vision that leads to poor mergers.

Instead of inventing schemes to buy your way into a monopoly situation (which will create a whole new set of problems), creating a competitive intelligence tracking system of developments in your industry or line of work will help you keep abreast of the changes or potential changes that could affect your business. This book has listed a number of ways in which you can learn industry news almost as fast as the journalists who break the stories. For those special situations when you need to know in advance what might happen, we have outlined a number of analysis tools, as well as diverse sources that can be of assistance.

Some companies resort to legal action or the threat of legal action to protect their vital interests and market position. This method has been used by both large and small businesses with mixed success. Often, the threat of legal action is enough to keep competitors from snooping around your office, copying your products or coaxing information out of your supply chain partners. We have already discussed the legal implications relating to stealing trade secrets and intellectual property, and other forms of corporate espionage. In these situations, the legal authorities usually make an appearance after the crime is a *fait accompli.* Yet consider the use of legal action to deter a competitor from making a strategic move that is not criminal.

At the time that this book was being written, GTE Corp, a US telephone company and Internet service provider, had accused two cable operators, AT&T Corp and Comcast Corp, of illegally forcing customers to buy Internet access from their affiliate, quashing any potential competition from rivals, including GTE's Internetworking unit. GTE's anti-trust lawsuit serves a number of purposes:

1. It creates a multitude of problems for AT&T and Comcast, including business interruptions, legal and other expenses, and potentially bad press.
2. It furthers GTE's ongoing campaign to force local cable television companies to open Internet access to all competitors, rather than just affiliated service providers.
3. It sends a message to regulators (the Federal Communications Commission), which had adopted a 'hands-off' approach to regulating cable Internet connections, that it is time to get involved in opening up the market.
4. GTE remains in the news, portrayed as the advocate for fair play and consumer protection.

The message that GTE creates with this aggressive strategy is that it has been victimized by the current situation. In fact, GTE has a monopoly in the market in question and has historically used legal action to try to protect its dominant position.

Protecting your company is an important part of any competitive intelligence your organization undertakes. The stakes are high for those companies that opt not to introduce some essential counter-intelligence techniques into the organization.

fourteen

Competitive **intelligence** in **action**

The great end of life is not knowledge but action.

TH HUXLEY

Throughout this book, we have provided examples of how companies have used competitive intelligence to their advantage and, conversely, how they have lost their competitive advantage by not implementing some of the tools, techniques and processes outlined in this book. This chapter will take a closer look at how CI is used to conduct business successfully. It will combine both real-life examples and some fictionalized cases to illustrate the value CI can bring to an intelligent organization that is looking to make the best strategic decisions.

There are so many possible uses for CI that no single book could provide an example of each; however, the following examples address significant decision-making areas that most businesses will recognize and be able to relate to. These studies will illustrate the step-by-step approach that is methodical, yet timely and efficient. They will also demonstrate that making CI an integral component or your business regime will reduce the number of unexpected crises, and make it easier to deal with the ones that you may still encounter from time to time.

The first example is a general overview of competitive intelligence in Corel Corporation, an established software company that competes successfully in the international market. The example is intended to give you 'the big picture' of how a company uses CI in different areas of its operations to improve its strategic decision-making abilities. It brings many of the concepts we have spoken about into the real world, and illustrates the value of CI for this particular company.

The subsequent examples focus on particular business situations: 'Discovering and evaluating a new competitor' identifies the areas in which you may want to apply the CI tools and techniques you have learnt in earlier chapters to answer critical questions about a new entrant. 'Deregulation of an industry' looks at an increasingly common phenomenon across the globe – the liberalizing of industries by governments looking to open up markets and economies to more competition. The opportunities resulting from deregulation can be substantial, but history has shown that both government bungling and lack of preparation on the part of existing players have resulted in many of these opportunities being squandered. This example serves also to identify the critical areas for improving your business's chances of success. Finally, 'Predicting successful mergers and acquisitions' provides some insight into how CI can be used to survive the world-wide epidemic of mergers, acquisitions and divestitures that has come to symbolize business in many different industries over the last few years.

Competitive intelligence at Corel Corporation

Corel Corporation is a Canadian-based software company with an international presence based on its CorelDraw and WordPerfect software applications, and its Office Suite software products. Corel is number one in the world in graphics with 70 per cent of the market. It is number two in the word-processing market. The company has experienced many ups and downs in its decade-long history, including a rather hostile and damaging challenge to Microsoft a few years ago. Corel has rebounded recently, and its Office Suite continues to compete worldwide against Microsoft's Office. The company's fortunes have looked even brighter as a result of its strategic decision to embrace Linux, the open source operating system that has amassed a growing following, as well as the 1999 ruling regarding Microsoft's monopoly status in the computer software industry. At the time of writing, Corel's shares have skyrocketed and it is being touted as a prime target for takeover by a 'wealthier' Linux software company based in the United States.

The Corel example illustrates how competitive intelligence can be carried out within a medium-sized company that has limited resources. Corel operates in the frantic and rapidly evolving high-technology world and has somehow managed to survive, scars and all, in an industry that sees companies come and go virtually overnight. David Hayes, Corel's vice-president of marketing, is involved in Corel's CI efforts in this highly competitive industry. On a scale of 1 to 10, with 10 being excellent and 1 being non-existent, Hayes rates Corel's current competitive intelligence efforts at an 8 or 9, and on their way to becoming a 10. He points to Corel's agility as one of the keys to its competitiveness, as well as its willingness to change or adjust to new industry directions. The vast improvement it has recently made in focusing on its core competencies has also helped the company become more effective and competitive.

Corel's CI efforts are directed at specific companies. It has identified who the key competitor companies are and assigns individuals from the marketing function the responsibility for ongoing intelligence gathering on those key competitors. For example, a Corel employee may be assigned Adobe, one of Corel's competitors. That employee becomes the 'custodian' of competitive intelligence on Adobe. 'Anything that comes from Adobe or has something to do with Adobe looking at another company, or Adobe is coming up with this type of product, or Adobe is doing this type of pricing switch, we make sure that person is communications central for that information,' says Hayes. He points out that the individual is responsible for bringing key points up in Corel's quarterly reviews of the market; however, if it is a 'burning issue, Corel acts on it right away'.

The fringe competitor, whom Hayes describes as the individual 'in the garage that creates the next potential big technology', is also researched, and identified as a 'competitive threat' and/or a 'competitive opportunity'. Corel does not diminish the relevance of this type of competitor. The company's goal is to get as great a feel for the industry as it can with the resources it has. As a result, while key people in the marketing function are watching the competition in its more public and visible form, the engineering group also has a system known as the 'virtual garage'. Under this system, employees who may have read something with technological relevance, or met somebody who shared a rumour on a new development, or heard about some obscure, new or lesser-known technology, take their nugget of information and put it in the garage. It is then analysed by key people to determine its relevance to Corel or within the current market environment. At that point Hayes' marketing group becomes involved again to analyse it from a marketing perspective, to forecast its appeal to consumers.

Hayes stresses the importance of staying on top of these fringe competitors. The established, well-known rivals are, according to Hayes, always in your face. Their products are on the shelf beside yours, the sales representatives know one other, sometimes work together and call on the same customers because they are competing for the same business. But the fringe companies come out of obscurity, and need to be monitored for the next Apple Computer or Milky Way Networks, two well known 'garage start-ups', as Hayes refers to them.

Once Corel employees have analysed the intelligence, they evaluate whether it is a threat in any way. If it is a threat, Hayes indicates that Corel assigns a key person who might be an expert in the particular area, or a team comprising individuals from sales, marketing and engineering to identify the risk to the business or the opportunity. For example, if the team discovers a new technology is being introduced in the industry, Corel could purchase it, develop it in house or respond in any number of ways. Hayes stresses that the key is first to identify it as an issue, and then ascertain how best to address that issue.

Corel uses competitive intelligence to address marketing issues, business development issues, engineering issues and distribution issues, and to forecast competitors' next moves. This is particularly important with the rapid pace of change in the software industry. Ultimately, the use of competitive intelligence filters up to the strategic decision-making level, where Hayes believes CI has the greatest value. 'Strategy is all about choice,' says Hayes. Corel's competitive analysis efforts give the company a choice by identifying, for example, that Corel should not be doing a certain thing, as it is not going to make money or, conversely, that something else is a great opportunity for Corel, as opposed to just doing it. 'It is easy to take the technology, wrap it up into a brand and put it out on the market, but the competitive intelligence gives you a bit more of the crystal ball gazing in terms of the success of the brand or the program.'

Within Corel, there is a group that concentrates primarily on strategic marketing and opportunity analysis. One specific project that this group undertook using competitive intelligence was to focus the whole organization on conducting reviews of the market. Corel went to all of its major competitors, gathered annual reports, evaluated Web sites, conducted primary research by talking to different players in the industry and talked to people who had used competing products. The company did as much as it could within reason and came back with enough ammunition to analyse and make recommendations about Corel's strategic direction.

In another instance, Corel used CI to determine that its main competitor in the area of software clip art, IMSI, was on a quest to purchase a number of companies to increase its clip art collection. Corel's analysis indicated that IMSI was missing a huge opportunity by not going after Graphic Corp, the world's largest designer and supplier of clip art. Corel purchased the company instead and, with that one acquisition, went from a relatively small clip art collection to the world's largest collection overnight. Now Corel has a number of companies, including Microsoft, buying this product from them. This one purchase paid for itself in two months, according to Hayes.

Corel also keeps an eye on its competitors' pre-campaigns for new clip art products so that when they release a value product with 375,000 pieces of clip art and a de luxe product with 1.2 million pieces, Corel is in a position to release comparably priced products with, for example, 380,000 and 1.3 million pieces respectively. With both products on the shelf at the same time, it is reasonable to expect that consumers will want more for the same price.

Hayes stresses the importance of communication amongst groups, such as engineering and marketing. The engineering group delivers presentations to the marketing group on new or developing technologies, explaining the technology's features and benefits. The marketing group is then better positioned to analyse and make recommendations on the technology from a marketing and sales perspective.

Another important role for competitive intelligence, in Hayes' mind, is using analysis methods to determine what competitors are doing wrong and ensuring that Corel does not duplicate these errors, whether they be in product development, marketing or customer service. The fact that CI can give a company a very good idea about what not to do is often overlooked. It gives you insight into the areas in which your rivals are simply throwing their money and other resources away. Corel also uses CI to preempt the strategies of its competitors.

In terms of financial analysis, Corel does enlist the help of financial experts to drill down into the financial data of competitors when it feels it needs a more thorough understanding of the competitors' financial strengths. For example, the company identified another player in the industry that, if acquired, would have greatly assisted Corel in meeting one of its strategic goals. While every element of the competitive analysis pointed to a great fit, the financial analysis was critical in determining that the acquisition would have been unwise.

For a technology company, Corel incorporates surprisingly little technology in its competitive intelligence efforts. While it conducts Web site analysis and is beginning to use some data mining applications, the company recognizes the true strength of human analysis and intervention in the strategic decision-making process. Hayes attributes Corel's early embracing of Linux to Corel's flamboyant and visionary CEO, Dr Michael Cowpland, who saw the powerful potential of the open source operating system very early in its development and had his company keep an eye on its progress. Within Hayes' marketing function is a group of people who keep an eye on emerging technologies and analyse the potential implications of these technologies for Corel. Linux has become the heart of this emerging technologies group, and it is becoming an increasingly large part of the company's future.

For Corel, the recipe for success includes using competitive intelligence to forecast the future of its industry and related industries, as well as being vigilant about what is going on in the marketplace in the present. It also includes protecting Corel from its competitors, through confidentiality agreements and disclaimers with employees, retailers and strategic partners, and limiting strategic information to key people prior to implementation. The employees, particularly those who give interviews or are involved in other types of communications, are advised about the type of information that is general and the type of information that must remain confidential.

Corel has had an exceptionally long life in an extremely volatile industry, and competitive intelligence has played a role in this success. While it rides high on the wave of the Microsoft finding and the stock markets' current love-affair with Linux, the company knows it must keep its CI efforts active. Hayes does not hesitate when he declares that companies not using competitive intelligence ignore its value at their peril.

Discovering and evaluating a new competitor

The discovery of a new competitor entering your market can be very disconcerting, particularly if you have been caught unawares and have little or no knowledge of the potential rival. Fortunately, this book has offered you many sources for gathering information, as well as analysis tools you can use to position yourself better to act on this threat. The more you know about the 'new kid on the block', the more effectively you can develop and implement strategies to counter its presence. Here are a few factors to consider:

1. Who is the new competitor? This question actually means a number of things, all of which can provide you with better insight into the company. For example, determining the business structure (proprietorship, partnership, limited partnership, incorporation) can often give you an indication of the size of the company and the people involved. You may also find out where the business is located, allowing you to evaluate the office or facility.

2. Where did the key people come from? A management profiling can provide very valuable information, helping an intelligent organization get a feel for the personality or personalities of its competitors. Your approach toward a new partnership guided by a couple of former university research assistants with life-sciences degrees using government funding may be distinctly different from that to a company that incorporates and lists as its president and CEO a well-known veteran executive with an established record of success at a couple of pharmaceutical firms. Take them all seriously, but adjust accordingly to the realities of their positions relative to yours. The two research assistants may have the greatest idea in the history of life sciences but may lack sufficient funding, contacts and business savvy to bring it to market.

3. Is it a direct competitor? You can answer this question by finding out what types of products or services the rival offers, dissecting them and comparing them to your own. How do your offerings stack up against this new player? Your analysis may bring you to the conclusion that this new business competes against some of your products but not all of them. At this point, it is also important to establish what that could mean to you. Have they created products to rival your most successful lines? You will probably want to act on this immediately to defend your position and your product. Will the new services they are introducing compete head to head with some of your company's less profitable services? Maybe it is time to divest yourself of these underperformers and pump the resources into a new, innovative service, or to consider improvements to give your existing stars more appeal. This analysis will also give you insight regarding the operational strategy of the new rival. By researching and analysing the competitor's offerings, you will undoubtedly discover whether they are copycats, improvers or innovators. Copycats, as the name implies, duplicate an existing product or service (ideally, a successful one!) with the hopes of gaining market share through advertising and lower prices, for

example. This is very common in the pharmaceutical industry after the patents on successful drugs expire. Improvers take an existing product or service, modify it in some way and market it as an improvement over existing offerings from the company from which the product or service originated. Innovators invest time and resources into something new to differentiate themselves from the current line-up in a given industry. Armed with this intelligence, you can also research what has traditionally succeeded in your industry by looking at the approach taken by the most successful firms. Hopefully, your intelligent organization is one of them. While you can also look at the methods they use to deliver the products and services to determine whether they are competing directly against you, this type of analysis has lost some of its value as a result of e-commerce and the Internet, and the ability to ship anything virtually anywhere in the world. Analysis of distribution methods is valuable when you are using competitive intelligence techniques to evaluate why competitors appear more cost-effective when delivering their products and services.

4. What compelled this new company to enter the market? Identifying and analysing the reasons that would compel a new company to start up in a business may give you insight into opportunities you are overlooking as a result of your current view from within the industry. For example, if you operated a national airline that was barely staying in the black, you might be surprised to hear of a new regional carrier preparing to go head to head with you on a number of routes. Your first reaction might be that if an experienced company like yours is struggling in a market you know inside out, a newcomer is going to find out the hard way. A more productive and proactive approach would be to find out as much about them as possible as soon as possible: what type of aircraft, what routes, what fees and air fares, what airports, what value-added services, what size of workforce, what level of pay and compensation? There are so many questions that can be answered that will not only give you more intelligence about your new rival but may also give you assistance with some of your own operational concerns. In reality, these are two sides of the same coin. Ultimately, you will be in a better position to compete.

5. What methods has it used to enter the market? An intelligent organization will be aware of the imminent arrival of a new competitor prior to its first day of business. It is quite likely that this new player

will be using specific methods to get its name out to the world. Advance advertising campaigns may lead to clues about the nature of the company's marketing strategies, and so too will announcements or press releases about partnerships and strategic alliances. Identifying and analysing the alliance partners helps your company understand what additional strengths (and weaknesses) will be at the disposal of this new player.

6. What are its strengths and weaknesses? As mentioned above, the more you can find out about the strengths and weaknesses of this new competitor, using SWOT analysis, the more you can prepare your company for action. These strengths and weaknesses must be evaluated relative to your own organization's, and relative to the industry as a whole. This could be effectively accomplished using competitor profiling. This type of analysis really helps to solidify the nature of the potential threat and, equally importantly, illustrates the opportunities that your intelligent organization can pursue. There are a number of areas that you can analyse for strengths and weaknesses. Many of these areas were discussed in Chapter 6, including methods to determine financial strength, availability of resources, use of technology and technological advances.

7. What are the sales, marketing and distribution strategies? In addition to pre-launch advertising, there are a number of options to find out more about the marketing direction of a new competitor. Using some of the techniques we discussed in earlier chapters, including field research, an intelligent organization can find out if a new entrant is choosing specific strategies to position itself. If it has been featured in a particular publication, it is possible that the journalist or editor has some insights into the industry as a whole, including this new player. It is unlikely, however, that an individual in this position would volunteer information about one company to another, and you might risk offending a potentially good source of information if you take such an approach. We would consider such research a success if it led us to another source, such as an industry insider or 'expert' with more specific information. Your existing clients or customers are also valuable sources of information. If you have a good relationship with them, asking about other firms that have contacted them should not pose any problems. They may be able to give you a detailed account of the 'sales pitch' they received, pricing structure, incentives and discounts, distribution

and channels, and even the target groups for this new rival. This type of field research can provide information that might help you with the next question.

8. How is the company positioning itself and who is it targeting? In Canada, the media have been very critical of banks and investment firms that charge exorbitant fees to 'manage' their clients' investment portfolios. It has brought both frustration and confusion to the average Canadian, who has also been inundated with both marketing campaigns and media stories about the urgent need to buy mutual funds and other investment vehicles to secure a financially comfortable future. All this publicity has led to an increase in the number of small, aggressive, discount brokerages, including online brokerages, which are hoping to prey on the 'conservative Canadian's' growing discontent with Canadian banks. Virtually all of the articles and advertisements contain some version of this theme – 'The banks do not care about you because you are just another account number to them; we are different and we are inexpensive.' The 'conservative Canadian' investor is a huge market indeed. Are the banks worried that their clients are being targeted? They do not seem to be (at least not publicly)... yet. While this is a fairly simple example, it does illustrate that a number of factors influence how a new player decides to position itself, and how it may prey on your very public weaknesses. If you can determine whether you or your clients are a target of the new rival's marketing strategy, you are better positioned to counter the perceived weaknesses upon which they plan to prey. We were able to help one of our clients pre-empt such a marketing campaign by a new competitor, by narrowing down the possible approaches it could use to position itself both in the market and, in this case, directly against our client, which was perceived as the most direct threat to the new entrant. Following the presentation of our analysis and recommendations, our client developed and launched a campaign that addressed a perceived weakness in the product it offered. The weakness was identified as a result of researching the new entrant, and the method it had adopted with the competing product. Simultaneously, our client dedicated additional resources on the operational side to ensure that the product would be out on the market if not before then at the same time as the competing product, or shortly thereafter. It was not the perfect situation for our client, but it was vastly better than it would have been if it had

remained ignorant of the whole marketing strategy of this new competitor. Knowing how a new competitor is positioning itself and who it is targeting as customers also helps your company analyse why a potential customer would pick it over you or, alternatively, why an existing customer might feel compelled to change. This is invaluable intelligence for protecting your organization, provided you act on it.

Deregulation of an industry

Deregulation is often the most significant way in which a government can affect industry. Globally, there has been a trend toward deregulation as national economic policies continue to embrace more open views on trade and investment, state-controlled business and industry evolves in increasingly 'free' markets and competition demands it. These are just a few of the reasons why the rules get loosened and the game changes. Regardless, the fallout from such a change in government policy can have significant repercussions. Energy markets offer a great example of the effects of deregulation. Germany made significant strides in making its energy market very competitive in less than a year, reaching a very liberalized state in a fraction of the time it took the UK. Increased competition, new entrants and attention to customer needs have led to significant price cuts and better service for consumers. North America has also been experiencing this phenomenon in the energy industry in recent years, as both US and Canadian governments deregulate the electricity market. The result has been crisis after crisis for many companies and regulatory authorities, which had become complacent after decades of stability, inertia, healthy profits and an anti-competitive environment in which consumers were being victimized by high energy costs. In the face of deregulation, utilities were forced to address a number of new questions. The companies that shifted their paradigm to embrace the new competitive environment found answers to these questions, developed and implemented a plan and were able to take advantage of the opportunities.

Each of the questions in the following section addresses a particular business element that must be considered when an industry is being deregulated. This is a broad competitive intelligence project and one that requires considerable co-ordination and effort.

Threats as a result of deregulation

The sources of potential threats are many. Identifying them is much easier for an intelligent organization that has a current and accurate assessment of its present position in the industry. This is the 'strengths and weaknesses' component of the SWOT analysis method discussed in Chapter 6. The assessment allows the company to analyse individual threats vis-à-vis its own capabilities and resources. This CI project would include finding answers to the following questions:

1. What is the timetable for deregulation? If your company starts addressing the deregulation issue from the day the first rumours start flying, it will be in an enviable position to prepare a strategy for the new competitive environment. Earlier in this book, we stressed that the government and regulators can be excellent sources of information. A regulated company should make every effort to understand the regulatory environment in which it operates, make reliable contacts at the government office or regulatory agency, and take advantage of the fact that these people are serving the public and businesses. As a businessperson, you can ask as many questions as you desire, as often as you want, to keep abreast of developments and changes to government and regulatory policy. You can even intervene in an attempt to slow the process, in some cases. Conversely, you can try to push regulatory change more rapidly if you believe this is a good strategic move for your organization. If you know the timetable for deregulation, you are in a better position to designate your resources and prepare a strategy.

2. Which players are the greatest threat in a deregulated environment and why? This question is also easier to answer for an intelligent organization that has been diligent about following its industry as well as related industries. Consider conducting ongoing competitor profiling to learn about the companies that pose the greatest threat to your competitiveness; however, be flexible enough to add new players to the analysis to account for the rapid changes in deregulated industries. One of the most likely occurrences of deregulation is the introduction of new players looking for a piece of the action because they have spotted growth opportunities, complementary business lines and fewer barriers to entry. Identifying and analysing existing and potential threats is crucial to developing a plan to maximize your company's opportunities. It is naïve to look just at the current industry leaders and assume they will be leading the

way under a new, more competitive system of conducting business. It is also inadequate just to identify the threats. You must understand why they are threats in a deregulated environment.

3. What will potential entrants require to develop a competitive advantage in the industry? If you have determined that deregulation will lead to new players, you will also need to analyse the ways in which they will try to become competitive against existing firms. Will they be acquiring existing companies to gain an immediate foothold? You might want to conduct a merger analysis. Will they offer bargain-basement rates for service? Event analysis might help with this question. Will they introduce incentives or innovative programmes to entice customers away from your company? Try event analysis combined with company profiling to address this concern. Again, it is important to know what they can do. The goal, however, is to know what they will do, before they do it.

4. What are the merger possibilities? This question builds on the earlier enquiries but is more specific. The intelligent organization wants to understand the potential for merger activity, both as a target and in terms of acquisition opportunities. Equally important is the need to determine who else may be considered a target, because mergers can very quickly change the business landscape and the competitive positions of many firms. In addition to mergers or acquisitions, deregulation can create opportunities for strategic alliances, particularly if the liberalized market is attracting new entrants. These alliances form with existing players as a means to solidify a dominant position against potential intruders and they form with complementary businesses in related or different industries where synergies can be created. To answer any questions relating to possible mergers or acquisitions, conduct merger analysis, financial ratio analysis and/or competitor analysis.

5. Does our approach to meeting customers' needs change as a result of deregulation? Answering the above questions, combined with an existing understanding of customer needs, will help an intelligent organization maintain its existing customer base and potentially increase it after the industry is deregulated. In the case of the German power markets, a price war became one of the dominant features of meeting customer needs. Prior to deregulation, Germany had the highest industrial power prices in Europe. Within a year, wholesale prices had been cut in half, and domestic consumers were expecting a similar decrease. These price cuts were

driven, not only by increased competition within Germany, but also by the fear of entry from other European utilities. This scenario leads to the next question.

6. If existing market definitions are not still valid, how does deregulation change the map? More often than not, geographic barriers tumble in a liberalized and lucrative industry. US and European companies have been jumping on opportunities in Mexico's energy sector and, even within countries, former regional utilities have been exploring new territory. Again, it is a question of analysing which barriers have been removed and which barriers, if any, still exist as a result of the deregulation. Conducting a market factors analysis will help you determine the possible outcome.

7. How will a deregulated industry evolve? Some might argue that the best analysis tool for this type of forecasting would be a crystal ball. While it is more difficult to predict the future in an industry that is undergoing a massive shift like deregulation, it is not impossible to identify where some competitive advantages may be cultivated. Analysing the potential threats allows you to identify particular characteristics about them that might stimulate change in the industry. Is the rival or potential rival innovative in specific functions? Are the new players more technologically advanced and, if so, will it be a competitive advantage for them? Such an evolution can lead to the introduction of new products and services, as well as new ways to deliver them. Solid analysis can help build a reasonable picture of what the future holds, even if it bears little resemblance to the past. You may want to consider a modified version of competitive benchmarking at either a company or an industry level for this situation. For example, you could direct your examination to another industry that has experienced deregulation to gain some insight into the implications for companies in this industry and see whether they might be valid to your current situation. Keep in mind that this is a difficult event to predict, and even skilled analysis may only present you with possible outcomes. Additionally, you should analyse events that take place following deregulation. Event analysis at an industry level may be useful in forecasting the repercussions.

Predicting successful mergers and acquisitions

The 1990s will be remembered in the business world as the decade of mergers and acquisitions. Very few industries were immune to the 'bigger is better' mentality that changed the face of the petroleum industry, the automobile industry and, especially, the high technology industry, where consolidation has become a way of life and companies form simply to be bought out by larger, wealthier players. There is no indication that the merger trend will change in the new millennium, and intelligent organizations will continue to measure their success and failure on how well they monitor their industry and related industries for key developments that will lead to opportunity.

Earlier in this book, we outlined Cisco Systems CEO John Chambers' checklist for a successful acquisition. It included some rather broad factors such as shared vision, similar cultures/chemistry, a winning proposition for acquired employees (at least over the short term), a winning proposition for shareholders, employees, customers and partners over the long term, and geographic proximity. Not one of these factors is apparent without doing the kind of research and analysis that competitive intelligence prescribes. Consider the financial forecasting involved in a merger of multi-billion-dollar firms and you will see the magnitude of these undertakings. While financial ratio analysis tools are fairly standard, analysing and forecasting the likelihood of shared vision or similar business cultures and chemistry is more enigmatic. Clearly, Chambers' formula works for Cisco, and they are in a position to acquire just about anyone they want, save for the anti-competition dilemma such a strategy might create. Yet this formula is not necessarily magical or accurate for all industries and business situations.

Daimler Chrysler has proven that geographic proximity and cultural likeness are not critical to a merger. On 7 May 1998, Daimler Benz and Chrysler Corporation merged to create Daimler Chrysler. This merger took place after four months of secret negotiations, and managed to remain a relative surprise to the industry. Within five or six months of the actual merger, the new company was officially created, a phenomenally quick pace for such a significant merger. At that time, the new company had 421,000 employees world-wide and plants in 34 countries. It was selling an estimated 4 million vehicles from 200 offices world-wide, putting it third in the world behind General Motors and Ford. So how did this all happen? Apparently the driving force was Jurgen Schrempp, the

German half of the current Daimler Chrysler leadership duo. Schrempp was quoted in *EuroBusiness* magazine as stating that, in the current merger-manic environment, he had to pounce or be pounced upon. His decision reflected his personality – he did not want to sit passively and become the object or by-product of someone else's decision.

The questions that need to be formulated and the answers required to merge two automotive giants confidently are many and complex. Undoubtedly, both Schrempp's team and Chrysler CEO Robert Eaton's team at Chrysler looked long and hard at many factors. They would already have known a fair bit about each other as players in the same industry. Although the product lines were not competing directly, they would have had a fairly reliable picture of each another. An industry analysis incorporating financial ratios and competitor profiling would have helped them determine the following:

1. How profitable is the industry as a whole?
2. What are the margins and fluctuations?
3. What segments are my competitors focusing on?
4. What segments should my company focus on?
5. What are the critical success factors (sales and marketing, research and development, distribution, for example)?
6. What are my competitors' strengths and weaknesses, and relative performance (SWOT analysis)?
7. How is the industry evolving and what factors will be crucial for future success?
8. Who will my company's competitors be in the future and how strong will they be?

The answers to these questions would have yielded a considerable amount of information. The decision-makers at both companies would have know that the automotive industry was already capable of manufacturing 15 million more cars than the world currently needs. Schrempp, for example, would also have learnt that Chrysler was the most profitable car maker in Detroit, generating more than US$1,000 profit on each vehicle it sold. Additionally, Schrempp would have been tantalized by the fact that there was virtually no product overlap between the two companies. Daimler Benz's strengths were in top-end luxury vehicles and heavy-duty trucks, while Chrysler's strengths rested in its family-value automobiles, mini vans, pick-up trucks and sport utility vehicles. What better way to enter the massive family/economy market without jeopardizing the premium Mercedes brand?

A competitive analysis of a merger must also consider competitive factors on an operational level. In Chapter 6, we discussed a number of elements to consider when conducting an analysis at this level, including technical elements such as financial summaries (sales, net income, assets, shareholder equity, debt, return on sales, asset turnover, return on assets, return on equity and debt to equity ratio, for example). This technical information gives you tools to forecast what is possible from a straightforward accounting perspective; however, it gives an incomplete picture without an analysis of the corporate personality. This analysis would provide additional clues about how a competitor or, as in this case, a merger candidate might perceive its situation and its business environment, and how it might respond to strategic changes like a merger opportunity. The areas to look at include:

- organizational structure;
- corporate culture;
- key managers' profiles;
- ownership;
- board of directors;
- goals/business strategies;
- marketing;
- history with acquisitions and divestitures.

An analysis of Chrysler Corporation, using the company analysis technique, would have included technical information such as revenues of US$61 billion in 1998, a 16 per cent market share of new vehicles sales in the US and a workforce of over 94,000 employees. Schrempp would also have known that Chrysler sold only 200,000 vehicles a year outside its home market in the United States. He would have noted, as mentioned above, that Chrysler was a high-margin automotive company, just like Daimler Benz. Apart from the technical data, the German group would have learnt a fair bit about Robert Eaton, including his salary of US$70 million. They would have learnt about Eaton's history as the European head of General Motors, and how he was selected by Lee Iacocca, the former chairperson of Chrysler, to lead the company. The Germans would probably have learnt of Eaton's reputation for modesty and for doing whatever was necessary to make Chrysler better for its shareholders. In terms of corporate culture, Daimler Benz's analysis would have revealed a group of decision-makers who move quickly when it comes to developing and implementing strategies. Schrempp would have had to consider the implications of this when analysing management integration issues, in the face of Daimler Benz's traditionally methodical, slow and risk-averse style of decision-making. While Chambers might have found such contrasting styles too significant to overcome for a Cisco acquisition candidate, Schrempp must have believed he could find a balance. No doubt his public admiration for certain leading US business leaders, and their influence on his personal management style, played a role in this decision.

Clearly, the task to research, analyse and, ultimately, implement this merger was enormous. The competitive intelligence process facilitates this kind of task by providing a systematic approach for proceeding at all stages and allowing an intelligent organization to act rather than react. The leaders at both Daimler Benz and Chrysler understood this. As a result of the competitive analysis that was already under way, they had enough intelligence to proceed with confidence and speed. The key to effective CI in mergers, as in other situations, is getting enough intelligence to make good decisions, not getting all the information that is available. Choosing the latter only increases your chance of losing control of your company's future. In business, time is money. Having the proper tools at your disposal and the capacity to use them effectively means the difference between success and failure.

References

Camp, RC (1989) *Benchmarking: The Search for Industry Best Practices that Lead to Superior Performance*, ASQ Quality Press, Milwaukee

Fuld, LM (1995) *The New Competitor Intelligence: The Complete Resource for Finding, Analyzing, and Using Information about your Competitors*, John Wiley & Sons, Inc, New York

Human Resource Management News (9 January 1999) Ethical Companies Show a Competitive Edge

Kahaner, L (1996) *Competitive Intelligence: From Black Ops to Boardrooms*, Simon & Schuster Inc, New York

Schrempp, J (1999) *EuroBusiness*, **1** (1)

Sirower, M (1997) *The Synergy Trap*, Free Press

Index

Give Your Organization the Competitive Edge...

Call the Competitive Intelligence and Business Development Specialists at Global Trade Solutions for:

Research and Analysis

Global Trade Solutions provides in-depth research and analysis on markets, industries, businesses, and governments – virtually anything required for private or public sector success. Our speciality is turning information into intelligence to give your organization the edge it needs. Some of these services include:

- Competitive Intelligence
- Market Research
- International Trade Research
- Industry Research and Analysis

Training and Seminars

Global Trade Solutions offers a wide selection of introductory, advanced, and customized seminars on everything your organization needs to become more competitive, some of which include:

- Setting Up and Managing Your Competitive Intelligence Department
- Competitive Intelligence for Executives
- Competitive Analysis
- Competitive Benchmarking
- Becoming an Intelligent Organization

Consulting

Global Trade Solutions works with organizations to find solutions to their unique concerns, helping them get the competitive edge. We will help your organization implement its competitive intelligence function, improve its competitiveness, benchmark your organization's strategies or operations, improve your competitive position in the global marketplace, or any other specific concern you may have.

Free Subscription

Learn why Fortune 500 executives, editors of leading business publications, and diplomats from around the world rely on *ciexperts.com*, the premier e-zine on competitive intelligence. For your free monthly subscription, delivered by e-mail to your desktop, visit www.ciexperts.com and click 'Subscribe'.

GLOBAL TRADE SOLUTIONS

Call Global Trade Solutions in Ottawa, Canada at +1 613-247-7007 to learn more about making your organization competitive.
Visit our Web site: www.go-global.net